Life, Liberty, and the Pursuit of Happiness:

Documents in American History, Volume II: 1861 to Present

Life, Liberty, and the Pursuit of Happiness

DOCUMENTS IN AMERICAN HISTORY, VOLUME II: 1861 TO PRESENT

FIRST EDITION

Edited by
P. Scott Corbett
Oxnard College

Ronald C. Naugle
Nebraska Wesleyan University

Boston   Burr Ridge, IL   Dubuque, IA   Madison, WI   New York
San Francisco   St. Louis   Bangkok   Bogotá   Caracas   Kuala Lumpur
Lisbon   London   Madrid   Mexico City   Milan   Montreal   New Delhi
Santiago   Seoul   Singapore   Sydney   Taipei   Toronto

The McGraw·Hill Companies

Mc Graw Hill Higher Education

LIFE, LIBERTY, AND THE PURSUIT OF HAPPINESS: DOCUMENTS IN AMERICAN HISTORY, VOLUME II: 1861 to PRESENT
Published by McGraw-Hill, a business unit of The McGraw-Hill Companies, Inc., 1221 Avenue of the Americas, New York, NY, 10020. Copyright © 2004 by The McGraw-Hill Companies, Inc. All rights reserved. No part of this publication may be reproduced or distributed in any form or by any means, or stored in a database or retrieval system, without the prior written consent of The McGraw-Hill Companies, Inc. including, but not limited to, in any network or other electronic storage or transmission, or broadcast for distance learning.
Some ancillaries, including electronic and print components, may not be available to customers outside the United States.

This book is printed on acid-free paper.

2 3 4 5 6 7 8 9 0 FGR/FGR 0 9 8 7 6 5 4 3

ISBN 0–07–284019-6

Publisher: *Lyn Uhl*
Senior sponsoring editor: *Steve Drummond, American History*
Developmental editor: *Kimberly McGrath*
Marketing manager: *Katherine Bates*
Senior project manager: *Jean Hamilton*
Production supervisor: *Carol A. Bielski*
Permissions editor: *Connie Dowcett*
Associate designer: *George Kokkonas*
Typeface: *10/12 Palatino*
Compositor: *GAC Indianapolis*
Printer: *Quebecor World Fairfield, Inc.*

Library of Congress Control Number: 2003106815

www.mhhe.com

BRIEF CONTENTS

INTRODUCTION

The range of documents appropriate for the study of American history is exceptionally rich. In assembling this volume, we have again been impressed both by the degree to which documents provide a deeper understanding of the times and context within which they were produced, and by how they connect with both preceding and succeeding events. The experience has reinforced our conviction that documentary study is an invaluable means to understand the American past. Yet, the study of primary documents for this purpose raises substantive issues ranging from historical interpretation to pedagogy. Where to begin and what to include become the most important questions.

We begin with what we believe many Americans already know and/or think they understand about the major events and themes of our nation's history. It is, after all, the recognition of names, events, and issues related to the past and the perception of knowledge and understanding of those elements that underlies American behavior and provides a foundation for American identity. Identifying a thematic framework for selecting documents that furnish insight into the American past became the first task. "Life, liberty, and the pursuit of happiness" quickly emerged as such a touchstone. It is a phrase omnipresent in the minds of Americans during the course of the recent past and one that has become a litany for what America was, is, and still aims to be. It has served frequently as a prism, even *the* prism to understand and interpret events and issues that have affected the entire course of the American republican experiment.

"Life, liberty, and the pursuit of happiness" also serves for many Americans as the bedrock of inalienable rights that channels the energies of citizens and their government into performing duties and shouldering responsibilities. Yet, for all that Americans pack into the phrase, the document from which it is derived, the Declaration of Independence, had its own unique and particular purpose grounded in a specific time and place. By going to the source, the document itself, it becomes clear that the Declaration of Independence did not create a mechanism or instrument of government, as many commonly assume. Rather than create freedoms and establish the role of government for Americans, the phrase "life, liberty, and the pursuit of happiness" in the Declaration was a rhetorical device to justify revolution and inspire people to dedicate their "lives," fortunes, and "sacred honor" to achieving an independent and self-sustaining government that would then and only then secure those rights. Nor did the Declaration of Independence create an independent United States of America; it merely served notice of the intention of the colonial revolutionaries to lead their neighbors and countrymen to that end.

As the central organizing theme for this collection of documents, "life, liberty, and the pursuit of happiness" provided the context for both selecting documents and for relating them to the unfolding events of American history. Some variation of the theme has certainly propelled people to this continent well before independence and every day since. In that process the theme has acquired a malleability that has enabled it to be reshaped at various times by various players in the nation's historical drama.

Various communities and subcommunities on the North American stage have defined "life, liberty, and the pursuit of happiness" differently or had different expectations of how it should be applied or used to guide behavior and policy. Native Americans, African Americans, women, various religious bodies or sects, and certain classes have all seized upon the phrase as ammunition for their battles and struggles to have those terms meaningfully articulated and implemented according to their specific visions and desires. Going to the source to understand the fabric of American history must therefore include consideration of the perspectives of such groups as they struggled to alter or preserve their American landscape.

Finally, it has become obvious over the years that the typical classroom contains persons who differ in how they learn, what they find interesting, and in how they formulate and articulate their knowledge. Work on multiple learning styles pioneered by Howard Gardner in numerous experiments over the past thirty or so years has identified nine multiple intelligences including verbal/linguistic, math/logical, visual/spatial, musical/rhythmic, bodily/kinesthetic, naturalist, intrapersonal, interpersonal, and existential. Accordingly though the selections in this book and the organization of the chapters will not strictly adhere to a format requiring equal representation of each of the nine intelligences. We have tried to include documents and other primary sources that might appeal to the broader range of intelligences that exist within today's classrooms. In some cases a single prompt may serve to release the energies and the inspiration of more than one of the intelligences. For example, the photographs from the Vietnam era (Chapter 30) might connect with anyone's visual/spatial intelligence, but they might also resonate with the interpersonal or the existential intelligences of students as they suggest, in more powerful ways, fundamental issues regarding human relations and the consequence of power.

The importance of learning what primary sources are and how their content becomes the choice historians make in formulating narratives and interpretations about the past may not seem self-evident these days. With so many historians laboring long and hard to create readable and stimulating accounts of the past, we may be lured into forgetting the importance of deriving some of our knowledge of our past from the original concepts and ideas grounded in their own time and place. It has been observed repeatedly over the years that the crucial rationale for the study of the nation's past is the need for citizens to become knowledgeable enough to utilize and shepherd their own freedoms and claims to the Declaration's inalienable rights of life, liberty, and the pursuit of happiness. Critical thinking, the desire and ability to go beyond the pat and convenient understandings placed before us, is an essential tool in effectively sustaining our democratic government and society. The importance of knowing something from firsthand experience and therefore being immune to attempts to delude or to shake that knowledge through subsequent interpretation and explanation of events was on General Dwight D. Eisenhower's mind in the spring of 1945. On April 12, 1945, Eisenhower, along with Generals George S. Patton and Omar Bradley, toured the death camp at Ohrdruf, a minor subcamp of Buchenwald. "The things I saw beggar description," said Eisenhower on first viewing the death camps. "I made the visit deliberately, in order to be in a position to give firsthand evidence of these things if ever, in the future, there develops a tendency to charge these allegations merely to propaganda." We hope these volumes and the study of the documents they include will enable readers to develop the knowledge and skills that will deepen their appreciation, strengthen their understanding of, and reinforce their commitment to the claims of the "self-evident truths" of life, liberty, and the pursuit of happiness.

To some degree the work that has gone into this volume, and its predecessor, Volume 1, represents the best of our combined experience and careers in studying and teaching history at various institutions and among different cultures across the United States and in other parts of the world. Sometimes the greatest insights into American history are derived from teaching it to non-Americans who ask questions and are puzzled about issues that would never arise in a classroom in Nebraska or California.

We are grateful for the time and effort our professors and mentors at the University of Kansas, in particular Norman Yetman, Walter Sedelow, Daniel Bays (now at Calvin College), David Katzman, and Theodore A. Wilson, invested in us and the good education we received there from them and others. We hope we have succeeded in passing the torch to the generations of students that have populated our classrooms.

As we have gathered, evaluated, and assembled the documents for this volume, we have been blessed with the support of various people and institutions. We thank Nebraska Wesleyan University, which has long supported creative scholarship and innovative teaching. We are also grateful to Oxnard College, which has provided a home and secure base of operation as well, and to Tomas Salinas of the History Department, who has been a valued friend and colleague.

In assembling these documents, a few individuals have assisted us in ways that were valued and appreciated. We owe a special debt of gratitude to Nebraska Wesleyan University Librarian, John Montag, skilled bibliographer, historian, and teaching colleague, who helped us identify and locate many of the documents we chose to include. At California State University, Northridge, two library assistants, Esperanza Bedolla and Milton Folk, were kind and cheerful in retrieving the documents and books we sought.

We are also grateful for the support and encouragement we have received from the people at McGraw-Hill. Steven Drummond, long-time friend and advocate for history throughout his distinguished career in the publishing industry, has remained firmly behind this project and continues to be a role model, mentor, and friend. Connie Dowcett's cheery disposition and tireless effort in handling much of the editing and permissions duties will always be appreciated and cherished, as will the grace and intelligence Kimberly McGrath lent to the project from beginning to end.

P. Scott Corbett
Camarillo, California

Ronald C. Naugle
Lincoln, Nebraska

16

His Terrible Swift Sword— the Civil War

The American Civil War was for many Americans a fiery forge that completed the democratic experiment. Others were less sure. At considerable cost, it had severed from the body politic the constitutionally protected system of African American slavery; yet fundamental issues surrounding "life, liberty, and the pursuit of happiness" remained. Did associations of people have the right or capacity to determine their political, economic, or cultural fate? What constituted the appropriate use of power by governments, both state and national? Imbedded into the American democratic experiment from its inception were several long fuses in the form of conflicts initially unresolved. Among these were fundamental disagreements between doctrines of states rights and "confederation" and nationalism and "federation." The shortest fuse, perhaps, was the conflict between the economic systems of slavery and free labor, in which North and South alike sought victory for their own peculiar ideology and vision of the future. In the process of reconciliation and nation-building, actions were taken that affected day-to-day a wide range of people, including many in the mainstream who had been in control of the American system and many previously on its fringes.

The initial documents in this chapter illustrate the attempt of the Confederacy to garner support from and forge an alliance with Native Americans. As the South desperately sought friends and support, olive branches and promises were extended to the Cherokee, among others, offering more life, liberty, and happiness than had previously been enjoyed at the hands of American state governments. At the same time the United States, on behalf of its northern and western territories and states, encouraged settlement of western lands and unleashed policies that would accelerate the clash between the Native American and Euro-American worlds. Seeking to spread both people and civilization across the continent, the Morrill Act reflected values that went back to the Puritan support for higher education. The association of knowledge and education with American political, religious, and cultural civilization represented a

1

unique element in the process of "winning" the West. In most trans-Mississippi states, the state university systems are the direct outgrowth of the Morrill Act.

The Civil War involved an infinite number of decisions that affected fundamental issues of life and death; not the least of which was the challenge of conducting a "civil" war in civil ways. That effort is revealed in a portion of General Order 100 that became the foundation of a developing belief about how Americans should behave in battle. The "Barlow/Gordon Incident" illustrates the fraternal nature of that war and suggests a subsequent issue for consideration. War veterans of both sides had to achieve reconciliation in order to regenerate the bonds of loyalty and patriotism to the United States of America. Before that could happen, the pain and sorrow associated with the most destructive war Americans had ever fought had to be addressed. Though there is considerable evidence that John B. Gordon's account of his encounter with Francis C. Barlow was amplified by his imagination, that "creative" process produced a symbolic story of reconciliation that was published and widely shared in the years after the guns of Gettysburg were silent. The "arithmetic of suffering" suggests the number of people personally touched by the war and the depth of the healing that had to take place. Some immediate consequences of the war are seen through the eyes of a 10-year-old girl—Carrie Berry. The life-long realities of the conflict are also suggested by Robert Frost in the character of the widow who lived in the black cottage, destined to spend the rest of her life a widow. Robert Frost himself represents, perhaps, the long shadow of the Civil War because he knew people like the widow. Their experiences influenced his life as he became a beloved American poet who recited one of his compositions at the inauguration of John F. Kennedy in 1960, one hundred years after the burdens of that civil strife had fallen on the shoulders of Abraham Lincoln and his generation.

DOCUMENT 16.1

Letter Recruiting the Cherokee Nation as Allies of the Confederacy

THE STATE OF ARKANSAS
EXECUTIVE DEPARTMENT

Little Rock
January 29, 1861

His Excellency JOHN ROSS
Principal Chief Cherokee Nation:

SIR:

It may now be regarded as almost certain that the States having slave property within their borders will, in consequence of repeated Northern aggression, separate themselves and withdraw from the Federal Government. South Carolina,

Alabama, Florida, Mississippi, Georgia, and Louisiana have already, by action of the people, assumed this attitude. Arkansas, Missouri, Tennessee, Kentucky, Virginia, North Carolina, and Maryland will probably pursue the same course by the 4th of March next.

Your people, in their institutions, productions, latitude, and natural sympathies, are allied to the common brotherhood of the slave-holding States.

Our people and yours are natural allies in war and friends in peace. Your country is salubrious and fertile, and possesses the highest capacity for future progress and development by the application of slave labor.

Besides this, the contiguity of our territory with yours induces relations of so intimate a character as to preclude the idea of discordant or separate action.

It is well established that the Indian country west of Arkansas is looked to by the incoming administration of Mr. Lincoln as fruitful fields, ripe for the harvest of abolitionism, free-soilers, and Northern mountebanks.

We hope to find in you friends willing to co-operate with the South in defense of her institutions, her honor, and her firesides, and with whom the slave-holding States are willing to share a common future, and afford protection commensurate with your exposed condition and your subsisting monetary interests with the Gen. Government.

As a direct means of expressing to you these sentiments I have dispatched to you my aide-de-camp, Lieut. Col. J. J. Gaines, to confer with you confidentially upon the subjects and to report to me any expressions of kindness and confidence that you may see proper to communicate to the Governor of Arkansas, who is your friend and the friend of your people.

Respectfully, your obedient servant,

H. M. RECTOR

Governor of Arkansas.

Source: Reprinted with permission from Ken Martin, *History of the Cherokee*, "Arkansas Governor Henry Rector to Principal Chief John Ross Encouraging the Cherokee to Ally Themselves with the Confederate States of America." © 2001 by Ken Martin. Available at cherokeehistory.com/index.html.

DOCUMENT 16.2

Declaration by the People of the Cherokee Nation of the Causes Which Have Impelled Them to Unite Their Fortunes with Those of the Confederate States of America

When circumstances beyond their control compel one people to sever the ties which have long existed between them and another state or confederacy, and to contract new alliances and establish new relations for the security of their rights and liberties, it is fit that they should publicly declare the reasons by which their action is justified.

The Cherokee people had its origin in the South; its institutions are similar to those of the Southern States, and their interests identical with theirs. Long since it accepted the protection of the United States of America, contracted with them treaties of alliance and friendship, and allowed themselves to be to a great extent governed by their laws.

In peace and war they have been faithful to their engagements with the United States. With much of hardship and injustice to complain of, they resorted to no other means than solicitation and argument to obtain redress. Loyal and obedient to the laws and the stipulations of their treaties, they served under the flag of the United States, shared the common dangers, and were entitled to a share in the common glory, to gain which their blood was freely shed on the battle-field.

When the dissentions between the Southern and Northern States culminated in a separation of State after State from the Union, they watched the progress of events with anxiety and consternation. While their institutions and the contiguity of their territory to the States of necessarily their own cause, their treaties had been made with the United States, and they felt the utmost reluctance even in appearance to violate their engagements or set at naught the obligations of good faith.

Conscious that they were a people few in numbers compared with either of the contending parties, and that their country might with no considerable force be easily overrun and devastated and desolation and ruin be the result if they took up arms for either side, their authorities determined that no other course was consistent with the dictates of prudence or could secure the safety of their people and immunity from the horrors of a war waged by an invading enemy than a strict neutrality, and in this decision they were sustained by a majority of the nation.

That policy was accordingly adopted and faithfully adhered to. Early in the month of June of the present year the authorities of the nation declined to enter into negotiations for an alliance with the Confederate States, and protested against the occupation of the Cherokee country by their troops, or any other violation of their neutrality. No act was allowed that could be construed by the United States to be a violation of the faith of treaties.

But Providence rules the destinies of nations, and events, by inexorable necessity, overrule human resolutions. The number of the Confederate States has increased to eleven, and their Government is firmly established and consolidated. Maintaining in the field an army of 200,000 men, the war became for them but a succession of victories. Disclaiming any intention to invade the Northern States, they sought only to repel invaders from their own soil and to secure the right of governing themselves. They claimed only the privilege asserted by the Declaration of American Independence, and on which the right of the Northern States themselves to self-government is founded, of altering their

Source: Ken Martin, *History of the Cherokee*, "Declaration of Ratification of the Treaty with the Confederate States of America by the Cherokee National Committee with Concurrence of the National Council and Approval of Chief John Ross." © 2001 by Ken Martin. Available at cherokeehistory.com/index.html.

form of government when it became no longer tolerable and establishing new forms for the security of their liberties.

Throughout the Confederate States we saw this great revolution effected without violence or the suspension of the laws or the closing of the courts. The military power was nowhere placed above the civil authorities. None were seized and imprisoned at the mandate of arbitrary power. All division among the people disappeared, and the determination became unanimous that there should never again be any union with the Northern States. Almost as one man all who were able to bear arms rushed to the defense of an invaded country, and nowhere has it been found necessary to compel men to serve or to enlist mercenaries by the offer of extraordinary bounties.

But in the Northern States the Cherokee people saw with alarm a violated Constitution, all civil liberty put in peril, and all the rules of civilized warfare and the dictates of common humanity and decency unhesitatingly disregarded. In States which still adhered to the Union a military despotism has displaced the civil power and the laws became silent amid arms. Free speech and almost free thought became a crime. The right to the writ of habeas corpus, guaranteed by the Constitution, disappeared at the nod of a Secretary or a general of the lowest grade. The mandate of the Chief Justice of the Supreme Court was set at naught by the military power, and this outrage on common right approved by a President sworn to support the Constitution. War on the largest scale was waged, and the immense bodies of troops called into the field in the absence of any law warranting it under the pretense of suppressing unlawful combination of men. The humanities of war, which even barbarians respect, were no longer thought worthy to be observed. Foreign mercenaries and the scum of cities and the inmates of prisons were enlisted and organized into regiments and brigades and sent into Southern States to aid in subjugating a people struggling for freedom, to burn, to plunder, and to commit the basest of outrages on women; while the heels of armed tyranny trod upon the necks of Maryland and Missouri, and men of the highest character and position were incarcerated upon suspicion and without process of law in jails, in forts, and in prison-ships, and even women were imprisoned by the arbitrary order of a President and Cabinet ministers; while the press ceased to be free, the publication of newspapers was suspended and their issues seized and destroyed; the officers and men taken prisoners in battle were allowed to remain in captivity by the refusal of their Government to consent to an exchange of prisoners; as they had left their dead on more than one field of battle that had witnessed their defeat to be buried and their wounded to be cared for by Southern hands.

Whatever causes the Cherokee people may have had in the past to complain of some of the Southern States, they cannot but feel that their interests and their destiny are inseparably connected with those of the South. The war now raging is a war of Northern cupidity and fanaticism against the institution of African servitude; against the commercial freedom of the South, and against the political freedom of the States, and its objects are to annihilate the sovereignty of those States and utterly change the nature of the Gen. Government.

The Cherokee people and their neighbors were warned before the war commenced that the first object of the party which now holds the powers of government of the United States would be to annul the institution of slavery in the whole Indian country, and make it what they term free territory and after a time a free State; and they have been also warned by the fate which has befallen those of their race in Kansas, Nebraska, and Oregon that at no distant day they too would be compelled to surrender their country at the demand of Northern rapacity, and be content with an extinct nationality, and with reserves of limited extent for individuals, of which their people would soon be despoiled by speculators, if not plundered unscrupulously by the State.

Urged by these considerations, the Cherokees, long divided in opinion, became unanimous, and like their brethren, the Creeks, Seminoles, Choctaws, and Chickasaws, determined, by the undivided voice of a Gen. Convention of all the people, held at Tahlequah, on the 21st day of August, in the present year, to make common cause with the South and share its fortunes.

In now carrying this resolution into effect and consummating a treaty of alliance and friendship with the Confederate States of America the Cherokee people declares that it has been faithful and loyal to its engagements with the United States until, by placing its safety and even its national existence in imminent peril, those States have released them from those engagements.

Menaced by a great danger, they exercise the inalienable right of self-defense, and declare themselves a free people, independent of the Northern States of America, and at war with them by their own act. Obeying the dictates of prudence and providing for the general safety and welfare, confident of the rectitude of their intentions and true to the obligations of duty and honor, they accept the issue thus forced upon them, unite their fortunes now and forever with those of the Confederate States, and take up arms for the common cause, and with entire confidence in the justice of that cause and with a firm reliance upon Divine Providence, will resolutely abide the consequences.

Tahlequah, C. N.
October 28, 1861.

THOMAS PEGG,
President National Committee.

JOSHUA ROSS,
Clerk National Committee.

Concurred.

LACY MOUSE,
Speaker of Council.

THOMAS B. WOLFE,
Clerk Council.

Approved.

JNO. ROSS.

DOCUMENT 16.3

The First Morrill Act

An Act Donating Public Lands to the several States and Territories which may provide Colleges for the Benefit of Agriculture and Mechanic Arts.

Be it enacted by the Senate and House of Representatives of the United States of America in Congress assembled, That there be granted to the several States, for the purposes hereinafter mentioned, an amount of public land, to be apportioned to each State a quantity equal to thirty thousand acres for each senator and representative in Congress to which the States are respectively entitled by the apportionment under the census of eighteen hundred and sixty: *Provided,* That no mineral lands shall be selected or purchased under the provisions of this Act.

* * *

Sec. 4

That all moneys derived from the sale of lands aforesaid by the States to which lands are apportioned and from the sales of land scrip hereinbefore provided for shall be invested in bonds of the United States or of the States or some other safe bonds; or the same may be invested by the States having no State bonds in any manner after the legislatures of such States shall have assented thereto and engaged that such funds shall yield a fair and reasonable rate of return, to be fixed by the State legislatures, and that the principal thereof shall forever remain unimpaired: *Provided,* That the moneys so invested or loaned shall constitute a perpetual fund, the capital of which shall remain forever undiminished (except so far as may be provided in section 5 of this Act), and the interest of which shall be inviolably appropriated, by each State which may take and claim the benefit of this Act, to the endowment, support, and maintenance of at least one college where the leading object shall be, without excluding other scientific and classical studies and including military tactics, to teach such branches of learning as are related to agriculture and the mechanic arts, in such manner as the legislatures of the States may respectively prescribe, in order to

Source: Excerpted from the *First Morrill Act,* Act of July 2, 1862, chap. 130, 12 Stat. 503, 7 U.S.C. 301 et seq.

promote the liberal and practical education of the industrial classes on the several pursuits and professions in life.

* * *

Sixth.

No State while in a condition of rebellion or insurrection against the government of the United States shall be entitled to the benefit of this act.

DOCUMENT 16.4

Laws of War: General Orders No. 100

Instructions for the Government of Armies of the United States in the Field

Prepared by Francis Lieber, promulgated as General Orders No. 100 by President Lincoln, 24 April 1863.

The text below is reprinted from the edition of the United States Government Printing Office of 1898; and reprinted in Schindler & Toman, eds., *The Laws of Armed Conflicts.*

* * *

Article 11.

The law of war does not only disclaim all cruelty and bad faith concerning engagements concluded with the enemy during the war, but also the breaking of stipulations solemnly contracted by the belligerents in time of peace, and avowedly intended to remain in force in case of war between the contracting powers.

It disclaims all extortions and other transactions for individual gain; all acts of private revenge, or connivance at such acts.

Offenses to the contrary shall be severely punished, and especially so if committed by officers.

* * *

Article 14.

Military necessity, as understood by modern civilized nations, consists in the necessity of those measures which are indispensable for securing the ends of the war, and which are lawful according to the modern law and usages of war. . . .

Instructions for the Government of Armies of the United States in the Field, prepared by Francis Lieber, LL.D., Originally Issued as General Orders No. 100, Adjutant General's Office, 1863, Washington 1898: Government Printing Office.

Article 15.

Military necessity admits of all direct destruction of life or limb of armed enemies, and of other persons whose destruction is incidentally unavoidable in the armed contests of the war; it allows of the capturing of every armed enemy, and every enemy of importance to the hostile government, or of peculiar danger to the captor; it allows of all destruction of property, and obstruction of the ways and channels of traffic, travel, or communication, and of all withholding of sustenance or means of life from the enemy, of the appropriation of whatever an enemy's country affords necessary for the subsistence and safety of the army, and of such deception as does not involve the breaking of good faith either positively pledged, regarding agreements entered into during the war, or supposed by the modern law of war to exist. Men who take up arms against one another in public war do not cease on this account to be moral beings, responsible to one another and to God.

Article 16.

Military necessity does not admit of cruelty—that is, the infliction of suffering for the sake of suffering or for revenge, nor of maiming or wounding except in fight, nor of torture to extort confessions. It does not admit of the use of poison in any way, nor of the wanton devastation of a district. It admits of deception, but disclaims acts of perfidy; and, in general, military necessity does not include any act of hostility which makes the return to peace unnecessarily difficult.

Article 17.

War is not carried on by arms alone. It is lawful to starve the hostile belligerent, armed or unarmed, so that it leads to the speedier subjection of the enemy.

* * *

Article 21.

The citizen or native of a hostile country is thus an enemy, as one of the constituents of the hostile state or nation, and as such is subjected to the hardships of the war.

Article 22.

Nevertheless, as civilization has advanced during the last centuries, so has likewise steadily advanced, especially in war on land, the distinction between the private individual belonging to a hostile country and the hostile country itself, with its men in arms. The principle has been more and more acknowledged that the unarmed citizen is to be spared in person, property, and honor as much as the exigencies of war will admit.

Article 23.

Private citizens are no longer murdered, enslaved, or carried off to distant parts, and the inoffensive individual is as little disturbed in his private relations as the commander of the hostile troops can afford to grant in the overruling demands of a vigorous war.

Article 24.

The almost universal rule in remote times was, and continues to be with barbarous armies, that the private individual of the hostile country is destined to suffer every privation of liberty and protection, and every disruption of family ties. Protection was, and still is with uncivilized people, the exception.

Article 25.

In modern regular wars of the Europeans, and their descendants in other portions of the globe, protection of the inoffensive citizen of the hostile country is the rule; privation and disturbance of private relations are the exceptions.

* * *

Article 27.

The law of war can no more wholly dispense with retaliation than can the law of nations, of which it is a branch. Yet civilized nations acknowledge retaliation as the sternest feature of war. A reckless enemy often leaves to his opponent no other means of securing himself against the repetition of barbarous outrage.

Article 28.

Retaliation will, therefore, never be resorted to as a measure of mere revenge, but only as a means of protective retribution, and moreover, cautiously and unavoidably; that is to say, retaliation shall only be resorted to after careful inquiry into the real occurrence, and the character of the misdeeds that may demand retribution.

Unjust or inconsiderate retaliation removes the belligerents farther and farther from the mitigating rules of regular war, and by rapid steps leads them nearer to the internecine wars of savages.

* * *

Article 43.

Therefore, in a war between the United States and a belligerent which admits of slavery, if a person held in bondage by that belligerent be captured by or come as a fugitive under the protection of the military forces of the United States, such person is immediately entitled to the rights and privileges of a freeman. To return such person into slavery would amount to enslaving a free person, and neither the United States nor any officer under their authority can enslave any human being. Moreover, a person so made free by the law of war is under the shield of the law of nations, and the former owner or State can have, by the law of postliminy, no belligerent lien or claim of service.

Article 44.

All wanton violence committed against persons in the invaded country, all destruction of property not commanded by the authorized officer, all robbery, all pillage or sacking, even after taking a place by main force, all rape, wounding, maiming, or killing of such inhabitants, are prohibited under the penalty of death, or such other severe punishment as may seem adequate for the gravity of the offense.

A soldier, officer or private, in the act of committing such violence, and disobeying a superior ordering him to abstain from it, may be lawfully killed on the spot by such superior.

* * *

Article 51.

If the people of that portion of an invaded country which is not yet occupied by the enemy, or of the whole country, at the approach of a hostile army, rise, under a duly authorized levy en masse to resist the invader, they are now treated as public enemies, and, if captured, are prisoners of war.

Article 52.

No belligerent has the right to declare that he will treat every captured man in arms of a levy en masse as a brigand or bandit. If, however, the people of a country, or any portion of the same, already occupied by an army, rise against it, they are violators of the laws of war, and are not entitled to their protection.

* * *

Article 60.

It is against the usage of modern war to resolve, in hatred and revenge, to give no quarter. No body of troops has the right to declare that it will not give, and therefore will not expect, quarter; but a commander is permitted to direct his troops to give no quarter, in great straits, when his own salvation makes it impossible to cumber himself with prisoners.

Article 61.

Troops that give no quarter have no right to kill enemies already disabled on the ground, or prisoners captured by other troops.

Article 62.

All troops of the enemy known or discovered to give no quarter in general, or to any portion of the army, receive none.

Article 63.

Troops who fight in the uniform of their enemies, without any plain, striking, and uniform mark of distinction of their own, can expect no quarter.

* * *

Article 68.

Modern wars are not internecine wars, in which the killing of the enemy is the object. The destruction of the enemy in modern war, and, indeed, modern war itself, are means to obtain that object of the belligerent which lies beyond the war.

Unnecessary or revengeful destruction of life is not lawful.

* * *

Article 81.

Partisans are soldiers armed and wearing the uniform of their army, but belonging to a corps which acts detached from the main body for the purpose of making inroads into the territory occupied by the enemy. If captured, they are entitled to all the privileges of the prisoner of war.

Article 82.

Men, or squads of men, who commit hostilities, whether by fighting, or inroads for destruction or plunder, or by raids of any kind, without commission, without being part and portion of the organized hostile army, and without sharing continuously in the war, but who do so with intermitting returns to their homes and avocations, or with the occasional assumption of the semblance of peaceful pursuits, divesting themselves of the character or appearance of soldiers—such men, or squads of men, are not public enemies, and, therefore, if captured, are not entitled to the privileges of prisoners of war, but shall be treated summarily as highway robbers or pirates.

* * *

SECTION X: INSURRECTION–CIVIL WAR–REBELLION

Article 149.

Insurrection is the rising of people in arms against their government, or a portion of it, or against one or more of its laws, or against an officer or officers of the government. It may be confined to mere armed resistance, or it may have greater ends in view.

Article 150.

Civil war is war between two or more portions of a country or state, each contending for the mastery of the whole, and each claiming to be the legitimate government. The term is also sometimes applied to war of rebellion, when the rebellious provinces or portions of the state are contiguous to those containing the seat of government.

Article 151.

The term rebellion is applied to an insurrection of large extent, and is usually a war between the legitimate government of a country and portions of provinces of the same who seek to throw off their allegiance to it and set up a government of their own.

Article 152.

When humanity induces the adoption of the rules of regular war to ward rebels, whether the adoption is partial or entire, it does in no way whatever imply a partial or complete acknowledgement of their government, if they have set up one, or of them, as an independent and sovereign power. Neutrals have no right to make the adoption of the rules of war by the assailed government toward rebels the ground of their own acknowledgment of the revolted people as an independent power.

Article 153.

Treating captured rebels as prisoners of war, exchanging them, concluding of cartels, capitulations, or other warlike agreements with them; addressing officers of a rebel army by the rank they may have in the same; accepting flags of truce; or, on the other hand, proclaiming Martial Law in their territory, or levying war-taxes or forced loans, or doing any other act sanctioned or demanded by the law and usages of public war between sovereign belligerents, neither proves nor establishes an acknowledgment of the rebellious people, or of the government which they may have erected, as a public or sovereign power. Nor does the adoption of the rules of war toward rebels imply an engagement with them extending beyond the limits of these rules. It is victory in the field that ends the strife and settles the future relations between the contending parties.

Article 154.

Treating, in the field, the rebellious enemy according to the law and usages of war has never prevented the legitimate government from trying the leaders of the rebellion or chief rebels for high treason, and from treating them accordingly, unless they are included in a general amnesty.

Article 155.

All enemies in regular war are divided into two general classes—that is to say, into combatants and noncombatants, or unarmed citizens of the hostile government.

The military commander of the legitimate government, in a war of rebellion, distinguishes between the loyal citizen in the revolted portion of the country and the disloyal citizen. The disloyal citizens may further be classified into those citizens known to sympathize with the rebellion without positively aiding it, and those who, without taking up arms, give positive aid and comfort to the rebellious enemy without being bodily forced thereto.

Article 156.

Common justice and plain expediency require that the military commander protect the manifestly loyal citizens, in revolted territories, against the hardships of the war as much as the common misfortune of all war admits.

The commander will throw the burden of the war, as much as lies within his power, on the disloyal citizens, of the revolted portion or province, subjecting them to a stricter police than the noncombatant enemies have to suffer in regular war; and if he deems it appropriate, or if his government demands of him that every citizen shall, by an oath of allegiance, or by some other manifest act, declare his fidelity to the legitimate government, he may expel, transfer, imprison, or fine the revolted citizens who refuse to pledge themselves anew as citizens obedient to the law and loyal to the government.

Whether it is expedient to do so, and whether reliance can be placed upon such oaths, the commander or his government have the right to decide.

Article 157.

Armed or unarmed resistance by citizens of the United States against the lawful movements of their troops is levying war against the United States, and is therefore treason.

DOCUMENT 16.5

The Barlow/Gordon Incident at Gettysburg

John B. Gordon

. . . The Confederates were stubbornly contesting every foot of ground, but the Southern left was slowly yielding. A few moments more and the day's battle might have been ended by the complete turning of Lee's flank. I was ordered to move at once to the aid of the heavily pressed Confederates. With a ringing yell, my command rushed upon the line posted to protect the Union right. Here occurred a hand-to-hand struggle. That protecting Union line once broken left my command not only on the right flank, but obliquely in rear of it. Any troops that were ever marshalled would, under like conditions, have been as surely and swiftly shattered. There was no alternative for Howard's men except to break and fly, or to throw down their arms and surrender. Under the concentrated fire from front and flank, the marvel is that any escaped. In the midst of the wild disorder in his ranks, and through a storm of bullets, a Union officer was seeking to rally his men for a final stand. He, too, went down, pierced by a Minié ball.

Riding forward with my rapidly advancing lines, I discovered that brave officer lying upon his back, with the July sun pouring its rays into his pale face. He was surrounded by the Union dead, and his own life seemed to be rapidly ebbing out. Quickly dismounting and lifting his head, I gave him water from my canteen, asked his name and the character of his wounds. He was Major-General Francis C. Barlow, of New York, and of Howard's corps. The ball had entered his body in front and passed out near the spinal cord, paralyzing him in legs and arms. Neither of us had the remotest thought that he could possibly survive many hours. I summoned several soldiers who were looking after the wounded, and directed them to place him upon a litter and carry him to the shade in the rear. Before parting, he asked me to take from his pocket a package of letters and destroy them. They were from his wife. He had but one request to make of me. That request was that if I should live to the end of the war and should ever meet Mrs. Barlow, I would tell her of our meeting on the field of Gettysburg and of his thoughts of her in his last moments. He wished me to assure her that he died doing his duty at the front, that he was willing to give his life for his country, and that his deepest regret was that he must die without looking upon her face again.

I learned that Mrs. Barlow was with the Union army, and near the battlefield. When it is remembered how closely Mrs. Gordon followed me, it will not be difficult to realize that my sympathies were especially stirred by the announcement that his wife was so near him. Passing through the day's battle unhurt, I despatched at its close, under flag of truce, the promised message to Mrs.

Source: Excerpted from General John B. Gordon, *Reminiscences of the Civil War.* © 1904. New York: Charles Scribner's Sons, pp. 151–153.

Barlow. I assured her that if she wished to come through the lines she should have safe escort to her husband's side.

In the desperate encounters of the two succeeding days, and the retreat of Lee's army, I thought no more of Barlow, except to number him with the noble dead of the two armies who had so gloriously met their fate. The ball, however, had struck no vital point, and Barlow slowly recovered, though this fact was wholly unknown to me. The following summer, in battle near Richmond, my kinsman with the same initials, General J. B. Gordon of North Carolina, was killed. Barlow, who had recovered, saw the announcement of his death, and entertained no doubt that he was the Gordon whom he had met on the field of Gettysburg. To me, therefore, Barlow was dead; to Barlow, I was dead.

Nearly fifteen years passed before either of us was undeceived. During my second term in the United States Senate, the Hon. Clarkson Potter, of New York, was a member of the House of Representatives. He invited me to dinner in Washington to meet a General Barlow who had served in the Union army. Potter knew nothing of the Gettysburg incident. I had heard that there was another Barlow in the Union army, and supposed, of course, that it was this Barlow with whom I was to dine. Barlow had a similar reflection as to the Gordon he was to meet. Seated at Clarkson Potter's table, I asked Barlow: "General, are you related to the Barlow who was killed at Gettysburg?" He replied: "Why, I am the man, sir. Are you related to the Gordon who killed me?" "I am the man, sir," I responded. No words of mine can convey any conception of the emotions awakened by those startling announcements. Nothing short of an actual resurrection from the dead could have amazed either of us more. Thenceforward, until his untimely death in 1896, the friendship between us which was born amidst the thunders of Gettysburg was greatly cherished by both.

Editors' note: Though there is considerable evidence that John B. Gordon's account of his encounter with Francis C. Barlow was amplified by his imagination, that "creative" process produced a symbolic story of reconciliation that was published and widely shared in the years after the guns of Gettysburg were silent.

DOCUMENT 16.6

The Arithmetic of Suffering

Some Numbers Associated with the Pain of the Civil War

For three days in July, 1863, one of the decisive battles of the war raged on the outskirts of Gettysburg, Pennsylvania. Though the exact number of casualties (both killed and wounded) may never be known, estimates commonly put Northern casualties at more than 23,000 and Southern casualties from 25,000 to 28,000. Working with simple averages and crude numbers, it would not be an overstatement to say that both armies together sustained 50,000 casualties.

Given that fighting was not continuous, and that roughly 30 hours of actual combat took place in those three days, what would be the rate of casualties per hour sustained by both sides? How many were killed or wounded per minute of combat?

In 1860 the population of the United States was roughly 31 million people, with an average household having 5.28 people. It is estimated that the total number of casualties (killed and wounded on both North and South) was as many as 892,397 people. Given the average size of families then, how many people and what percentage of the total population might have been related to someone killed or wounded in the war?

DOCUMENT 16.7

The Diary of Carrie Berry

Editors' note: The following passages were taken from the diary of Carrie Berry, a 10-year-old resident of Atlanta, August 1, 1864–January 4, 1865. They provide a firsthand account of war through the eyes of a child.

Aug. 3. Wednesday. This was my birthday. I was ten years old, But I did not have a cake times were too hard so I celebrated with ironing. I hope by my next birthday we will have peace in our land so that I can have a nice dinner.

* * *

Fri. Nov. 4. Nothing of interest has happened to day. It is the repote that the federals are going to have to leave Atlanta and we are afraid that we will have to leave too.

* * *

Sun Nov. 7. Every boddie seems to be in confusion. The black wimmen are running around trying to get up north for fear that the Rebels will come in and take them.

* * *

Sat. Nov. 12. We were fritened almost to death last night. Some mean soldiers set several houses on fire in different parts of the town. I could not go to sleep for fear that they would set our house on fire. We all dred the next few days to come for they said that they would set the last house on fire if they had to leave this place.

Source: Diary of Carrie Berry, Atlanta History Center, manuscript. Available at americancivilwar.com/women/carrie_berry.html. This is part of a larger excerpt taken from the *Diary of Carrie Berry*, a 10-year-old resident of Atlanta, Aug. 1, 1864–Jan. 4, 1865. It was derived from a typed copy of the original manuscript, provided by the Atlanta History Center to Duke University.

Sun. Nov. 13. The federal soldiers have ben coming to day and burning houses and I have ben looking at them come in nearly all day.

Mon. Nov. 14. They came burning Atlanta to day. We all dread it because they say that they will burn the last house before they stop. We will dread it.

Tues. Nov. 15. This has ben a dreadful day. Things have ben burning all around us. We dread to night because we do not know what moment that they will set our house on fire. We have had a gard a little while after dinner and we feel a little more protected.,

Wed. Nov. 16. Oh what a night we had. They came burning the store house and about night it looked like the whole town was on fire. We all set up all night. If we had not set up our house would have ben burnt up for the fire was very near and the soldiers were going around setting houses on fire where they were not watched. They behaved very badly. They all left the town about one o'clock this evening and we were glad when they left for no body know what we have suffered since they came in.

* * *

Tues. Nov. 22. It is just a week to day since the federals were burning. Papa and Mama say that they feel very poor. We have not got anything but our little house. It is still very cold.

* * *

Wed. Nov. 30. We have ben resting to day. The cittizens are still coming in and it wont be very long untill they get the railroad fixed up from here to Macon and then I hope I can see Grandma.

* * *

Wed. Dec. 7. This has ben a election day for Mayor and council men but the election was broken up. I had a little sister this morning at eight o'clock and Mama gave her to me. I think its very pretty. I had to cook breakfast and dinner and supper.

* * *

Tues. Dec. 20. I have ben buisy making presents all day. I went down to Mrs. Lesters to make Mamas. Miss Matt helped me. I think it is so pretty. I fear we will not get through with our presents Christmas is getting so near.

Wed. Dec. 21. Papa has to go back to Macon next week and we fear he will be put in servis. He has ben buisy all day making me a pair of shoes. I do hope he will get off, the people are treating the citizens so mean that stayed here with the yankees.

Thurs. Dec. 22. We went to get our Christmas tree this evening. It was very cold but we did not feel it we were so excited about it.

Fri. Dec. 23. I went down to Mrs. Lesters and Ella and me planted the tree and finished making the last presents. I came home and strained some pumpkins to make some pies for Christmas.

Sat. Dec. 24. I have been buisy to day making cakes to trim the tree and Ella and I have it all ready trimed and we are all going to night to see it. I think it looks very pretty. We will be sorry when it is all over.

Sun. Dec. 25, 1864. We all went down last night to see the tree and how pretty it looked. The room was full of ladies and children and Cap. gave us music on the pianno and tried to do all he could to make us enjoy our selves and we did have a merry time. All came home perfectly satisfied.

This has ben a cold dark day but we all went down to see how the tree looked in the day time but it was not as pretty as at night.

* * *

Sunday. Jan. 1. 1865. This is New Year day. I woke up this morning and cant Mama New Years gift but did not get anything the times is too hard. I stayed at home untill evening and then I went down to Mrs. Lesters and I found there and we played around there and then we came around home and we sat down and wrote a little letter and then Ella and Anna went home.

Mon. Jan. 2. We all started to school this morning to Miss Mattie. Ella, me and Buddie are studying arithmetic, spelling, reading and geography. We are all trying to see which will learn the most.

DOCUMENT 16.8

The Black Cottage

Robert Frost

That was the father as he went to war.
She always, when she talked about the war,
Sooner or later came and leaned, half knelt,
Against the lounge beside it, though I doubt
If such unlifelike lines kept power to stir
Anything in her after all the years.
He fell at Gettysburg or Fredericksburg,
I ought to know—it makes a difference which:
Fredericksburg wasn't Gettysburg, of course.
But what I'm getting to is how forsaken
A little cottage this has always seemed;
Since she went, more than ever, but before—

Source: Excerpted from Robert Frost, "The Black Cottage," *The Poetry of Robert Frost: The Collected Poems, Complete and Unabridged,* ed., Edward C. Lathem, (New York: Holt, Rinehart & Winston, 1969), pp. 55–59.

I don't mean altogether by the lives
That had gone out of it, the father first,
Then the two sons, till she was left alone.
(Nothing could draw her after those two sons.
She valued the considerate neglect
She had at some cost taught them after years.)
I mean by the world's having passed it by—
As we almost got by this afternoon.
It always seems to me a sort of mark
To measure how far fifty years have brought us.
Why not sit down if you are in no haste?
These doorsteps seldom have a visitor.
The warping boards pull out their own old nails
With none to tread and put them in their place.
She had her own idea of things, the old lady.
And she liked talk. She had seen Garrison
And Whittier, and had her story of them.
One wasn't long in learning that she thought,
Whatever else the Civil War was for,
It wasn't just to keep the States together,
Nor just to free the slaves, though it did both
She wouldn't have believed those ends enough
To have given outright for them all she gave.
Her giving somehow touched the principle
That all men are created free and equal.
And to hear her quaint phrases—so removed
From the world's view today of all those things.
That's a hard mystery of Jefferson's.
What did he mean? Of course the easy way
Is to decide it simply isn't true.
It may not be. I heard a fellow say so.
But never mind, the Welshman got it planted
Where it will trouble us a thousand years.
Each age will have to reconsider it.
You couldn't tell her what the West was saying,
And what the South, to her serene belief.
She had some art of hearing and yet not
Hearing the latter wisdom of the world.
White was the only race she ever knew.
Black she had scarcely seen, and yellow never.
But how could they be made so very unlike
By the same hand working in the same stuff?
She had supposed the war decided that.
What are you going to do with such a person?
Strange how such innocence gets its own way. . . .

17

Binding the Wounds

In the early days of the Civil War, there were a few persons so confident of a Union victory they began to consider appropriate policies to deal with rebellious states and citizens. The preservation of life, liberty, and the pursuit of happiness for both the victorious and the vanquished and the entity known as the United States presented problematic issues.

The first document in this chapter suggests there were those inclined to be stern with the rebellious South. The selection from the "Southern Homestead Act" raises issues regarding the extension to the south of previously enacted and applied federal policies, the possible punishment of Southern plantation owners, and opportunities for newly freed slaves to acquire land. African Americans received citizenship through the provisions of the 13th and 14th Amendments. It is important to understand that in the early days of the American Republic, Congress passed the first federal naturalization act (1790), which barred nonwhites from American citizenship and relegated citizenship policies in general to the individual states. Hence, the 14th Amendment broke tradition in two ways—creating an American citizenship by federal law and central government activity as well as conferring citizenship on nonwhites en masse.

Federal land policies had long been based on making relatively cheap land available to farmers as both a positive economic and social benefit. With few exceptions African Americans had been shackled to a tenuous dependent status and excluded from the process or the ability to become landowners. The relationship between land and independence had become so obvious, it was only natural that, in the aftermath of the Civil War, many could embrace the ability to acquire land and become independent farmers as the bridge by which Black Americans could join the American democratic experiment as equal partners. General Rufus Saxton had been assigned responsibilities by General Sherman to find ways of implanting freed slaves on southern soil to empower and sustain themselves as freemen. Could the experiment succeed or was it doomed to failure? Despite the smoothness of Henry W. Grady's views for a new southern society, an older South, with deep political, social and cultural roots, envisioned a less-than-equal partnership between the new Southerner and African American citizens.

DOCUMENT 17.1

The Treatment of the South

William T. Sherman

September 1863

. . . It seems to me in contemplating the past two years history, all the people of our country north, south, east & west have been undergoing a Salutary Political Schooling, learning lessons which might have been taught by the History of other People; but we had all become so wise in our own conceit, that we would only learn by actual experience of our own.

The people even of small & unimportant localities north as well as south, had reasoned themselves into the belief that their opinions were superior to the aggregated interest of the whole nation. Half our territorial nation rebelled on a doctrine of secession that they themselves now scorn, and a real numerical majority actually believed, that a little state was endowed with such sovereignty, that it could defeat the Policy of the Great Whole. I think the present war has exploded that notion, and were this war to cease now, the experience gained though dear would be worth the expense.

Another Great & important natural Truth is still in contest and can only be solved by War. Numerical majorities by vote is our Great Arbiter. Heretofore all have submitted to it in questions left open, but numerical majorities are not necessarily physical majorities. The South though numerically inferior, contend they can whip the Northern superiority of numbers, and therefore by natural Law are not bound to submit. This issue is the only real one, and in my judgment all else should be deferred to it. War alone can decide it, and it is the only question left to us as a People.

Can we whip the South? If we can, our numerical majority has both the natural and constitutional right to govern. If we cannot whip them they contend for the natural right to Select their own Government, and they have the argument. Our Armies must prevail over theirs, our officers, marshals and courts must penetrate into the innermost recesses of their Land before we have the natural right to demand their submission. I would banish all minor questions, and assert the broad doctrine that as a nation the United States has the Right and also the Physical Power to penetrate to every part of the National domain,

Source: From Brooks D. Simpson and Jean V. Berlin, eds., *Sherman's Civil War: Selected Correspondence of William T. Sherman, 1860–1865* (Chapel Hill: University of North Carolina Press, 1999), pp. 547–49.

and that we will do it—that we will do it in our own time and in our own way, that it makes no difference whether it be in one year, or two, or ten or twenty: that we will remove & destroy every obstacle, if need be take every life, every acre of land, every particle of property, every thing that to us seems proper, that we will not cease till the end is attained, that all who do not aid are enemies, and we will not account to them for our acts. If the People of the South oppose they do so at their peril, and if they stand by mere lookers on the domestic tragedy, they have no right to immunity, protection or share in the final Result.

I even believe and contend further, that in the North every member of the Nation is bound by both natural & constitutional Law to "maintain and defend the Government against all its opposers whomsoever." If they fail to do it, they are derelict, and can be punished, or deprived of all advantage arising from the labors of those who do—If any man north or south withholds his share of taxes, or physical assistance in this crisis of our History, he could and should be deprived of all voice in the future Elections of this country and might be banished or reduced to the condition of a Denizen of the Land.

War is upon us. None can deny it. It is not the act of the Government of the United States but of a Faction. The Government was forced to accept the issue or submit to a degradation fatal & disgraceful to all the Inhabitants. In accepting war it should be pure & simple as applied to the Belligerents. I would Keep it so, till all traces of war are effaced, till those who appealed to it are sick & tired of it, and come to the emblem of our Nation and Sue for Peace. I would not coax them, or even meet them half way, but make them so sick of war that Generations would pass before they would again appeal to it.

I know what I say, when I repeat that the insurgents of the South sneer at all overtures looking to their interest. They Scorn the alliance with Copperheads: they tell me to my face that they respect Grant, McPherson and our brave associates who fight manfully & well for a principle, but despise the Copperheads & sneaks, who profess friendship for the South, and opposition to the War, as mere covers to their Knavery & poltroonery.

God knows that I deplored this fratricidal war as much as any man living, but it is upon us a physical fact; and there is only one honorable issue from it. We must fight it out, army against army, and man against man, and I know and you Know, and civilians begin to realize the fact, that reconciliation and reconstruction will be easier through and by means of strong, well equipped & organised armies than through any species of conventions that can be framed. The issues are made & all discussion is out of place and ridiculous.

The Section of 30 pounder Parrott Rifles now drilling before my tent is a more convincing argument than the largest Democratic or Union meeting the State of New York could assemble at Albany: and a simple order of the War Department to draft enough men to fill our Skeleton Regiments would be more convincing as to our national perpetuity, than an humble pardon to Jeff Davis and all his misled host.

The only Government now needed or deserved by the States of Louisiana, Arkansas and Mississippi now exists in Grants Army. It needs simply enough privates to fill its Ranks, all else will follow in due season. This army has its well defined code of Laws and Practice, and can adapt itself to the wants and necessities of a city; the country, the Rivers, the Sea, indeed to all parts of this Land. It better subserves the interest and Policy of the General Government and the People prefer it to any weak or servile combination, that would at once from force of habit revive & perpetuate local prejudices and passions. The People of this country have forfeited all Right to a voice in the Councils of the Nation. They Know it and feel it, and in after years they will be the better citizens from the dear bought experience of the present Crisis. Let them learn now, and learn it well that good citizens must obey as well as command. Obedience to law, absolute yea even abject is the lesson that this war under Providence will teach the Free & enlightened American Citizen. As a Nation we will be the better for it.

DOCUMENT 17.2

The Southern Homestead Act

An Act for the Disposal of the Public Lands for Homestead Actual Settlement in the States of Alabama, Mississippi, Louisiana, Arkansas, and Florida

Be it enacted by the Senate and House of Representatives of the United States of America, in Congress assembled, That from and after the passage of this act all the public lands in the States of Alabama, Mississippi, Louisiana, Arkansas, and Florida shall be disposed of according to the stipulations of the homestead law of twentieth May, eighteen hundred and sixty-two, entitled "An act to secure homesteads to actual settlers on the public domain," and the act supplemental thereto, approved twenty-first of March, eighteen hundred and sixty-four, but with this restriction, that until the expiration of two years from and after the passage of this act, no entry shall be made for more than a half-quarter section, or eighty acres; and in lieu of the sum of ten dollars required to be paid by the second section of said act, there shall be paid the sum of five dollars at the time of the issue of each patent; and that the public lands in said States shall be disposed of in no other manner after the passage of this act: *Provided,* That no distinction or discrimination shall be made in the construction or execution of this act on account of race or color: *And provided further,* That no mineral lands shall be liable to entry and settlement under its provisions.

Section 2.

And be it further enacted, That section second of the above-cited homestead law, entitled " An act to secure homesteads to actual settlers on the public

Source: The Southern Homestead Act, Thirty-ninth Congress, Session 1, Chap. 127, 1866, "An Act for the Disposal of the Public Lands for Homestead Actual Settlement in the States of Alabama, Mississippi, Louisiana, Arkansas, and Florida" (U.S. Statutes at Large), pp. 66–67.

domain," approved May twentieth, eighteen hundred and sixty-two, be so amended as to read as follows: That the person applying for the benefit of this act shall, upon application to the register of the land office in which he or she is about to make such entry, make affidavit before the said register or receiver that he or she is the head of a family, or is twenty-one years or more of age, or shall have performed service in the army or navy of the United States, and that such application is made for his or her exclusive use and benefit, and that said entry is made for the purpose of actual settlement and cultivation, and not either directly or indirectly for the use or benefit of any other person or persons whomsoever; and upon filing the said affidavit with the register or receiver, and on payment of five dollars, when the entry is of not more than eighty acres, he or she shall thereupon be permitted to enter the amount of land specified: *Provided, however,* That no certificate shall be given, or patent issued therefor, until the expiration of five years from the date of such entry; and if, at the expiration of such time, or at any time within two years thereafter, the person making such entry, or, if he be dead, his widow; or in case of her death, his heirs or devisee; or in case of a widow making such entry, her heirs or devisee, in case of her death, shall prove by two credible witnesses that he, she, or they have resided upon or cultivated the same for the term of five years immediately succeeding the time of filing the affidavit aforesaid, and shall make affidavit that no part of said land has been alienated, and that he will bear true allegiance to the government of the United States; then, in such case, he, she, or they, if at that time a citizen of the United States, shall be entitled to a patent, as in other cases provided by law: *And provided further,* That in case of the death of both father and mother, leaving an infant child or children under twenty-one years of age, the right and fee shall enure to the benefit of said infant child or children; and the executor, administrator, or guardian may, at any time within two years after the death of the surviving parent, and in accordance with the laws of the State in which such children, for the time being, have their domicile, sell said land for the benefit of said infants, but for no other purpose; and the purchaser shall acquire the absolute title by the purchase, and be entitled to a patent from the United States on the payment of the office fees and sum of money herein specified: *Provided,* That until the first day of January, eighteen hundred and sixty-seven, any person applying for the benefit of this act shall, in addition to the oath, hereinbefore required, also make oath that he has not borne arms against the United States, or given aid and comfort to its enemies.

Section 3.

And be it further enacted, That all the provisions of the said homestead law, and the act amendatory thereof, approved March twenty-first, eighteen hundred and sixty-four, so far as the same may be applicable, except so far as the same are modified by the preceding sections of this act, are applied to and made part of this act as fully as if herein enacted and set forth.

Approved, June 21, 1866.

DOCUMENT 17.3

Fourteenth Amendment

Section 1.

All persons born or naturalized in the United States, and subject to the jurisdiction thereof, are citizens of the United States and of the state wherein they reside. No state shall make or enforce any law which shall abridge the privileges or immunities of citizens of the United States; nor shall any state deprive any person of life, liberty, or property, without due process of law; nor deny to any person within its jurisdiction the equal protection of the laws.

Section 2.

Representatives shall be apportioned among the several states according to their respective numbers, counting the whole number of persons in each state, excluding Indians not taxed. But when the right to vote at any election for the choice of electors for President and Vice President of the United States, Representatives in Congress, the executive and judicial officers of a state, or the members of the legislature thereof, is denied to any of the male inhabitants of such state, being twenty-one years of age, and citizens of the United States, or in any way abridged, except for participation in rebellion, or other crime, the basis of representation therein shall be reduced in the proportion which the number of such male citizens shall bear to the whole number of male citizens twenty-one years of age in such state.

Section 3.

No person shall be a Senator or Representative in Congress, or elector of President and Vice President, or hold any office, civil or military, under the United States, or under any state, who, having previously taken an oath, as a member of Congress, or as an officer of the United States, or as a member of any state legislature, or as an executive or judicial officer of any state, to support the Constitution of the United States, shall have engaged in insurrection or rebellion against the same, or given aid or comfort to the enemies thereof. But Congress may by a vote of two-thirds of each House, remove such disability.

Section 4.

The validity of the public debt of the United States, authorized by law, including debts incurred for payment of pensions and bounties for services in suppressing insurrection or rebellion, shall not be questioned. But neither the United States nor any state shall assume or pay any debt or obligation incurred in aid of insurrection or rebellion against the United States, or any claim for the loss or emancipation of any slave; but all such debts, obligations and claims shall be held illegal and void.

Section 5.

The Congress shall have power to enforce, by appropriate legislation, the provisions of this article.

DOCUMENT 17.4

Rufus Saxton, Testimony before Congress, 1866

Q. What is [the freedmen's] disposition in regard to purchasing land, and what is the disposition of the landowners in reference to selling land to Negroes?

A. The object which the freedman has most at heart is the purchase of land. They all desire to get small homesteads and to locate themselves upon them, and there is scarcely any sacrifice too great for them to make to accomplish this object. I believe it is the policy of the majority of the farm owners to prevent Negroes from becoming landholders. They desire to keep the Negroes landless, and as nearly in a condition of slavery as it is possible for them to do. I think that the former slaveholders know really less about the freedmen than any other class of people. The system of slavery has been one of concealment on the part of the Negro of all his feelings and impulses; and that feeling of concealment is so ingrained with the very constitution of the Negro that he deceives his former master on almost every point. The freedman has no faith in his former master, nor has his former owner any faith in the capacity of the freedman. A mutual distrust exists between them. But the freedman is ready and willing to contract to work for any northern man. One man from the North, a man of capital, who employed large numbers of freedmen, and paid them regularly, told me, as others have, that he desired no better laborers; that he considered them fully as easy to manage as Irish laborers. That was my own experience in employing several thousands of them in cultivating the soil. I have also had considerable experience in employing white labor, having, as quartermaster, frequently had large numbers of laborers under my control.

* * *

Q. If the Negro is put in possession of all his rights as a man, do you apprehend any danger of insurrection among them?

A. I do not; and I think that is the only thing which will prevent difficulty. I think if the Negro is put in possession of all his rights as a citizen and as a man, he will be peaceful, orderly, and self-sustaining as any other man or class of men, and that he will rapidly advance. . . .

* * *

Q. It has been suggested that, if the Negro is allowed to vote, he will be likely to vote on the side of his former master, and be inveigled in the support of a policy hostile to the government of the United States; do you share in that apprehension?

Source: "Testimony of Rufus Saxton," *Report of the Joint Committee on Reconstruction* (Washington, 1866).

A. I have positive information from Negroes, from the most intelligent freed-men in those States, those who are leaders among them, that they are thor-oughly loyal, and know their friends, and they will never be found voting on the side of oppression. . . . I think it vital to the safety and prosperity of the two races in the south that the Negro should immediately be put in pos-session of all his rights as a man; and that the word "color" should be left out of all laws, constitutions, and regulations for the people; I think it vital to the safety of the Union that this should be done.

DOCUMENT 17.5

The Perspective of Henry W. Grady

What shall the South do to be saved? Through what paths shall she reach the end? Through what travail, or what splendors, shall she give to the Union this section, its wealth garnered, its resources utilized, and its rehabilitation complete—and restore to the world this problem solved in such justice as the finite mind can measure, or finite hands administer?

In dealing with this I shall dwell on two points.

First, the duty of the South in its relation to the race problem.

Second, the duty of the South in relation to its no less unique and important industrial problem. . . .

What of the negro? This of him. I want no better friend than the black boy who was raised by my side, and who is now trudging patiently with downcast eyes and shambling figure through his lowly way in life. I want no sweeter mu-sic than the crooning of my old "mammy," now dead and gone to rest, as I heard it when she held me in her loving arms, and bending her old black face above me stole the cares from my brain, and led me smiling into sleep. I want no truer soul than that which moved the trusty slave, who for four years while my father fought with the armies that barred his freedom, slept every night at my mother's chamber door, holding her and her children as safe as if her hus-band stood guard, and ready to lay down his humble life on her threshold. His-tory has no parallel to the faith kept by the negro in the South during the war. Often five hundred negroes to a single white man, and yet through these dusky throngs the women and children walked in safety, and the unprotected homes rested in peace. Unmarshaled, the black battalions moved patiently to the fields in the morning to feed the armies their idleness would have starved, and at night gathered anxiously at the big house to "hear the news from marster," though conscious that his victory made their chains enduring. Everywhere humble and kindly; the bodyguard of the helpless; the rough companion of the little ones; the observant friend; the silent sentry in his lowly cabin; the shrewd counselor. And when the dead came home, a mourner at the open grave. A

Source: Joel Chandler Harris, *Life of Henry W. Grady, Including His Writings and Speeches, Memorial Volume* (New York: Cassell Publishing, 1890).

thousand torches would have disabled every Southern army, but not one was lighted. When the master going to a war in which slavery was involved said to his slave, "I leave my home and loved ones in your charge," the tenderness between man and master stood disclosed. And when the slave held that charge sacred through storm and temptation, he gave new meaning to faith and loyalty. I rejoice that when freedom came to him after years of waiting, it was all the sweeter because the black hands from which the shackles fell were stainless of a single crime against the helpless ones confided to his care.

My countrymen, right here the South must make a decision on which very much depends. Many wise men hold that the white vote of the South should divide, the color line be beaten down, and the southern States ranged on economic or moral questions as interest or belief demands. I am compelled to dissent from this view. The worst thing in my opinion that could happen is that the white people of the South should stand in opposing factions, with the vast mass of ignorant or purchasable negro votes between. Consider such a status. If the negroes were skillfully led,—and leaders would not be lacking,—it would give them the balance of power—a thing not to be considered. If their vote was not compacted, it would invite the debauching bid of factions, and drift surely to that which was the most corrupt and cunning. With the shiftless habit and irresolution of slavery days still possessing him, the negro voter will not in this generation, adrift from war issues, become a steadfast partisan through conscience or conviction. In every community there are colored men who redeem their race from this reproach, and who vote under reason. Perhaps in time the bulk of this race may thus adjust itself. But, through what long and monstrous periods of political debauchery this status would be reached, no tongue can tell.

The clear and unmistakable domination of the white race, dominating not through violence, not through party alliance, but through the integrity of its own vote and the largeness of its sympathy and justice through which it shall compel the support of the better classes of the colored race,—that is the hope and assurance of the South. Otherwise, the negro would be bandied from one faction to another. His credulity would be played upon, his cupidity tempted, his impulses misdirected, his passions inflamed. He would be forever in alliance with that faction which was most desperate and unscrupulous. Such a state would be worse than reconstruction, for then intelligence was banded, and its speedy triumph assured. But with intelligence and property divided— bidding and overbidding for place and patronage—irritation increasing with each conflict—the bitterness and desperation seizing every heart—political debauchery deepening, as each faction staked its all in the miserable game—there would be no end to this, until our suffrage was hopelessly sullied, our people forever divided, and our most sacred rights surrendered.

This problem is not only enduring, but it is widening. The exclusion of the Chinese is the first step in the revolution that shall save liberty and law and religion to this land, and in peace and order, not enforced on the gallows or at the bayonet's end, but proceeding from the heart of an harmonious people, shall secure in the enjoyment of these rights, and the control of this republic, the homogeneous people that established and has maintained it. The next step will be taken when some brave statesman, looking Demagogy in the face, shall move to call to the stranger at our gates, "Who comes here?" admitting every man who seeks a home, or honors our institutions, and whose habit and blood will run with the native current; but excluding all who seek to plant anarchy or to establish alien men or measures on our soil; and will then demand that the standard of our citizenship be lifted and the right of acquiring our suffrage be abridged. When that day comes, and God speed its coming, the position of the South will be fully understood, and everywhere approved. Until then, let us—giving the negro every right, civil and political, measured in that fullness the strong should always accord the weak—holding him in closer friendship and sympathy than he is held by those who would crucify us for his sake—realizing that on his prosperity ours depends—let us resolve that never by external pressure, or internal division, shall he establish domination, directly or indirectly, over that race that everywhere has maintained its supremacy. Let this resolution be cast on the lines of equity and justice. Let it be the pledge of honest, safe and impartial administration, and we shall command the support of the colored race itself, more dependent that any other on the bounty and protection of government. Let us be wise and patient, and we shall secure through its acquiescence what otherwise we should win through conflict, and hold in insecurity.

All this is no unkindness to the negro—but rather that he may be led in equal rights and in peace to his uttermost good. Not in sectionalism—for my heart beats true to the Union, to the glory of which your life and heart is pledged. Not in disregard of the world's opinion—for to render back this problem in the world's approval is the sum of my ambition, and the height of human achievement. Not in reactionary spirit—but rather to make clear that new and grander way up which the South is marching to higher destiny, and on which I would not halt her for all the spoils that have been gathered unto parties since Catiline conspired, and Caesar fought. Not in passion, my countrymen, but in reason—not in narrowness, but in breadth—that we may solve this problem in calmness and in truth, and lifting its shadows let perpetual sunshine pour down on two races, walking together in peace and contentment. Then shall this problem have proved our blessing, and the race that threatened our ruin work our salvation as it fills our fields with the best peasantry the world has ever seen. Then the South—putting behind her all the achievements of her past—and in war and in peace they beggar eulogy—may stand upright among the nations and challenge the judgment of man and the approval of God, in having worked out in their sympathy, and in His guidance, this last and surpassing miracle of human government. . . .

The South, under the rapid diversification of crops and diversification of industries, is thrilling with new life. As this new prosperity comes to us, it will bring no sweeter thought to me, and to you, my countrymen, I am sure, than that it adds not only to the comfort and happiness of our neighbors, but that it makes broader the glory and deeper the majesty, and more enduring the strength, of the Union which reigns supreme in our hearts. In this republic of ours is lodged the hope of free government on earth. Here God has rested the ark of his covenant with the sons of men. Let us—once estranged and thereby closer bound,—let us soar above all provincial pride and find our deeper inspirations in gathering the fullest sheaves into the harvest and standing the staunchest and most devoted of its sons as it lights the path and makes clear the way through which all the people of this earth shall come in God's appointed time. . . .

The world is a battle-field strewn with the wrecks of government and institutions, of theories and of faiths that have gone down in the ravage of years. On this field lies the South, sown with her problems. Upon the field swings the lanterns of God. Amid the carnage walks the Great Physician. Over the South he bends. "If ye but live until to-morrow's sundown ye shall endure, my countrymen." Let us for her sake turn our faces to the east and watch as the soldier watched for the coming sun. Let us staunch her wounds and hold steadfast. The sun mounts the skies. As it descends to us, minister to her and stand constant at her side for the sake of our children, and of generations unborn that shall suffer if she fails. And when the sun has gone down and the day of her probation has ended, and the stars have rallied her heart, the lanterns shall be swung over the field and the Great Physician shall lead her up, from trouble into content, from suffering into peace, from death to life. Let every man here pledge himself in this high and ardent hour, as I pledge myself and the boy that shall follow me; every man himself and his son, hand to hand and heart to heart, that in death and earnest loyalty, in patient painstaking and care, he shall watch her interest, advance her fortune, defend her fame and guard her honor as long as life shall last. Every man in the sound of my voice, under the deeper consecration he offers to the Union, will consecrate himself to the South. Have no ambition but to be first at her feet and last at her service. No hope but, after a long life of devotion, to sink to sleep in her bosom, and as a little child sleeps at his mother's breast and rests untroubled in the light of her smile.

With such consecrated service, what could we not accomplish; what riches we should gather for her; what glory and prosperity we should render to the Union; what blessings we should gather unto the universal harvest of humanity. As I think of it, a vision of surpassing beauty unfolds to my eyes. I see a South, the home of fifty millions of people, who rise up every day to call from blessed cities, vast hives of industry and of thrift; her country-sides the treasures from which their resources are drawn; her streams vocal with whirring spindles; her valleys tranquil in the white and gold of the harvest; her mountains showering down the music of bells, as her slow-moving flocks and herds go forth from their folds; her rulers honest and her people loving, and her homes happy and their hearthstones bright, and their waters still, and their pastures green, and her conscience clear; her wealth diffused and poor-houses empty, her churches earnest and all creeds lost in the gospel. Peace and sobriety walking hand in hand through her borders; honor in her homes; uprightness in her midst; plenty in her fields; straight and simple faith in the hearts of her sons and daughters; her two races walking together in peace and contentment; sunshine everywhere and all the time, and night falling on her generally as from the wings of the unseen dove.

DOCUMENT 17.6

Testimony of Benjamin Singleton

Washington, D.C., April 17, 1880, before the Senate Select Committee Investigating the "Negro Exodus from the Southern States"

Q. You have brought out 7,432 people from the South to Kansas?
A. Yes, sir; brought and sent.

* * *

Q. Yes; What was the cause of your going out, and in the first place how did you happen to go there, or to send these people there?
A. Well, my people, for the want of land—we needed land for our children—and their disadvantages—that caused my heart to grieve and sorrow; pity for my race, sir, that was coming down, instead of going up—that caused me to go to work for them. I sent out there perhaps in '66—perhaps so; or in '65, any way—my memory don't recollect which; and they brought back tolerable favorable reports; then I jacked up three or four hundred, and went into Southern Kansas, and found it was a good country, and I thought Southern Kansas was congenial to our nature, sir; and I formed a colony there, and bought about a thousand acres of ground—the colony did—my people.

* * *

Q. Tell us how these people are getting on in Kansas?
A. I am glad to tell you, sir.
Q. Have they any property now?
A. Yes; I have carried some people in there that when they got there they didn't have fifty cents left, and now they have got in my colony—Singleton colony—a house, nice cabins, their milch cows, and pigs, and sheep, perhaps a span of horses, and trees before their yeards, and some three or four or ten acres broken up, and all of them has got little houses that I carried there. They didn't go under no relief assistance; they went on their own resources; and when they went in there first the country was not overrun with them; you see they could get good wages; the country was not overstocked with people; they went to work, and I never helped them as soon as I put them on the land.

* * *

. . . There is good white men in the Southern country, but it ain't the minority [majority]; they can't do nothing; the bulldozers has got possession of the country, and they have got to go in there and stop them; if they don't the last colored man will leave them. I see colored men testifying to a positive lie, for they told me out there all their interests were in Louisiana and Mississippi. Said I, "You are right to protect you own country," and they would tell me, "I am obliged to do what I am doing." Of course I have done the same, but I am clear footed.

Q. Now you say that during these years you have been getting up this colony you have spent, yourself, some six hundred dollars in circulars, and in sending them out; where did you send them, Mr. Singleton?

A. Into Mississippi, Alabama, South Carolina, Georgia, Kentucky, Virginia, North Carolina, Texas, Tennessee, and all those countries.

* * *

Q. And you attribute this movement to the information you gave in your circulars?

A. Yes, sir; I am the whole cause of the Kansas immigration!

Q. You take all that responsibility on yourself?

A. I do, and I can prove it; and I think I have done a good deal of good, and I feel relieved!

Q. You are proud of your work?

A. Yes, sir; I am! (Uttered emphatically.)

18

Rising Phoenix; Dying Thunderbird

While the challenge of "binding up its wounds" offered opportunities for vision and innovation and large measures of idealism, the nation that emerged owed its character largely to earlier patterns of economic development and territorial growth. Opportunities in the West—for sod farmers and "cowboys" as well as entrepreneurs—attracted thousands in the years following the Civil War. Farmers and cowboys increasingly shrunk the landscape of the Native Americans' world and restricted the lifestyle and freedoms they deemed fundamental to their survival. There were those like Standing Bear who faced the dilemma of relating to white-imposed structures and rules, rules often based on conflicting goals and policies or, as illustrated by the Dawes Severalty Act, alternating between ideals of preserving a limited degree of Native culture and transforming it completely into a variation of the dominant Anglo-American world.

As Anglo-American governments and individuals in the West were sorting out policies regarding one group of nonwhites who shared the continent, similar issues arose regarding African Americans in the South and eventually Asians both in the United States and in Asia. Ida B. Wells devoted her life to exposing the explicit and at times subtle ways the southern racial system was constructed and maintained. Certainly part of the process required constructing an ideology that could mediate and blend inconsistencies and illogical and irrational belief systems. Southerners saw little contradiction between thinking of themselves as law-abiding citizens reverently committed to the preservation of law and order and condoning, perhaps encouraging, the frequent activity of lynch mobs to achieve those goals. At the same time, racial concerns of western states led to the adoption of the Chinese Exclusion Act of 1882 that sought to severely limit, if not eliminate, the immigration of Chinese to America.

From the first settlements in the New World, Anglo-Americans had been pulled, or pushed, to the "West," a directional imperative endemic to their history and culture. The experience in America was no different. It should come as no surprise that, in the nearly worldwide, turn-of-the-century, feeding frenzy of imperialism, the United States would continue its westward orientation in the form of Asian imperialism. For some thirty years after the Civil War, within the context of racist values and policies within the United States, American soldiers were expected to fight a surprisingly tenacious foe in the Philippines—a foe that merely desired the same independence and self-determination that the former American colonies had achieved a century before. The rules of war would again become an important issue, and the application of General Order 100 seemed to ensure humane and civilized conduct by American officers and enlisted men. But did it? More importantly, did the system of justice to deal with wrongdoing and preserve national honor work any better in these instances than it did regarding the lives, liberties, and pursuits of happiness of African Americans or Native Americans within the continental United States?

DOCUMENT 18.1

Letter from Uriah W. Oblinger to Matie V. Oblinger and Ella Oblinger

Fillmore Co Neb
Sabbath Feb 9th 1873

Dear Wife & Baby

I have just been looking over all or nearly all the letters received since we separated and it seems as though today we ought to be together talking instead of using the silent but ever faithful pen but so it is Ma we are apart and the pen will ever do its faithful work whether to record blessings or curses but thank high Heaven ours does not record anything but love and blessings for one another, and may it never be otherwise. . . . Ma I would love to be with you and baby and go to church today but our lot is cast otherwise. It seems as though we are destined to help make (what was once called the great american desert) blossom as the rose.

Within the memory of men now living, all this vast extent of land from the Missouri river to the foot of the Rocky Mountains was covered with nothing but what is called buffalo grass and inhabited by nothing but wild beasts and wilder men. But now for nearly 200 miles west of the Missouri River the occasional spot of buffalo grass is pointed out by the pioneer as the waymark of a vegetation that but a few years ago flourished luxuriantly but now is being replaced by that more useful prairie grass called bluejoint which is the pioneers hay & fodder. And the wild animals and wild men that but a few years ago reigned supreme all over this beautiful extent of country are fast passing away before the approaching civilization of the 'pale face' . . . and in a few years will be numbered among the things that were. And what was once known as the great 'American desert' will blossom as the rose. Surely the hand of Providence

Source: Handwritten text in collections of the Nebraska State Historical Society, Lincoln, Nebraska. Collection RG 1346. Transcription edited from Library of Congress, American Memory website memory.loc.gov/ammem/award98/nbhihtml/pshome.html.

must be in this, as it seems this desert as it has been termed so long has been specially reserved for the poor of our land to find a place to dwell in and where they can find a home for themselves and families and where they can enjoy the companionship of their loved ones undisturbed by those that have heretofore held them under their almost exclusive control. But enough of this and we will now set about answering some of the questions I can remember of your asking in your previous letters. . . .

DOCUMENT 18.2

Life in the Saddle

Frank Collinson

My First Trail Trip

When I recall that first long cattle drive to the Northwest and think of the hardships we experienced, I wonder if there was really much glamour or adventure to the trip. It was 98 per cent hard work, but I am glad I had the experience, and we helped make cattle history on that drive. We beat out a trail over sections of the country that had not been traveled before, and over which thousands of cattle would later be driven to the ranges in Montana, North and South Dakota, Wyoming, and Colorado.

I started working for Lytle in December, 1873, and during January and February we rounded up 2,500 big steers, most of them being bought in small bunches from various ranchmen. Most of those steers had been branded before, as they ranged in age from four to ten years. A few of the older animals had been branded as far back as the Civil War, but the majority had been marked in the late sixties. . . .

The work was rough, and it took rough men to handle those brush steers. Our work was mostly holding and driving in. We started early each morning. We would work the country and round up a bunch, then drive to the herd that was already being held. Then we'd work back to the corral, pen the ones we wanted to keep, and let the others go. Some of us usually stood guard around the corral. After a day or two, when we had a herd gathered, we would move five or ten miles to another corral. Several hundred steers would be gathered in a week's time, and we'd work back to the pasture and spend a day road-branding. We would crowd a rough pole chute full of those steers and commence to brand. A 7D, branded lengthwise on the left loin, was Lytle's road brand. After the cattle were branded they were turned into pasture, and we'd start out the next day in another direction to begin rounding up another herd.

I expected the cattle to be wilder than they really were, but they were accustomed to seeing men on horses and were fairly easily handled. Some of the aged steers were hard to hold. They would run together and make a beeline for

Source: Excerpted from Frank Collinson, *Life in the Saddle* (Norman: University of Oklahoma Press, 1963), pp. 31–43.

the brush. This problem was solved by driving the holding herd to where these wild steers would be likely to run out. When they were back in the herd again, they usually cooled down. One or two real outlaws had to be roped and held until the herd was driven to them before they were turned loose again. A steer that was run and roped and jerked around was called a "windsucker." The wildest steers usually settled down upon finding themselves back with the herd after their first run.

We had several Indian scares when gathering those steers, but luckily no one was killed. Once Willie Lytle, a nephew of John T. Lytle, and I were making a trip from our camp to the Lytle ranch. Deer were thick and he shot a fat yearling doe with his Colt. After cleaning the animal, we tied it behind my saddle and rode on. A small bunch of Indians suddenly broke out of the brush and started after us, yelling at the top of their voices. "Cut that deer loose and let it go," Lytle said. This I did, and the fresh venison fell to the ground as we dashed on. When the Indians reached the meat they stopped. They must have been hungry. That was the last we saw of them. . . .

Our greatest trouble with the herd was stampedes, and it always took several days for them to settle down afterward. They seemed to stampede more on the drive from Fort Griffin to Camp Supply than anywhere along the trail. Maybe it was the atmosphere. Sometimes on a clear night the cattle would be bedded down, when the air would suddenly become warm and still. Then distant thunder could be heard and phosphorous would shine on the long horns of the cattle and on the horses' ears. Then we knew a storm was brewing. Suddenly like a streak of lightning every steer jumped to its feet and was away on the run. The entire herd seemed to move like one huge animal.

In such instances the cowboys tried to keep in the lead so that the steers could eventually be turned in a circle. If the lightning and thunder and rain continued, the frightened animals would keep running for several miles.

Finally when they were herded there was water standing everywhere, and it was difficult or impossible to bed them again. Then the cowboys, cold and miserable, and often wet to the skin, stood guard the remainder of the night. Maybe one or two broke into song, but it took a brave lad to sing under such conditions. . . .

We were all glad to be at the trail's end, and pitched camp on the Niobrara River. Lytle soon rode over to talk to General George Custer, then in command at Fort Robinson, about receiving the cattle.

In the entire distance from Medina County, Texas—1,500 miles—we had not experienced too many difficulties. We had not seen an Indian, had enjoyed buffalo meat from Griffin to Dodge, and before that, after leaving Mason, Texas, had killed antelope whenever we wanted fresh meat. The antelope were curious animals. They often came right up to our herd and sometimes ran into it. They were easy to kill.

General Custer and the quartermaster rode out the next day to look over the herd, and they were real pleased with the stock and commented on their good condition. When the final count was made we had about two hundred more steers than the contract called for, but they were glad to buy those animals also. They paid Lytle an average of thirty-six dollars per head. At that price the government was able to feed the Indians very reasonably indeed.

August 1 was set as receiving day. When we had turned the cattle over to the agency the quartermaster offered any of the hands the same pay they had gotten on the trail to stay and help issue the cattle to the Indians. If they stayed as long as three months on the reservation, he would pay their return fare to Texas. I thought this sounded interesting and I decided to stay. So did several others. Lytle then settled with us, sold some of his horses to the quartermaster, and with the rest of his outfit, pulled out for Texas.

The steers were divided into three herds; two thousand of them were kept on the Niobrara where grazing was good, and where they could be issued to the Indians when needed. Eight hundred were held ten miles east, and eight hundred were driven to a range about two miles from the agency. I helped look after the latter herd, and we were ordered to corral them at night and herd them through the day. Our home was a camp house near the corrals, and we were to look after ourselves, do our own cooking and housekeeping. The government would furnish our supplies. We could carry guns as we had done along the trail, but never in any instance were we to trade with the Indians.

There were about ten thousand Indians on the reservation at that time, and Red Cloud, chief of the southern Sioux, was head chief over them all. He had subchiefs and these in turn had subchiefs, and each one was responsible for so many lodges.

The Sioux were the best looking of any Indians I ever saw. I often wondered where they got their strong, handsome features. I had an opportunity to see a great deal of this tribe when I was at Fort Robinson. The men were tall and well built. Many of them stood six feet or more, and weighed fully two hundred pounds.

When young the women were fine specimens of womanhood. They aged early because they worked so hard. They set up the tipis, moved camp, made clothing and moccasins, cooked, looked after the children and waited on the men. I noticed that the women never had over two or three children. I never saw any large families among them.

There were more women in camp than men. A warrior could have as many wives as he could feed. There were numerous widows because so many men had been killed in battle.

I often saw Red Cloud, the chief, who had learned that it was useless to fight against the white man. He was a fine-looking warrior but not as large as some of the men in his tribe. Some folks said he was a better leader than Sitting Bull. He was said to have led the fight at the Fort Phil Kearny Massacre when Captain W. J. Fetterman's entire force of men was destroyed on December 21, 1866.

During my stay on the reservation many of Red Cloud's young braves slipped off to join Sitting Bull. I am sure there were many of these southern Sioux in the Little Big Horn fight.

Once a week all of the Indians were issued beef on the hoof. We worked six days a week, and from our herd we issued about 125 head weekly. At the end of October the steers had diminished until there were not over 500 head left.

DOCUMENT 18.3

The Trial of Standing Bear

During the fifteen years in which I have been engaged in administering the laws of my country, I have never been called upon to hear or decide a case that appealed so strongly to my sympathy as the one now under consideration. On the one side, we have a few of the remnants of a once numerous and powerful, but now weak, insignificant, unlettered, and generally despised race; on the other, we have the representative of one of the most powerful, most enlightened, and most Christianized nations of modern times. On the one side, we have the representatives of this wasted race coming into this national tribunal of ours, asking for justice and liberty to enable them to adopt our boasted civilization, and to pursue the arts of peace, which have made us great and happy as a nation; on the other side, we have this magnificent, if not magnanimous, government, resisting this application with the determination of sending these people back to the country which is to them less desirable than perpetual imprisonment in their own native land. . . .

The petition alleges, in substance, that the relators are Indians who have formerly belonged to the Ponca tribe of Indians, now located in the Indian Territory; that they had some time previously withdrawn from the tribe, and completely severed their tribal relations therewith, and had adopted the general habits of the whites, and were then endeavoring to maintain themselves by their own exertions, and without aid or assistance from the general government; that whilst they were thus engaged, and without being guilty of violating any of the laws of the United States, they were arrested and restrained of their liberty by order of the respondent, George Crook. . . .

Every "person" who comes within our jurisdiction, whether he be European, Asiatic, African, or "native to the manor born," must obey the laws of the United States. Every one who violates them incurs the penalty provided thereby. When a "person" is charged, in a proper way, with the commission of crime, we do not inquire upon the trial in what country the accused was born, nor to what sovereign or government allegiance is due, nor to what race he belongs. The questions of guilt and innocence only form the subjects of inquiry. An Indian, then, especially off from his reservation, is amenable to the criminal laws of the United States, the same as all other persons. They being subject to arrest for the violation of our criminal laws, and being "persons" such as the law contemplates and includes in the description of parties who may sue out the writ, it would indeed be a sad commentary on the justice and impartiality of our laws to hold that Indians, though natives of our own country, cannot test the validity of an alleged illegal imprisonment in this manner, as well as a subject of a foreign government who may happen to be sojourning in this country, but owing it no sort of allegiance. I cannot doubt that congress intended to give

Source: The Trial of Standing Bear, Case No. 14,891: United States ex rel. Standing Bear v. Crook, [5 Dill 453] Circuit Court, D Nebraska, 1979. [25 Fed. Case].

to every person who might be unlawfully restrained of liberty under color of authority of the United States, the right to the writ and a discharge thereon. I conclude, then, that, so far as the issuing of the writ is concerned, it was properly issued, and that the relators are within the jurisdiction conferred by the habeas corpus act. . . .

The Poncas lived upon their reservation in southern Dakota, and cultivated a portion of the same, until two or three years ago, when they removed therefrom, but whether by force or otherwise does not appear. At all events, we find a portion of them, including the relators, located at some point in the Indian Territory. There, the testimony seems to show, is where the trouble commenced. Standing Bear, the principal witness, states that out of five hundred and eighty-one Indians who went from the reservation in Dakota to the Indian Territory, one hundred and fifty-eight died within a year or so, and a great proportion of the others were sick and disabled, caused, in a great measure, no doubt, from change of climate; and to save himself and the survivors of his wasted family, and the feeble remnant of his little band of followers, he determined to leave the Indian Territory and return to his old home, where, to use his own language, "he might live and die in peace, and be buried with his fathers." He also states that he informed the agent of their final purpose to leave, never to return, and that he and his followers had finally, fully, and forever severed his and their connection with the Ponca tribe of Indians, and had resolved to disband as a tribe, or band, of Indians, and to cut loose from the government, go to work, become self-sustaining, and adopt the habits and customs of a higher civilization. To accomplish what would seem to be a desirable and laudable purpose, all who were able so to do went to work to earn a living. The Omaha Indians, who speak the same language, and with whom many of the Poncas have long continued to intermarry, gave them employment and ground to cultivate, so as to make them self-sustaining. And it was when at the Omaha reservation, and when thus employed, that they were arrested by order of the government, for the purpose of being taken back to the Indian Territory. They claim to be unable to see the justice, or reason, or wisdom, or necessity, of removing them by force from their own native plains and blood relations to a far-off country, in which they can see little but new-made graves opening for their reception. The land from which they fled in fear has no attractions for them. The love of home and native land was strong enough in the minds of these people to induce them to brave every peril to return and live and die where they had been reared. The bones of the dead son of Standing Bear were not to repose in the land they hoped to be leaving forever, but were carefully preserved and protected, and formed a part of what was to them a melancholy procession homeward. Such instances of parental affection, and such love of home and native land, may be heathen in origin, but it seems to me that they are not unlike Christian in principle. . . .

I have searched in vain for the semblance of any authority justifying the commissioner in attempting to remove by force any Indians, whether belonging to a tribe or not, to any place, or for any other purpose than what has been stated. Certainly, without some specific authority found in an act of congress, or in a treaty with the Ponca tribe of Indians, he could not lawfully force the relators back to the Indian Territory, to remain and die in that country, against their will. In the absence of all treaty stipulations of laws of the United States authorizing such removal, I must conclude that no such arbitrary authority exists. It is true, if the relators are to be regarded as a part of the great nation of Ponca Indians, the government might, in time of war, remove them to any place of safety so long as the war should last, but perhaps no longer, unless they were charged with the commission of some crime. This is a war power merely, and exists in time of war only. Every nation exercises the right to arrest and detain an alien enemy during the existence of a war, and all subjects or citizens of the hostile nations are subject to be dealt with under this rule . . .

The reasoning advanced in support of my views, leads me to conclude:

1. That an Indian is a "person" within the meaning of the laws of the United States, and has, therefore, the right to sue out a writ of habeas corpus in a federal court, or before a federal judge, in all cases where he may be confined or in custody under color of authority of the United States, or where he is restrained of liberty in violation of the constitution or laws of the United States.
2. That General George Crook, the respondent, being commander of the military department of the Platte, has the custody of the relators, under color of authority of the United States, and in violation of the laws thereof.
3. That no rightful authority exists for removing by force any of the relators to the Indian Territory, as the respondent has been directed to do.
4. That the Indians possess the inherent right of expatriation, as well as the more fortunate white race, and have the inalienable right to "life, liberty, and the pursuit of happiness," so long as they obey the laws and do not trespass on forbidden ground. And,
5. Being restrained of liberty under color of authority of the United States, and in violation of the laws thereof, the relators must be discharged from custody, and it is so ordered.

Ordered accordingly.

DOCUMENT 18.4

The Dawes Severalty Act: An Indian Homestead Act

An Act to Provide for the Allotment of Lands in Severalty to Indians on the Various Reservations . . .

Be it enacted by the Senate and House of Representatives of the United States of America in Congress assembled, That in all cases where any tribe or band of Indians has been, or shall hereafter be, located upon any reservation created for their use, either by treaty stipulation or by virtue of an act of Congress or executive order

Source: Excerpted from *The Dawes Severalty Act: An Indian Homestead Act.* Forty-ninth Congress, Session 2, Chap. 119, 1887, U.S. Statutes at Large, pp. 388–91.

setting apart the same for their use, the President of the United States be, and he hereby is, authorized, whenever in his opinion any reservation or any part thereof of such Indians is advantageous for agricultural and grazing purposes, to cause said reservation, or any part thereof, to be surveyed, or resurveyed if necessary, and to allot the lands in said reservation in severalty to any Indian located thereon in quantities as follows:

To each head of a family, one-quarter of a section;

To each single person over eighteen years of age, one-eighth of a section;

To each orphan child under eighteen years of age, one-eighth of a section; and

To each other single person under eighteen years now living, or who may be born prior to the date of the order of the President directing an allotment of the lands embraced in any reservation, one-sixteenth of a section. . . .

Section 2.

That all allotments set apart under the provisions of this act shall be selected by the Indians, heads of families selecting for their minor children, and the agents shall select for each orphan child, and in such manner as to embrace the improvements of the Indians making the selection. . . .

* * *

Section 4.

That where any Indian not residing upon a reservation, or for whose tribe no reservation has been provided by treaty, act of Congress, or executive order, shall make settlement upon any surveyed or unsurveyed lands of the United States not otherwise appropriated, he or she shall be entitled, upon application to the local land-office for the district in which the lands are located, to have the same allotted to him or her, and to his or her children, in quantities and manner as provided in this act for Indians residing upon reservations; and when such settlement is made upon unsurveyed lands, the grant to such Indians shall be adjusted upon the survey of time lands so as to conform thereto; and patents shall be issued to them for such lands in the manner and with the restrictions as herein provided. . . .

Section 5.

That upon the approval of the allotments provided for in this act by the Secretary of the Interior, he shall cause patents to issue therefor in time name of the allottees, which patents shall be of the legal effect, and declare that the United States does and will hold the land thus allotted, for the period of twenty-five years, in trust for the sole use and benefit of the Indian to whom such allotment shall have been made, or, in case of his decease, of his heirs according to the laws of the State or Territory where such land is located, and that at the expiration of said period the United States will convey the same by patent to said Indian, or his heirs as aforesaid, in fee, discharged of said trust and free of all charge or incumbrance whatsoever. . . .

Section 6.

That upon the completion of said allotments and the patenting of the lands to said allottees, each and every member of the respective bands or tribes of Indians to whom allotments have been made shall have the benefit of and be subject to the laws, both civil and criminal, of the State or Territory in which they may reside; and no Territory shall pass or enforce any law denying any such Indian within its jurisdiction the equal protection of the law. And every Indian born within the territorial limits of the United States to whom allotments shall have been made under the provisions of this act, or under any law or treaty, and every Indian born within the territorial limits of the United States who has voluntarily taken up, within said limits, his residence separate and apart from any tribe of Indians therein, and has adopted the habits of civilized life, is hereby declared to be a citizen of the United States, and is entitled to all the rights, privileges, and immunities of such citizens, whether said Indian has been or not, by birth or otherwise, a member of any tribe of Indians within the territorial limits of the United States without in any manner impairing or otherwise affecting the right of any such Indian to tribal or other property.

* * *

Section 8.

That the provision of this act shall not extend to the territory occupied by the Cherokees, Creeks, Choctaws, Chickasaws, Seminoles, and Osage, Miamies and Peorias, and Sacs and Foxes, in the Indian Territory, nor to any of the reservations of the Seneca Nation of New York Indians in the State of New York, nor to that strip of territory in the State of Nebraska adjoining the Sioux Nation on the south added by executive order.

* * *

Section 10.

That nothing in this act contained shall be so construed as to affect the right and power of Congress to grant the right of way through any lands granted to an Indian, or a tribe of Indians, for railroads or other highways, or telegraph lines, for the public use, or to condemn such lands to public uses, upon making just compensation.

Section 11.

That nothing in this act shall be so construed as to prevent the removal of the Southern Ute Indians from their present reservation in Southwestern Colorado to a new reservation by and with the consent of a majority of the adult male members of said tribe.

Approved, February 8, 1887.

DOCUMENT 18.5

Ida B. Wells on Lynching

Of these thousands of men and women who have been put to death without judge or jury, less than one-third of them have been even accused of criminal assault. The world at large has accepted unquestionably the statement that Negroes are lynched only for assaults upon white women. Of those who were lynched from 1882 to 1891, the first ten years of the tabulated lynching record, the charges are as follows:

Two hundred and sixty-nine were charged with rape; 253 with murder; 44 with robbery; 37 with incendiarism; 4 with burglary; 27 with race prejudice; 13 quarreled with white men; 10 with making threats; 7 with rioting; 5 with miscegenation; in 32 cases no reasons were given, the victims were lynched on general principles.

During the past five years the record is as follows:

Of the 171 persons lynched in 1895 only 34 were charged with this crime. In 1896, out of 131 persons who were lynched, only 34 were said to have assaulted women. Of the 156 in 1897, only 32. In 1898, out of 127 persons lynched, 24 were charged with the alleged "usual crime." In 1899, of the 107 lynchings, 16 were said to be for crimes against women. These figures, of course, speak for themselves, and to the unprejudiced, fair-minded person it is only necessary to read and study them in order to show that the charge that the Negro is a moral outlaw is a false one, made for the purpose of injuring the Negro's good name and to create public sentiment against him.

If public sentiment were alive, as it should be upon the subject, it would refuse to be longer hoodwinked, and the voice of conscience would refuse to be stilled by these false statements. If the laws of the country were obeyed and respected by the white men of the country who charge that the Negro has no respect for law, these things could not be, for every individual, no matter what the charge, would have a fair trial and an opportunity to prove his guilt or innocence before a tribunal of law.

That is all the Negro asks—that is all the friends of law and order need to ask, for once the law of the land is supreme, no individual who commits crime will escape punishment.

Individual Negroes commit crimes the same as do white men, but that the Negro race is peculiarly given to assault upon women, is a falsehood of the deepest dye. The tables given above show that the Negro who is saucy to white men is lynched as well as the Negro who is charged with assault upon women. Less than one-sixth of the lynchings last year, 1899, were charged with rape.

The Negro points to his record during the war in rebuttal of this false slander. When the white women and children of the South had no protector save only these Negroes, not one instance is known where the trust was betrayed. It

Source: From Jacqueline Jones Royster, ed., *Southern Horrors and Other Writings: The Anti-Lynching Campaign of Ida B. Wells, 1892–1900* (Boston: Bedford/St. Martin's, 1997).

is remarkably strange that the Negro had more respect for womanhood with the white men of the South hundreds of miles away, than they have to-day, when surrounded by those who take their lives with impunity and burn and torture, even worse than the "unspeakable Turk."

Again, the white women of the North came South years ago, threaded the forests, visited the cabins, taught the schools and associated only with the Negroes whom they came to teach, and had no protectors near at hand. They had no charge or complaint to make of the danger to themselves after association with this class of human beings. Not once has the country been shocked by such recitals from them as come from the women who are surrounded by their husbands, brothers, lovers and friends. If the Negro's nature is bestial, it certainly should have proved itself in one of these two instances. The Negro asks only justice and an impartial consideration of these facts.

DOCUMENT 18.6

The Conquest of the Philippines by the United States

. . . On April 15, 1902, however, we find an order for the court martial of General Smith. Here was a sensational case surely. What do the records show?

General Smith had been in charge of subduing the island of Samar and his first step had been to install a system of reconcentration. For the benefit of those unfamiliar with this drastic term, it should be explained that reconcentration (as practised by Weyler in Cuba and American commanders in the Philippines) means the establishment of a certain prescribed zone or place where the people of a district may be herded together. The establishment of this zone is announced by proclamation or otherwise some days in advance and all persons must leave their homes and come within this area, there to remain until further orders. All persons found outside that zone are then treated as public enemies.

Such a method of putting down a rebellion is naturally attended with great hardships. Crops are left to ruin, homes are deserted, and the peaceful as well as the active suffer alike. It was the establishment of such camps in Cuba with the attendant horrors that finally led to the Spanish American War. How the practice of reconcentration affected McKinley when the Spaniards practised it in Cuba, may be expressed in his own words: "It was not civilized warfare [he told Congress], but a new and inhuman phase happily unprecedented in the modern history of civilized Christian people. . . . It was extermination. The only peace it could beget was that of the wilderness and the grave." . . .

But General Smith was not tried for establishing these camps, for they were also used in other provinces of the archipelago. . . .

The real gravity of the Smith offense would apparently seem to be worse than that pictured in the newspaper item. To quote from Secretary Root's letter to the President on July 12, he stated that Smith had given *the following oral instructions:*

Source: From Moorfield Storey and Marcial P. Lichauco, *The Conquest of the Philippines by the United States 1898–1925* (Freeport, NY: Books for Libraries Press, 1926).

"I want no prisoners. I wish you to kill and burn: the more you kill and burn the better you will please me," and further, that he wanted all persons killed who were capable of bearing arms and in actual hostilities against the United States, and did in reply to a question by Major Waller asking for an age limit, designate the limit as ten years of age.

It will be observed that in this accusation by the Secretary, which is grave enough on its face, the Secretary interpolated the words, "in actual hostilities against the United States," after the phrase "capable of bearing arms." But the dispatches which came from Manila in the course of the trial which were never questioned clearly refute that mitigating phrase. For General Smith's counsel was quoted as saying,

General Smith did give instructions to Major Waller to "kill and burn" and "make Samar a howling wilderness" and he admits that he wanted everybody killed capable of bearing arms, and that he did specify all over ten years of age, as the Samar boys of that age were equally as dangerous as their elders.

The accused bore his trial like a man. He admitted giving the orders. He did not seek to excuse them on the ground that his words were reckless talk,—on the contrary, he sought to justify them. On the solitary question, therefore, of whether or no he had given the order the reviewing officers of high rank found him guilty and sentenced him *"to be admonished."*

19

The Goose That Lays Golden Eggs

The steam and energy that drove Americans across the continent and eventually the Pacific Ocean was produced by the engine of rapid economic growth after the Civil War. Getting back to business after the Civil War, American entrepreneurs, businessmen, and workers crafted the foundation of the modern American industrial state and its status as a world power. In the process, the status of various characters on the American stage changed, illustrated by two songs of the era. One suggests the decline in status of the farmer, once considered the bedrock of society; the second notes the dangers associated with industrial occupations. The alteration of how Americans earned their living and the proportionate role of various occupations in the economy is further revealed in the two pie charts depicting the distribution of various occupations in 1880 and 1920.

Russell H. Conwell reveals excitement and exhilaration regarding the possibilities for advancement and financial success in those years. Moreover, the people who seemed to be leading the nation toward prosperity and power became new heroes and role models for successive generations of Americans—perhaps even to today. If a ten-year-old boy were asked in 1860 what he wanted to be when he grew up, he could very well have answered: "A farmer!" People hearing that answer might have nodded with approval. But if a 10 year-old boy were asked that same question in 1900 the answer more than likely would have been: "A factory owner or a railroad magnate!" Again, approving heads would have nodded, accentuating the answer and the cultural changes it revealed.

A railroad timetable seems a mundane document. Yet it reveals a myriad of assumptions and transformations wrought by the process of industrialization. Railroads were among the first large corporations that had to organize money, personnel, and material nationally. That organization depended, in part, on agreed-upon terms and definitions—not the least of which was the time of day. Prior to the institution of national timetables by railroads, which allowed customers a general sense of when goods and people would depart or arrive, there was no compelling reason for the time system or that the time in one city or state be coordinated with the time of day in another city or state. For farmers, clock time was irrelevant—they had the sun. But for railroads, clock time was essential—and the sun, for the most part, irrelevant.

The power and need to organize in order to meet national market demands (and reap huge national fortunes) so essential to organizers and entrepreneurs, often proved a disadvantage for individual workers. The concerns of workers, floating atop the waves of industrialization and frequently swamped if not drowned by them, were raised by labor leaders and advocates of the rights of private citizens. There were also those like Edward Bellamy who hoped for a future somewhere between that advocated by union organizer Eugene V. Debs and the world of scientific management proposed by Frederick Winslow Taylor. Bellamy envisioned a utopian world capable of producing enough wealth for all to live in comfort, peace, and harmony with each other.

DOCUMENT 19.1

Songs of Work

The Farmer Is the Man

Source: John Anthony Scott, *Living Documents in American History*, vol. 2: *From Reconstruction to the Outbreak of World War I* (New York: Washington Square Press, 1968).

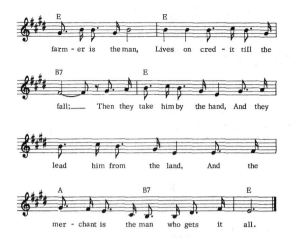

farm - er is the man, Lives on cred - it till the

fall;___ Then they take him by the hand, And they

lead him from the land, And the

mer - chant is the man who gets it all.

Oh, the farmer comes to town
With his wagon broken down,
    But the farmer is the man who feeds them all.
If you'll only look and see,
I think you will agree,
    That the farmer is the man who feeds them all.

    The farmer is the man,
    The farmer is the man,
    Lives on credit till the fall;
    Then they take him by the hand,
    And they lead him from the land,
    And the merchant is the man who gets it all.

When the lawyer hangs around,
While the butcher cuts a pound,
    Oh, the farmer is the man who feeds them all.
When the preacher and the cook
Go strolling by the brook
    Oh, the farmer is the man who feeds them all.

    The farmer is the man, etc.

When the banker says he's broke
And the merchant's up in smoke,
    They forget that it's the farmer feeds them all.
It would put them to the test
If the farmer took a rest;
    Then they'd know that it's the farmer feeds them all.

    The farmer is the man,
    The farmer is the man,
    Lives on credit till the fall;
    With the interest rate so high,
    It's a wonder he don't die,
    For the mortgage man's the one who gets it all.

The Avondale Mine Disaster

THE AVONDALE MINE DISASTER

Good Chris-tians all, both great and small, I pray you lend an ear, And lis-ten with at-ten-tion while The truth I will de-clare; When you hear this lam-en-ta-tion 'Twill cause you to weep and wail A-bout the suf-fo-ca-tion In the mines of Av-on-dale.

Transcribed by permission from record AAFS L16, American Archive of Folk Song, Library of Congress.

Good Christians all, both great and small,
  I pray you lend an ear,
And listen with attention while
  The truth I will declare;
When you hear this lamentation,
  'Twill cause you to weep and wail
About the suffocation
  In the mines of Avondale.
On the Sixth day of September,
  Eighteen sixty-nine,
Those miners all then got a call
  To go to work in the mine;
But little did they think that day
  That death would soon prevail
Before they would return again
  From the mines of Avondale.

The women and their children,
  Their hearts were filled with joy,

To see their men go to their work
    Likewise every boy;
But a dismal sight in broad daylight
    Soon made them turn pale,
When they saw the breaker burning
    O'er the mines of Avondale.

From here and there and everywhere,
    They gathered in a crowd,
Some tearing off their clothes and hair,
    And crying out aloud—
"Get out our husbands and our sons,
    Death he's going to steal
Their lives away without delay
    In the mines of Avondale."

But all in vain, there was no hope
    One single soul to save,
For there is no second outlet
    From the subterranean cave.
No pen can write the awful fright
    And horror that prevailed,
Among those dying victims,
    In the mines of Avondale.

A consultation then was held,
    T'was asked who'd volunteer,
For to go down the dismal shaft,
    To seek their comrades dear;
Two Welshmen brave, without dismay,
    And courage without fail,
Went down the shaft, without delay
    In the mines of Avondale.

When at the bottom they arrived
    And thought to make their way,
One of them died for want of air,
    While the other in great dismay,
He gave a sign to hoist him up,
    To tell the dreadful tale,
That all was lost forever
    In the mines of Avondale.

Now to conclude, and make an end,
    Their number I'll set down—
A hundred and ten of brave strong men
    Were smothered underground;
They're in their graves till this last day,
    Their widows may bewail,
And the orphan cries they rend the skies
    All round through Avondale!

(slightly abridged)

DOCUMENT 19.2

Occupational Distribution, 1880 and 1920

Between 1880 and 1920, management and industrial work—employing white- and blue-collar workers—grew at the expense of farm work.

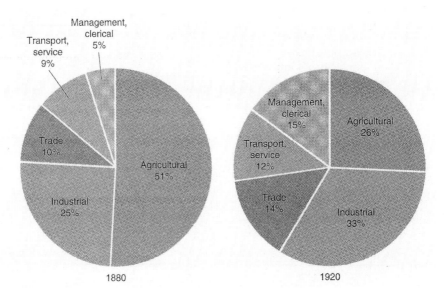

Source: From Davidson, J. W. et al. (New York: McGraw-Hill, 2001) *Nation of Nations,* 4th Ed. , p. 617.

DOCUMENT 19.3

Acres of Diamonds

Russell H. Conwell

Now then, I say again that the opportunity to get rich, to attain unto great wealth, is here in Philadelphia now, within the reach of almost every man and woman who hears me speak tonight, and I mean just what I say. I have not come to this platform even under these circumstances to recite something to you. I have come to tell you what in God's sight I believe to be the truth, and if the years of life have been of any value to me in the attainment of common sense, I know I am right; that the men and women sitting here, who found it difficult perhaps to buy a ticket to this lecture or gathering to-night, have within their reach "acres of diamonds," opportunities to get largely wealthy. There never was a place on earth more adapted than the city of Philadelphia to-day, and never in the history of the world did a poor man without capital have such

Source: From Russell H. Conwell, *Acres of Diamonds* (New York: Harper & Brothers, 1915), pp. 18–21.

an opportunity to get rich quickly and honestly as he has now in our city. I say it is the truth, and I want you to accept it as such; for if you think I have come to simply recite something, then I would better not be here. I have no time to waste in any such talk, but to say the things I believe, and unless some of you get richer for what I am saying to-night my time is wasted.

I say that you ought to get rich, and it is your duty to get rich. How many of my pious brethren say to me, "Do you, a Christian minister, spend your time going up and down the country advising young people to get rich, to get money?" "Yes, of course I do." They say, "Isn't that awful! Why don't you preach the gospel instead of preaching about man's making money?" "Because to make money honestly is to preach the gospel." That is the reason. The men who get rich may be the most honest men you find in the community.

"Oh," but says some young man here to-night, "I have been told all my life that if a person has money he is very dishonest and dishonorable and mean and contemptible." My friend, that is the reason why you have none, because you have that idea of people. The foundation of your faith is altogether false. Let me say here clearly, and say it briefly, though subject to discussion which I have not time for here, ninety-eight out of one hundred of the rich men of America are honest. That is why they are rich. That is why they are trusted with money. That is why they carry on great enterprises and find plenty of people to work with them. It is because they are honest men.

Says another young man, "I hear sometimes of men that get millions of dollars dishonestly." Yes, of course you do, and so do I. But they are so rare a thing in fact that the newspapers talk about them all the time as a matter of news until you get the idea that all the other rich men got rich dishonestly.

My friend, you take and drive me—if you furnish the auto—out into the suburbs of Philadelphia, and introduce me to the people who own their homes around this great city, those beautiful homes with gardens and flowers, those magnificent homes so lovely in their art, and I will introduce you to the very best people in character as well as in enterprise in our city, and you know I will. A man is not really a true man until he owns his own home, and they that own their homes are made more honorable and honest and pure, and true and economical and careful, by owning the home.

For a man to have money, even in large sums, is not an inconsistent thing. We preach against covetousness, and you know we do, in the pulpit, and oftentimes preach against it so long and use the terms about "filthy lucre" so extremely that Christians get the idea that when we stand in the pulpit we believe it is wicked for any man to have money—until the collection-basket goes around, and then we almost swear at the people because they don't give more money. Oh, the inconsistency of such doctrines as that!

Money is power, and you ought to be reasonably ambitious to have it. You ought because you can do more good with it than you could without it. Money printed your Bible, money builds your churches, money sends your missionaries, and money pays your preachers, and you would not have many of them, either, if you did not pay them. I am always willing that my church should raise my salary, because the church that pays the largest salary always raises it the easiest. You never knew an exception to it in your life. The man who gets the largest salary can do the most good with the power that is furnished to him. Of course he can if his spirit be right to use it for what it is given to him.

I say, then, you ought to have money. If you can honestly attain unto riches in Philadelphia, it is your Christian and godly duty to do so.

DOCUMENT 19.4

A Railroad Timetable

Source: A Railroad Timetable. From An American Time Capsule: Three Centuries of Broadsides and Other Printed Ephemera at http://memory.loc.gov/ammem/rbpehtml/pehome.html.

DOCUMENT 19.5

The Appeal to Reason

Eugene V. Debs

Now, my friends, I am opposed to the system of society in which we live today, not because I lack the natural equipment to do for myself, but because I am not satisfied to make myself comfortable knowing that there are thousands upon thousands of my fellow men who suffer for the barest necessities of life. We were taught under the old ethic that man's business upon this earth was to look out for himself. That was the ethic of the jungle; the ethic of the wild beast. Take care of yourself, no matter what may become of your fellow man. Thousands of years ago the question was asked: "Am I my brother's keeper?" That question has never yet been answered in a way that is satisfactory to civilized society. . . .

I am in revolt against capitalism (and that doesn't mean to say, my friends, that I am hating you—not the slightest). I am opposed to capitalism because I love my fellow men, and if I am opposing you I am opposing you for what I believe to be your good, and though you spat upon me with contempt I should still oppose you to the extent of my power. . . .

If there is a man on this earth who is entitled to all the comforts and luxuries of this life in abundance it is the man whose labor produces them. If he is not, who is? Does he get them in the present system? . . .

As long as a relatively few men own the railroads, the telegraph, the telephone, own the oil fields and the gas fields and the steel mills and the sugar refineries and the leather tanneries—own, in short, the sources and means of life—they will corrupt our politics, they will enslave the working class, they will impoverish and debase society, they will do all things that are needful to perpetuate their power as the economic masters and the political rulers of the people. Not until these great agencies are owned and operated by the people can the people hope for any material improvement in their social condition.

Is the condition fair today, and satisfactory to the thinking man? . . .

Now, we Socialists propose that society in its collective capacity shall produce, not for profit, but in abundance to satisfy human wants; that every man shall have the inalienable right to work, and receive the full equivalent of all he produces; that every man may stand fearlessly erect in the pride and majesty of his own manhood.

Every man and every woman will then be economically free. They can, without let or hindrance, apply their labor, with the best machinery that can be devised, to all the natural resources, do the work of society and produce for all; and then receive in exchange a certificate of value equivalent to that of their production. Then society will improve its institutions in proportion to the progress of invention. Whether in the city or on the farm, all things productive will be carried forward on a gigantic scale. All industry will be completely

Source: Excerpted from Eugene V. Debs, "The Appeal to Reason," *Debs: His Life, Writings, and Speeches*, (Kansas: Girad, 1908).

organized. Society for the first time will have a scientific foundation. Every man, by being economically free, will have some time for himself. He can then take a full and perfect breath. He can enjoy life with his wife and children, because then he will have a home.

We are not going to destroy private property. We are going to establish private property—all the private property necessary to house man, keep him in comfort and satisfy his wants. Eighty per cent of the people of the United States have no property today. A few have got it all. They have dispossessed the people, and when we get into power we will dispossess them. We will reduce the workday and give every man a chance. We will go to the parks, and we will have music, because we will have time to play music and desire to hear it.

Is it not sad to think that not one in a thousand knows what music is? Is it not pitiable to see the poor, ignorant, dumb human utterly impervious to the divine influences of music? If humanity could only respond to the higher influences! And it would if it had time.

Release the animal, throw off his burden; give him a chance and he rises as if by magic to the plane of a man. Man has all of the divine attributes. They are in a latent state. They are not yet developed. It does not pay now to love music. Keep your eye on the almighty dollar and your fellowman. Get the dollar and keep him down. Make him produce for you. You are not your brother's keeper. Suppose he is poor! Suppose his wife is forced into prostitution! Suppose his child is deformed! And suppose he shuffles off by destroying himself! What is that to you?

But you ought to be ashamed. Take the standard home and look it in the face. If you know what that standard means, and you are a success, God help the failure!

Our conduct is determined by our economic relations. If you and I must fight each other to exist, we will not love each other very hard. We can go to the same church and hear the same minister tell us in good conscience that we ought to love each other, and the next day we approach some business transaction. Do we remember what the minister told us? No; it is gone until next Sunday. Six days in the week we are following the Golden Rule reversed. Now, when we approach a business transaction in competition, what is more natural than that we should try to get the better of it?—get the better of our fellowman?—cheat him if we can?

And if you succeed that fixes you as a business man. You have all the necessary qualifications. Don't let your conscience disturb you—that would interfere with business.

DOCUMENT 19.6

Frederick Winslow Taylor on the Principles of Scientific Management

The committee met at 10:36 o'clock a.m., Hon. William B. Wilson (chairman) presiding.

TESTIMONY OF MR. FREDERICK WINSLOW TAYLOR

. . . *The Chairman.* Mr. Taylor, are you the author or compiler of the system of shop management generally known as the "Taylor system?"

Mr. Taylor. I have had a very great deal to do with the development of the system of management which has come to be called by certain people the "Taylor system," but I am only one of many men who have been instrumental in the development of this system. . . .

* * *

The number of shovel loads which each handled in the course of the day was counted and written down. At the end of the day the total tonnage of the material handled by each man was weighed and this weight was divided by the number of shovel loads handled, and the average shovel load handled was 38 pounds, and that with this load on the shovel the man handled, say, about 25 tons per day. We then cut the shovel off, making it somewhat shorter, so that instead of shoveling a load of 38 pounds it held a load of approximately 34 pounds. The average, then, with the 34 pound load, of each man went up, and instead of handling 25 he had handled 30 tons per day. These figures are merely relative, used to illustrate the general principle, and I do not mean that they were the exact figures. The shovel was again cut off, and the load made approximately 30 pounds, and again the tonnage ran up, and again the shovel load was reduced and the tonnage handled per day increased, until at about 21 or 22 pounds per shovel we found that these men were doing their largest day's work. If you cut the shovel load off still more, say until it averages 18 pounds instead of 21½, the tonnage handled per day will begin to fall off, and at 16 pounds it will be still lower, and so on right down. Very well; we now have developed the scientific fact that a workman well suited to his job, what we call a first-class shoveler, will do his largest day's work when he has a shovel load of 21½ pounds. . . .

Now, what does that fact amount to? At first it may not look to be a fact of much importance, but let us see what it amounted to right there in the yard of the Bethlehem Steel Co. Under the old system . . . the workmen owned their shovels, and the shovel was the same size whatever the kind of work. Now, as a matter of common sense, we saw at once that it was necessary to furnish each workman each day with a shovel which would hold just 21½ pounds of the particular material which he was called upon to shovel. A small shovel for the heavy material, such as ore, and a large scoop for light material, such as ashes. That meant, also, the building of a large shovel room, where all kinds of

Source: Excerpted from Frederick Winslow Taylor's Congressional Testimony. "Testimony of Mr. Frederick Winslow Taylor," Hearings before the Special Committee of the House of Representatives to Investigate the Taylor and Other Systems of Shop Management Under the Authority of House Resolution 90 (1911), Hearings, vol. 3 (Washington: GPO,1912), 1377–1378, 1397–1405.

laborers' implements were stored. It meant having an ample supply of each type of shovel, so that all the men who might be called upon to use a certain type in any one day could be supplied with a shovel of the size desired that would hold just 21½ pounds. It meant, further, that each day each laborer should be given a particular kind of work to which he was suited, and that he must be provided with a particular shovel suited to that kind of work, whereas in the past all the laborers in the yard of the Bethlehem Steel Co. had been handled in masses, or in great groups of men, by the old-fashioned foreman, who had from 25 to 100 men under him and walked them from one part of the yard to another. You must realize that the yard of the Bethlehem Steel Co. at that time was a very large yard. I should say that it was at least 1½ or 2 miles long and, we will say, a quarter to a half mile wide, so it was a good large yard; and in that yard at all times an immense variety of shoveling was going on.

* * *

Now, gentlemen, I want you to see clearly that, because that is one of the characteristic features of scientific management; . . . The old way of treating with workmen, on the other hand, even with a good foreman, would have been something like this: "See here, Pat, I have sent for you to come up here to the office to see me; four or five times now you have not earned your 60 per cent increase in wages; you know every workman in this place has got to earn 60 per cent more wages than they pay in any other place around here, but you're no good and that's all there is to it; now, get out of this." That's the old way. . . .

The new way is to teach and help your men as you would a brother; to try to teach him the best way and show him the easiest way to do his work. This is the new mental attitude of the management toward the men, and that is the reason I have taken so much of your time in describing this cheap work of shoveling. It may seem to you a matter of very little consequence, but I want you to see, if I can, this new mental attitude is the very essence of scientific management; that the mechanism is nothing if you have not got the right sentiment, the right attitude in the minds of the men, both on the management's side and on the workman's side. Because this helps to explain the fact that until this summer there has never been a strike under scientific management. . . .

At the end of some three and a half years we had the opportunity of proving whether or not scientific management did pay in its application to yard labor. When we went to the Bethlehem Steel Co. we found from 400 to 600 men at work in that yard, and when we got through 140 men were doing the work of the 400 to 600, and these men handled several million tons of material a year.

We were very fortunate to be able to get accurate statistics as to the cost of handling a ton of materials in that yard under the old system and under the new. Under the old system the cost of handling a ton of materials had been running between 7 and 8 cents, and all you gentlemen familiar with railroad work know that this is a low figure for handling material. Now, after paying for all the clerical work which was necessary under the new system for the time study and the teachers, for building and running the labor office and the implement room, for constructing a telephone system for moving men about the yard, for a great variety of duties not performed under the old system, after paying for all these things incident to the development of the science of shoveling and managing the men the new way, and including the wages of the workmen, the cost of handling a ton of material was brought down from between 7 and 8 cents to between 3 and 4 cents, and the actual saving, during the last six months of the three and one-half years I was there, was at the rate of $78,000 a year. That is what the company got out of it; while the men who were on the labor gang received an average of sixty per cent more wages than their brothers got or could get anywhere around that part of the country. And none of them were overworked, for it is no part of scientific management ever to overwork any man; certainly overworking these men could not have been done with the knowledge of anyone connected with scientific management, because one of the first requirements of scientific management is that no man shall ever be given a job which he can not do and thrive under through a long term of years. It is no part of scientific management to drive anyone. At the end of the three years we had men talk to and investigate all of these yard laborers and we found that they were almost universally satisfied with their jobs.

DOCUMENT 19.7

Looking Backward

Edward Bellamy

By way of attempting to give the reader some general impression of the way people lived together in those days, and especially of the relations of the rich and poor to one another, perhaps I cannot do better than to compare society as it then was to a prodigious coach which the masses of humanity were harnessed to and dragged toilsomely along a very hilly and sandy road. The driver was hunger, and permitted no lagging, though the pace was necessarily very slow. Despite the difficulty of drawing the coach at all along so hard a road, the top was covered with passengers who never got down, even at the steepest ascents. These seats on top were very breezy and comfortable. Well up out of the dust, their occupants could enjoy the scenery at their leisure, or critically discuss the merits of the straining team. Naturally such places were in great demand and the competition for them was keen, every one seeking as the first end in life to secure a seat on the coach for himself and to leave it to his child after him. By the rule of the coach a man could leave his seat to whom he wished, but on the other hand there were many accidents by which it might at any time be wholly lost. For all that they were so easy, the seats were very insecure, and at every sudden jolt of the coach persons were slipping out of them and falling to the ground, where they were instantly compelled to take hold of the rope and help

Source: Excerpted from Edward Bellamy, *Looking Backward, 2000–1887* (Houghton Mifflin, 1887).

to drag the coach on which they had before ridden so pleasantly. It was natu-rally regarded as a terrible misfortune to lose one's seat, and the apprehension that this might happen to them or their friends was a constant cloud upon the happiness of those who rode.

But did they think only of themselves? you ask. Was not their very luxury rendered intolerable to them by comparison with the lot of their brothers and sisters in the harness, and the knowledge that their own weight added to their toil? Had they no compassion for fellow beings from whom fortune only dis-tinguished them? Oh, yes; commiseration was frequently expressed by those who rode for those who had to pull the coach, especially when the vehicle came to a bad place in the road, as it was constantly doing, or to a particularly steep hill. At such times, the desperate straining of the team, their agonized leaping and plunging under the pitiless lashing of hunger, the many who fainted at the rope and were trampled in the mire, made a very distressing spectacle, which often called forth highly creditable displays of feeling on the top of the coach. At such times the passengers would call down encouragingly to the toilers of the rope, exhorting them to patience, and holding out hopes of possible compensa-tion in another world for the hardness of their lot, while others contributed to buy salves and liniments for the crippled and injured. It was agreed that it was a great pity that the coach should be so hard to pull, and there was a sense of general relief when the specially bad piece of road was gotten over. This relief was not, indeed, wholly on account of the team, for there was always some dan-ger at these bad places of a general overturn in which all would lose their seats.

It must in truth be admitted that the main effect of the spectacle of the mis-ery of the toilers at the rope was to enhance the passengers' sense of the value of their seats upon the coach, and to cause them to hold on to them more des-perately than before. If the passengers could only have felt assured that neither they nor their friends would ever fall from the top, it is probable that, beyond contributing to the funds for liniments and bandages, they would have troubled themselves extremely little about those who dragged the coach.

I am well aware that this will appear to the men and women of the twenti-eth century an incredible inhumanity, but there are two facts, both very curious, which partly explain it. In the first place, it was firmly and sincerely believed that there was no other way in which Society could get along, except the many pulled at the rope and the few rode, and not only this, but that no very radical improvement even was possible, either in the harness, the coach, the roadway, or the distribution of the toil. It had always been as it was, and it always would be so. It was a pity, but it could not be helped, and philosophy forbade wasting compassion on what was beyond remedy.

The other fact is yet more curious, consisting in a singular hallucination which those on the top of the coach generally shared, that they were not exactly like their brothers and sisters who pulled at the rope, but of finer clay, in some way belonging to a higher order of beings who might justly expect to be drawn. This seems unaccountable, but, as I once rode on this very coach and shared that very hallucination, I ought to be believed. The strangest thing about the hallucination was that those who had but just climbed up from the ground, before they had outgrown the marks of the rope upon their hands, began to fall under its influence. As for those whose parents and grandparents before them had been so fortunate as to keep their seats on the top, the conviction they cherished of the essential difference between their sort of humanity and the common article was absolute. The effect of such a delusion in moderating fellow feeling for the sufferings of the mass of men into a distant and philosophical compassion is obvious. To it I refer as the only extenuation I can offer for the indifference which, at the period I write of, marked my own attitude toward the misery of my brothers.

20

Urban Canyons

The urbanization of America was a major transformation for our social landscape. The migration of people from both the countryside and other countries created areas of dense population concentration that contributed to both the productive and consumptive behavior of people. The change was irrevocable; cities are an obvious and ordinary part of the landscape today. In the 21st century, it is easy to forget that the aggregation of people into cities in the 19th century required prior technological advances that made it physically possible to stack people atop one another and to move vast quantities of goods and services in and out of the urban beehives that resulted. The first selection in this chapter is a picture of one of the first skyscrapers in New York—the Flatiron building, representing the beginning of the construction of urban canyons. The relationship between technology and urbanization can also be seen in the graphic illustrating the growth of New Orleans, because city expansion and the growth of the city's streetcar system were mutually dependent and reinforcing developments.

Along with the physical machines and mechanisms that made cities possible, social machinery arose to bring order out of the potential chaos of so many souls rubbing shoulders every day. As with industry itself, the "captains" of the social industries in cities discovered that volume, numbers, and mass behaviors could create vast fortunes and formidable power. Very quickly, as the next few selections reveal, struggles between good and evil spiced up daily life among the urban masses and influenced local, state, and even national politics.

Bold politicians could be proud of the services they rendered despite the costs of those services. Since cities represented larger aggregations of people, there were more people to be reached, entertained, and possibly inspired by popular communication systems such as daily newspapers and what became known as "muckraking" journalism. Editorial cartoons represented a possible vehicle for awakening the people to the realities of urban life. Finally, if much of the social life and fabric of the country were be-

ing transformed, changes could be anticipated in religious institutions and practices as some sought to adapt religion to better serve Americans in their new circumstances.

DOCUMENT 20.1

Photograph of the Flatiron Building

Photograph by Daniel Burnham, at New York, New York, 1902. The image is actually a photograph by Howard Davis, Artifice PCD.2260.1012.1702.058. © Howard Davis posted at GreatBuildings.com. Daniel Burnham was the architect of the building.

DOCUMENT 20.2

Growth of New Orleans to 1900

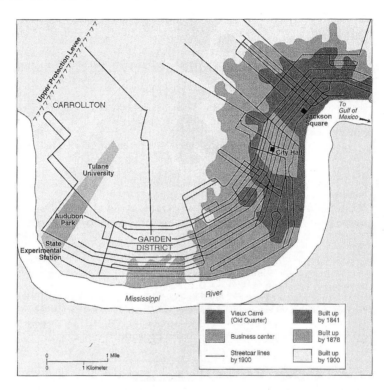

Streetcars helped cities spread beyond business districts while still functioning as organic wholes. By 1900, streetcar lines in New Orleans reached all the way to Audubon Park and Tulane University, bringing these once distant points within the reach of city dwellers and creating "streetcar suburbs."

From Davidson, J. W. et al. (2001). *Nation of Nations*, 4th Ed. New York: McGraw-Hill, p. 646.

DOCUMENT 20.3

"I Seen My Opportunities and I Took 'Em"
George W. Plunkitt

Honest Graft and Dishonest Graft

EVERYBODY is talkin' these days about Tammany men growin' rich on graft, but nobody thinks of drawin' the distinction between honest graft and dishonest graft. There's all the difference in the world between the two. Yes, many of our men have grown rich in politics. I have myself. I've made a big fortune out of the game, and I'm gettin' richer every day, but I've not gone in for dishonest graft—blackmailin' gamblers, saloonkeepers, disorderly people, etc.—and neither has any of the men who have made big fortunes in politics.

There's an honest graft, and I'm an example of how it works. I might sum up the whole thing by sayin': "I seen my opportunities and I took 'em."

Just let me explain by examples. My party's in power in the city, and it's goin' to undertake a lot of public improvements. Well, I'm tipped off, say, that they're going to lay out a new park at a certain place.

I see my opportunity and I take it. I go to that place and I buy up all the land I can in the neighborhood. Then the board of this or that makes its plan public, and there is a rush to get my land, which nobody cared particular for before.

Ain't it perfectly honest to charge a good price and make a profit on my investment and foresight? Of course, it is. Well, that's honest graft.

Or supposin' it's a new bridge they're goin' to build. I get tipped off and I buy as much property as I can that has to be taken for approaches. I sell at my own price later on and drop some more money in the bank.

Wouldn't you? It's just like lookin' ahead in Wall Street or in the coffee or cotton market. It's honest graft, and I'm lookin' for it every day in the year. I will tell you frankly that I've got a good lot of it, too.

I'll tell you of one case. They were goin' to fix up a big park, no matter where. I got on to it, and went lookin' about for land in that neighborhood.

I could get nothin' at a bargain but a big piece of swamp, but I took it fast enough and held on to it. What turned out was just what I counted on. They couldn't make the park complete without Plunkitt's swamp, and they had to pay a good price for it. Anything dishonest in that?

Up in the watershed I made some money, too. I bought up several bits of land there some years ago and made a pretty good guess that they would be bought up for water purposes later by the city.

Somehow, I always guessed about right, and shouldn't I enjoy the profit of my foresight? It was rather amusin' when the condemnation commissioners came along and found piece after piece of the land in the name of George Plunkitt of the Fifteenth Assembly District, New York City. They wondered how I knew just what to buy. The answer is—I seen my opportunity and I took it. I haven't confined myself to land; anything that pays is in my line.

For instance, the city is repavin' a street and has several hundred thousand old granite blocks to sell. I am on hand to buy, and I know just what they are worth.

How? Never mind that. I had a sort of monopoly of this business for a while, but once a newspaper tried to do me. It got some outside men to come over from Brooklyn and New Jersey to bid against me.

Was I done? Not much. I went to each of the men and said: "How many of these 250,000 stones do you want?" One said 20,000, and another wanted

Source: From George Washington Plunkitt (recorded by William L. Riordon), *Plunkitt of Tammany Hall* (New York: E. P. Dutton, 1963).

15,000, and other wanted 10,000. I said: "All right, let me bid for the lot, and I'll give each of you all you want for nothin'."

They agreed, of course. Then the auctioneer yelled: "How much am I bid for these 250,000 fine pavin' stones?"

"Two dollars and fifty cents," says I.

"Two dollars and fifty cents!" screamed the auctioneer. "Oh, that's a joke! Give me a real bid."

He found the bid was real enough. My rivals stood silent. I got the lot for $2.50 and gave them their share. That's how the attempt to do Plunkitt ended, and that's how all such attempts end.

I've told you how I got rich by honest graft. Now, let me tell you that most politicians who are accused of robbin' the city get rich the same way.

They didn't steal a dollar from the city treasury. They just seen their opportunities and took them. That is why, when a reform administration comes in and spends a half million dollars in tryin' to find the public robberies they talked about in the campaign, they don't find them.

The books are always all right. The money in the city treasury is all right. Everything is all right. All they can show is that the Tammany heads of departments looked after their friends, within the law, and gave them what opportunities they could to make honest graft. Now, let me tell you that's never goin' to hurt Tammany with the people. Every good man looks after his friends, and any man who doesn't isn't likely to be popular. If I have a good thing to hand out in private life, I give it to a friend. Why shouldn't I do the same in public life?

Another kind of honest graft. Tammany has raised a good many salaries. There was an awful howl by the reformers, but don't you know that Tammany gains ten votes for every one it lost by salary raisin'?

The Wall Street banker thinks it shameful to raise a department clerk's salary from $1500 to $1800 a year, but every man who draws a salary himself says: "That's all right. I wish it was me." And he feels very much like votin' the Tammany ticket on election day, just out of sympathy.

Tammany was beat in 1901 because the people were deceived into believin' that it worked dishonest graft. They didn't draw a distinction between dishonest and honest graft, but they saw that some Tammany men grew rich, and supposed they had been robbin' the city treasury or levyin' blackmail on disorderly houses, or workin' in with the gamblers and lawbreakers.

As a matter of policy, if nothing else, why should the Tammany leaders go into such dirty business, when there is so much honest graft lyin' around when they are in power? Did you ever consider that?

Now, in conclusion, I want to say that I don't own a dishonest dollar. If my worst enemy was given the job of writin' my epitaph when I'm gone, he couldn't do more than write:

"George W. Plunkitt. He Seen His Opportunities, and He Took 'Em."

DOCUMENT 20.4

The Shame of the Cities

Lincoln Steffins

Whenever anything extraordinary is done in American municipal politics, whether for good or for evil, you can trace it almost invariably to one man. The people do not do it. Neither do the "gangs," "combines," or political parties. These are but instruments by which bosses (not leaders; we Americans are not led, but driven) rule the people, and commonly sell them out. But there are at least two forms of the autocracy which has supplanted the democracy here as it has everywhere democracy has been tried. One is that of the organized majority by which, as with the Republican machine in Philadelphia, the boss has normal control of more than half the voters. The other is that of the adroitly managed minority. The "good people" are herded into parties and stupefied with convictions and a name, Republican or Democrat; while the "bad people" are so organized or interested by the boss that he can wield their votes to enforce terms with party managers and decide elections. St. Louis is a conspicuous example of this form. Minneapolis is another. Colonel Ed Butler is the unscrupulous opportunist who handled the non-partisan minority which turned St. Louis into a "boodle town." In Minneapolis "Doc" Ames was the man.

Source: From Lincoln Steffins, *The Shame of the Cities* (New York: Hill and Wang, 1904), pp. 42–43.

DOCUMENT 20.5

Cartoons of Thomas Nast

The Tammany Kingdom

Source: Morton Keller, *The Art and Politics of Thomas Nast* (New York: Oxford University Press, 1968), p. 115 (Thomas Nast's cartoon of October 29, 1870).

Wholesale and Retail

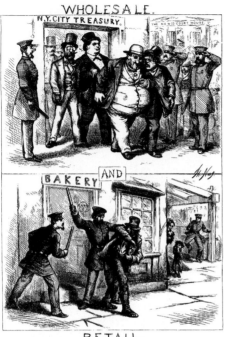

Source: Morton Keller, *The Art and Politics of Thomas Nast* (New York: Oxford University Press, 1968), p. 120 (Thomas Nast's cartoon of September 16, 1871).

DOCUMENT 20.6

How the Other Half Lives

Jacob Riis

"We wuz six," said an urchin of twelve or thirteen I came across in the News-boys' Lodging House, "and we ain't got no father. Some on us had to go." And so he went, to make a living by blacking boots. The going is easy enough. There is very little to hold the boy who has never known anything but a home in a ten-ement. Very soon the wild life in the streets holds him fast, and thenceforward by his own effort there is no escape. Left alone to himself, he soon enough finds a place in the police books, and there would be no other answer to the second question: "what becomes of the boy?" than that given by the criminal courts every day in the week.

But he is not left alone. Society in our day has no such suicidal intention. Right here, at the parting of the ways, it has thrown up the strongest of all its de-fences for itself and for the boy. What the Society for the Prevention of Cruelty

Source: From Jacob Riis, *How the Other Half Lives* (Williamston, Mass.: Corner House Publishers, 1972), p.201.

to Children is to the baby-waif, the Children's Aid Society is to the homeless boy at this real turning-point in his career. The good it has done cannot easily be overestimated. Its lodging-houses, its schools and its homes block every avenue of escape with their offer of shelter upon terms which the boy soon accepts, as on the whole cheap and fair. In the great Duane Street lodging-house for newsboys, they are succinctly stated in a "notice" over the door that reads thus: "Boys who swear and chew tobacco cannot sleep here." There is another unwritten condition, viz.: that the boy shall be really without a home; but upon this the managers wisely do not insist too obstinately, accepting without too close inquiry his account of himself where that seems advisable, well knowing that many a home that sends forth such lads far less deserves the name than the one they are able to give them.

DOCUMENT 20.7

In His Steps

Charles Monroe Sheldon

There was some reason, perhaps, . . . for Henry Maxwell's feeling of satisfaction whenever he considered his parish as he had the previous Sunday. There was an unusually large number of strong, individual characters who claimed membership there. But as he noted their faces this morning he was simply wondering how many of them would respond to the strange proposition he was about to make. He continued slowly, taking time to choose his words carefully, and giving the people an impression they had never felt before, even when he was at his best with his most dramatic delivery.

"What I am going to propose now is something which ought not to appear unusual or at all impossible of execution. Yet I am aware that it will be so regarded by a large number, perhaps, of the members of this church. But in order that we may have a thorough understanding of what we are considering, I will put my proposition very plainly, perhaps bluntly. I want volunteers from the First Church who will pledge themselves, earnestly and honestly for an entire year, not to do anything without first asking the question, 'What would Jesus do?' And after asking that question, each one will follow Jesus as exactly as he knows how, no matter what the result may be. I will of course include myself in this company of volunteers, and shall take for granted that my church here will not be surprised at my future conduct, as based upon this standard of action, and will not oppose whatever is done if they think Christ would do it. Have I made my meaning clear? At the close of the service I want all those members who are willing to join such a company to remain and we will talk over the details of the plan. Our motto will be, 'What would Jesus do?' Our aim will be to

Source: From Charles Monroe Sheldon, *In His Steps* (Old Tappan, N.J.: Fleming H. Revel Co., 1977), pp. 15–17, 183–85.

act just as He would if He was in our places, regardless of immediate results. In other words, we propose to follow Jesus' steps as closely and as literally as we believe He taught His disciples to do. And those who volunteer to do this will pledge themselves for an entire year, beginning with today, so to act."

* * *

"What would be the result if all the church members of this city tried to do as Jesus would do? It is not possible to say in detail what the effect would be. But it is easy to say, and it is true, that instantly the human problem would begin to find an adequate answer.

"What is the test of Christian discipleship? Is it not the same as in Christ's own time? Have our surroundings modified or changed the test? If Jesus were here today would He not call some of the members of this very church to do just what He commanded the young man, and ask them to give up their wealth and literally follow Him? I believe He would do that if He felt certain that any church member thought more of his possessions than of the Saviour. The test would be the same today as then. I believe Jesus would demand—He does demand now—as close a following, as much suffering, as great self-denial as when He lived in person on the earth and said, 'Except a man renounce all that he hath he cannot be my disciple.' That is, unless he is willing to do it for my sake, he cannot be my disciple.

"What would be the result if in this city every church member should begin to do as Jesus would do? It is not easy to go into details of the result. But we all know that certain things would be impossible that are now practiced by church members. What would Jesus do in the matter of wealth? How would He spend it? What principle would regulate His use of money? Would He be likely to live in great luxury and spend ten times as much on personal adornment and entertainment as He spent to relieve the needs of suffering humanity? How would Jesus be governed in the making of money? Would He take rentals from saloons and other disreputable property, or even from tenement property that was so constructed that the inmates had no such things as a home and no such possibility as privacy or cleanliness?

"What would Jesus do about the great army of unemployed and desperate who tramp the streets and curse the church, or are indifferent to it, lost in the bitter struggle for the bread that tastes bitter when it is earned on account of the desperate conflict to get it? Would Jesus care nothing for them? Would He go His way in comparative ease and comfort? Would He say that it was none of His business? Would He excuse Himself from all responsibility to remove the causes of such a condition?

"What would Jesus do in the center of a civilization that hurries so fast after money that the very girls employed in great business houses are not paid enough to keep soul and body together without fearful temptations so great that scores of them fall and are swept over the great boiling abyss; where the demands of trade sacrifice hundreds of lads in a business that ignores all Christian duties toward them in the way of education and moral training and personal affection? Would Jesus, if He were here today as a part of our age and commercial industry, feel nothing, do nothing, say nothing, in the face of these facts which every business man knows?

"What would Jesus do? Is not that what the disciple ought to do? Is he not commanded to follow in His steps? How much is the Christianity of the age suffering for Him? Is it denying itself at the cost of ease, comfort, luxury, elegance of living? What does the age need more than personal sacrifice? Does the church do its duty in following Jesus when it gives a little money to establish missions or relieve extreme cases of want? Is it any sacrifice for a man who is worth ten million dollars simply to give ten thousand dollars for some benevolent work? Is he not giving something that cost him practically nothing so far as any personal suffering goes? Is it true that the Christian disciples today in most of our churches are living soft, easy, selfish lives, very far from any sacrifice that can be called sacrifice? What would Jesus do?

"It is the personal element that Christian discipleship needs to emphasize. 'The gift without the giver is bare.' The Christianity that attempts to suffer by proxy is not the Christianity of Christ. Each individual Christian business man, citizen, needs to follow in His steps along the path of personal sacrifice to Him. There is not a different path today from that of Jesus' own times. It is the same path. The call of this dying century and of the new one soon to be, is a call for a new discipleship, a new following of Jesus, more like the early, simple, apostolic Christianity, when the disciples left all and literally followed the Master. Nothing but a discipleship of this kind can face the destructive selfishness of the age with any hope of overcoming it. There is a great quantity of nominal Christianity today. There is need of more of the real kind. We need revival of the Christianity of Christ. We have, unconsciously, lazily, selfishly, formally grown into a discipleship that Jesus himself would not acknowledge. He would say to many of us when we cry, 'Lord, Lord,' 'I never knew you!' Are we ready to take up the cross? Is it possible for this church to sing with exact truth,

> 'Jesus, I my cross have taken,
> All to leave and follow Thee?'

If we can sing that truly, then we may claim discipleship. But if our definition of being a Christian is simply to enjoy the privileges of worship, be generous at no expense to ourselves, have a good, easy time surrounded by pleasant friends and by comfortable things, live respectably and at the same time avoid the world's great stress of sin and trouble because it is too much pain to bear it—if this is our definition of Christianity, surely we are a long way from following the steps of Him who trod the way with groans and tears and sobs of anguish for a lost humanity; who sweat, as it were, great drops of blood, who cried out on the upreared cross, 'My God, my God, why hast thou forsaken me?'

"Are we ready to make and live a new discipleship? Are we ready to reconsider our definition of a Christian? What is it to be a Christian? It is to imitate Jesus. It is to do as He would do. It is to walk in His steps."

21

More Hell and Less Corn

With the changes in the rural areas of the country from the end of the Civil War to the turn of the century, it was only a matter of time before key interests would manifest themselves in a flurry of political activity. Unrest resulted in reform movements within the two major parties, as well as the formation of issue-oriented third parties, as it did in the case of the People's Party, also known as the Populist Movement. In part, agrarian Americans responded to the recognition that their fate and prosperity had less to do with their own energies and talents as farmers and more with the machinations of speculators buying and selling grain futures. Other links in the chain of production from the fields to the consumers became implicated as well, such as the elevators, banks, railroads, and state legislatures.

The social status of farmers and the political power of rural America had all but vanished as the United States became more industrial and urban. As a result, fiery rhetoric and lively songs were often used by the Populists attempting to either regain lost status and power or to reacquaint America with the worth and the value of farmers. African American farmers also sought to organize themselves in an effort to mitigate their inability to wrest a better deal from both economic and political systems. The political potential was obvious, and some Populists shifted their appeals across former racial caverns to align the poor against the rich.

Within the milieu of unrest, various strains of discontented, disenfranchised, and disinherited Americans were able to make the case for government regulation of certain utilities in the interests of the general public. The process of creating an agency within the government charged with protecting the public from unscrupulous behavior and to whom the people could turn for redress of wrongs is illustrated in the legislation creating the Interstate Commerce Commission. It is a process that has become deeply woven into American civic culture. Dissatisfied with what began as mild forms of regulation and control, the Populists made a formidable bid to take over the political system *through the candidacy of William Jennings Bryan. In that election the forces of old politics, appealing to people directly and personally, and new politics, riding waves of media-generated support, battled it out toe-to-toe. The victory of McKinley and well-financed campaigns has affected the nature of American politics ever since.*

DOCUMENT 21.1

The Pit

Frank Norris

Since that day when—acting upon the foreknowledge of the French import duty—Jadwin had sold his million of bushels short, the price of wheat had been steadily going down. From ninety-three and ninety-four it had dropped to the eighties. Heavy crops the world over had helped the decline. No one was willing to buy wheat. The Bear leaders were strong, unassailable. Lower and lower sagged the price; now it was seventy-five, now seventy-two. From all parts of the country in solid, waveless tides wheat—the mass of it incessantly crushing down the price—came rolling in upon Chicago and the Board of Trade Pit. All over the world the farmers saw season after season of good crops. They were good in the Argentine Republic, and on the Russian steppes. In India, on the little farms of Burmah, of Mysore, and of Sind the grain, year after year, headed out fat, heavy, and well-favoured. In the great San Joaquin valley of California the ranches were one welter of fertility. All over the United States, from the Dakotas, from Nebraska, Iowa, Kansas, and Illinois, from all the wheat belt came steadily the reports of good crops.

But at the same time the low price of grain kept the farmers poor. New mortgages were added to farms already heavily "papered"; even the crops were mortgaged in advance. No new farm implements were bought. Throughout the farming communities of the Middle West there were no longer purchases of buggies and parlour organs. Somewhere in other remoter corners of the world the cheap wheat, that meant cheap bread, made living easy and induced prosperity, but in the United States the poverty of the farmer worked upward through the cogs and wheels of the whole great machine of business. It was as though a lubricant had dried up. The cogs and wheels worked slowly and with dislocations. Things were a little out of joint. Wall Street stocks were down. In a word, "times were bad." Thus for three years. It became a proverb on the Chicago Board of Trade that the quickest way to make money was to sell wheat short. One could with almost absolute certainty be sure of buying cheaper than one had sold. And that peculiar, indefinite thing known—among the most unsentimental men in the world—as "sentiment," prevailed more and more strongly in favour of low prices. "The 'sentiment,'" said the market reports,

Source: From Frank Norris, *The Pit: A Story of Chicago,* 1903; Internet Wiretap electronic edition, prepared by John Hamm, 1993. Available at wiretap.area.com/Gopher/Library/Classic/pit.txt.

"was bearish"; and the traders, speculators, eighth-chasers, scalpers, brokers, bucket-shop men, and the like—all the world of La Salle Street—had become so accustomed to these "Bear conditions," that it was hard to believe that they would not continue indefinitely.

Jadwin, inevitably, had been again drawn into the troubled waters of the Pit. Always, as from the very first, a Bear, he had once more raided the market, and had once more been successful. Two months after this raid he and Gretry planned still another coup, a deal of greater magnitude than any they had previously hazarded. Laura, who knew very little of her husband's affairs—to which he seldom alluded—saw by the daily papers that at one stage of the affair the "deal" trembled to its base.

But Jadwin was by now "blooded to the game." He no longer needed Gretry's urging to spur him. He had developed into a strategist, bold, of inconceivable effrontery, delighting in the shock of battle, never more jovial, more daring than when under stress of the most merciless attack. On this occasion, when the "other side" resorted to the usual tactics to drive him from the Pit, he led on his enemies to make one single false step. Instantly—disregarding Gretry's entreaties as to caution—Jadwin had brought the vast bulk of his entire fortune to bear, in the manner of a general concentrating his heavy artillery, and crushed the opposition with appalling swiftness.

DOCUMENT 21.2

The Bloodhounds of Money

Mary E. Lease

This is a nation of inconsistencies. The Puritans fleeing from oppression became in turn oppressors. We fought England for our liberty and put chains on four millions of blacks. We wiped out slavery and by our tariff laws and national banks began a system of white wage slavery worse than the first. Wall Street owns the country. It is no longer a government of the people, by the people and for the people, but a government of Wall Street, by Wall Street and for Wall Street. The great common people of this country are slaves, and monopoly is the master. The West and South are bound and prostrate before the manufacturing East. Money rules, and our Vice President is a London banker. Our laws are the output of a system which clothes rascals in robes and honesty in rags. The parties lie to us and the political speakers mislead us. We were told two years ago to go to work and raise a big crop, that was all we needed. We went to work and plowed and planted; the rains fell, the sun shone, nature smiled, and we raised the big crop that they told us to; and what came of it? Eight-cent corn, ten-cent oats, two-cent beef and no price at all for butter and eggs—that's what came of it. Then the politicians said we suffered from over-production. Over-production,

Source: Mary E. Lease, "The Bloodhounds of Money," quoted in Elizabeth N. Barr, "The Populist Uprising," in W. E. Connelley, ed., *History of Kansas, State, and People* (Topeka, KS: Lewis Publishing Co., Topeka, Kansas, 1928), 2:1167.

when 10,000 little children, so statistics tell us, starve to death every year in the United States, and over 100,000 shop-girls in New York are forced to sell their virtue for the bread their niggardly wages deny them. Tariff is not the paramount question. The main question is the money question. John J. Ingalls never smelled gunpowder in all his cowardly life. His war record is confined to the court-marshalling of a chicken thief. Kansas suffers from two great robbers, the Santa Fe Railroad and the loan companies. The common people are robbed to enrich their masters. There are 30,000 millionaires in the United States. Go home and figure out how many paupers you must have to make one millionaire with the circulation only $10 per capita. There are thirty men in the United States whose aggregate wealth is over one and one-half billion dollars. There are half a million men looking for work. There are 60,000 soldiers of the Union in poor-houses, but no bondholders. It would have been better if Congress had voted pensions to those 60,000 paupers who wore the blue and dyed it red with their blood in the country's defense than to have voted to make the banker's bonds non-taxable, and payable, interest and principal, in gold. We want money, land and transportation. We want the abolition of the National Banks, and we want the power to make loans direct from the Government. We want the accursed foreclosure system wiped out. Land equal to a tract thirty miles wide and ninety miles long has been foreclosed and bought in by loan companies of Kansas in a year. We will stand by our homes and stay by our firesides by force if necessary, and we will not pay our debts to the loan-shark companies until the Government pays its debts to us. The people are at bay, let the blood-hounds of money who have dogged us thus far beware.

DOCUMENT 21.3

A Populist Song: Good-bye, My Party, Good-bye

Air: "Good-bye, My Lover, Good-bye"

It was no more than a year ago,
   Good-bye, my party, good-bye.
That I was in love with my party so,
   Good-bye, my party, good-bye.
To hear aught else I never would go;
   Good-bye, my party, good-bye.
Like the rest I made a great blow;
   Good-bye, my party, good-bye.

Chorus:

Bye, party, bye, lo; bye, party, bye, lo;
Bye, party, bye, lo; good-bye, my party, good-bye.

Source: From John D. Hicks, *The Populist Revolt: A History of the Farmer's Alliance and the People's Party* (Minneapolis: University of Minnesota Press, 1931), pp. 169–70.

I was often scourged with the party lash,
    Good-bye, my party, good-bye.
The bosses laid on with demands for cash;
    Good-bye, my party, good-bye.
To do aught else I deemed it rash,
    Good-bye, my party, good-bye.
So I had to take it or lose my hash,
    Good-bye, my party, good-bye.

Chorus:

I was raised up in the kind of school,
    Good-bye, my party, good-bye.
That taught to bow to money rule,
    Good-bye, my party, good-bye.
And it made of me a "Kansas Fool,"
    Good-bye, my party, good-bye.
When they found I was a willing tool,
    Good-bye, my party, good-bye.

Chorus:

The old party is on the downward track,
    Good-bye, my party, good-bye.
Picking its teeth with a tariff tack,
    Good-bye, my party, good-bye.
With a placard pinned upon his back,
    Good-bye, my party, good-bye.
That plainly states, "I will never go back";
    Good-bye, my party, good-bye.

Chorus:

DOCUMENT 21.4

Race and Populism: You Can't Come In

The argument against the independent political movement in the South may be boiled down into one word—NIGGER!

Fatal word!

Why, for thirty years before our war, did the North and South hate each other?

NIGGER.

What brought disunion and war?

NIGGER.

Source: Barton C. Shaw, *The Wool-Hat Boys: Georgia's Populist Party* (Baton Rouge: Louisiana State University Press, 1984), pp. 80–81.

With what did Abraham Lincoln break the backbone of the Confederacy?
NIGGER.
What impeded reconstruction?
NIGGER.
How did the Republicans rule the South for years after Appomattox?
NIGGER.
What has kept the South in a cast iron straight jacket?
NIGGER.
What will be the slogan of our old politicians until Gabriel calls them home?
NIGGER.
Pious Southern people never dreaded death so much as they do now. They fear that when they knock at the pearly gates of the New Jerusalem St. Peter will peep through the key-hole and say:
"You can't come in."
"Why?"
"NIGGER!"

DOCUMENT 21.5

Interstate Commerce Act

. . . All charges made for any service rendered or to be rendered in the transportation of passengers or property as aforesaid, or in connection therewith, or for the receiving, delivering, storage, or handling of such property, shall be reasonable and just; and every unjust and unreasonable charge for such service is prohibited and declared to be unlawful.

Section 12

That the Commission hereby created shall have authority to inquire into the management of the business of all common carriers subject to the provisions of this act, and shall keep itself informed as to the manner and method in which the same is conducted, and shall have the right to obtain from such common carriers full and complete information necessary to enable the Commission to perform the duties and carry out the objects for which it was created; and for the purposes of this act the Commission shall have power to require the attendance and testimony of witnesses and the production of all books, papers, tariffs, contracts, agreements, and documents relating to any matter under investigation, and to that end may invoke the aid of any court of the United States in requiring the attendance and testimony of witnesses and the production of books, papers, and documents under the provisions of this section. . . .

Source: Available at www.civics-online.org/library/formatted/texts/interstate_commerce.html.

Section 13

That any person, firm, corporation, or association, or any mercantile, agricultural, or manufacturing society, or any body politic or municipal organization complaining of anything done or omitted to be done by any common carrier subject to the provisions of this act, in contravention of the provisions thereof, may apply to said Commission by petition, which shall briefly state the facts; whereupon a statement of the charges thus made shall be forwarded by the Commission to such common carrier, who shall be called upon to satisfy the complaint or to answer the same in writing within a reasonable time, to be specified by the Commission. . . . If there shall appear to be any reasonable ground for investigating said complaint, it shall be the duty of the Commission to investigate the matters complained of in such manner and by such means as it shall deem proper.

Said Commission shall in like manner investigate any complaint forwarded by the railroad commissioner or railroad commission of any State or Territory, at the request of such commissioner or commission, and may institute any inquiry on its own motion in the same manner and to the same effect as though complaint had been made. . . .

* * *

Section 16

That whenever any common carrier, . . . shall violate or refuse to neglect to obey any lawful order or requirement of the Commission on this act named, it shall be the duty of the Commission, and lawful for any company or person interested in such order or requirement, to apply, in a summary way, by petition, to the circuit court of the United States sitting in equity in the judicial district in which the common carrier complained of has its principal office, or in which the violation or disobedience of such order or requirements shall happen, alleging such violation or disobedience, as the case may be; and the said court shall have power to hear and determine the matter, on such short notice to the common carrier complained of as the court shall deem reasonable. . . .

* * *

Section 20

That the Commission is hereby authorized to require annual reports from all common carriers subject to the provisions of this act, fix the time and prescribe the manner in which such reports shall be made, and to require from such carriers specific answers to all questions upon which the Commission may need information. Such reports shall also contain such information in relation to rates or regulations concerning fares or freights, or agreements, arrangements, or contracts with other common carriers, as the Commission may require; and the said Commission may, within its discretion, for the purpose of enabling it the better to carry out the purposes of this act, prescribe (if in the opinion of the Commission it is practicable to prescribe such uniformity and methods of keeping accounts) a period of time within which all common carriers subject to the provisions of this act shall have, as near as may be, a uniform system of accounts, and the manner in which such accounts shall be kept. . . .

Approved 1887.

DOCUMENT 21.6

A Cross of Gold

William Jennings Bryan

. . . Never before in the history of this country has there been witnessed such a contest as that through which we have just passed. Never before in the history of American politics has a great issue been fought out as this issue has been, by the voters of a great party. On the fourth of March, 1895, a few Democrats, most of them members of Congress, issued an address to the Democrats of the nation, asserting that the money question was the paramount issue of the hour; declaring that a majority of the Democratic party had the right to control the action of the party on this paramount issue; and concluding with the request that the believers in the free coinage of silver in the Democratic party should organize, take charge of, and control the policy of the Democratic party. Three months later, at Memphis, an organization was perfected, and the silver Democrats went forth openly and courageously proclaiming their belief, and declaring that, if successful, they would crystallize into a platform the declaration which they had made. Then began the conflict. With a zeal approaching the zeal which inspired the crusaders who followed Peter the Hermit, our silver Democrats went forth from victory unto victory until they are now assembled, not to discuss, not to debate, but to enter up the judgment already rendered by the plain people of this country. In this contest brother has been arrayed against brother, father against son. The warmest ties of love, acquaintance and association have been disregarded; old leaders have been cast aside when they have refused to give expression to the sentiments of those whom they would lead, and new leaders have sprung up to give direction to this cause of truth. Thus has the contest been waged, and we have assembled here under as binding and solemn instructions as were ever imposed upon representatives of the people. . . .

And now, my friends, let me come to the paramount issue. If they ask us why it is that we say more on the money question than we say upon the tariff question, I reply that, if protection has slain its thousands, the gold standard has slain its tens of thousands. If they ask us why we do not embody in our platform all the things that we believe in, we reply that when we have restored the money of the Constitution all other necessary reforms will be possible; but that until this is done there is no other reform that can be accomplished.

Source: From William Jennings Bryan, *The First Battle: A Story of the Campaign of 1896* (Chicago, W. B. Conkey Co., 1896), pp. 199–206.

Why is it that within three months such a change has come over the country? Three months ago, when it was confidently asserted that those who believe in the gold standard would frame our platform and nominate our candidates, even the advocates of the gold standard did not think that we could elect a president. And they had good reason for their doubt, because there is scarcely a State here today asking for the gold standard which is not in the absolute control of the Republican party. But note the change. Mr. McKinley was nominated at St. Louis upon a platform which declared for the maintenance of the gold standard until it can be changed into bimetallism by international agreement. Mr. McKinley was the most popular man among the Republicans, and three months ago everybody in the Republican party prophesied his election. How is today? Why, the man who was once pleased to think that he looked like Napoleon—that man shudders today when he remembers that he was nominated on the anniversary of the battle of Waterloo. Not only that, but as he listens he can hear with ever-increasing distinctness the sound of the waves as they beat upon the lonely shores of St. Helena.

Why this change? Ah, my friends, is not the reason for the change evident to any one who will look at the matter? No private character, however pure, no personal popularity, however great, can protect from the avenging wrath of an indignant people a man who will declare that he is in favor of fastening the gold standard upon this country, or who is willing to surrender the right of self-government and place the legislative control of our affairs in the hands of foreign potentates and powers.

We go forth confident that we shall win. Why? Because upon the paramount issue of this campaign there is not a spot of ground upon which the enemy will dare to challenge battle. If they tell us that the gold standard is a good thing, we shall point to their platform and tell them that their platform pledges the party to get rid of the gold standard and substitute bimetallism. If the gold standard is a good thing, why try to get rid of it? I call your attention to the fact that some of the very people who are in this convention today and who tell us that we ought to declare in favor of international bimetallism—thereby declaring that the gold standard is wrong and that the principle of bimetallism is better—these very people four months ago were open and avowed advocates of the gold standard, and were then telling us that we could not legislate two metals together, even with the aid of all the world. If the gold standard is a good thing, we ought to declare in favor of its retention and not in favor of abandoning it; and if the gold standard is a bad thing why should we wait until other nations are willing to help us to let go? Here is the line of battle, and we care not upon which issue they force the fight; we are prepared to meet them on either issue or on both. If they tell us that the gold standard is the standard of civilization, we reply to them that this, the most enlightened of all the nations of the earth, has never declared for a gold standard and that both the great parties this year are declaring against it. If the gold standard is the standard of civilization, why, my friends, should we not have it? If they come to meet us on that issue we can present the history of our nation. More than that; we can tell them that they will search the pages of history in vain to find a single instance where the common people of any land have ever declared themselves in favor of the gold standard. They can find where the holders of fixed investments have declared for a gold standard, but not where the masses have. . . .

My friends, we declare that this nation is able to legislate for its own people on every question, without waiting for the aid or consent of any other nation on earth; and upon that issue we expect to carry every State in the Union. I shall not slander the inhabitants of the fair State of Massachusetts nor the inhabitants of the State of New York by saying that, when they are confronted with the proposition, they will declare that this nation is not able to attend to its own business. It is the issue of 1776 over again. Our ancestors, when but three millions in number, had the courage to declare their political independence of every other nation; shall we, their descendants, when we have grown to seventy millions, declare that we are less independent than our forefathers? No, my friends, that will never be the verdict of our people. Therefore, we care not upon what lines the battle is fought. If they say bimetallism is good, but that we cannot have it until other nations help us, we reply that, instead of having a gold standard because England has, we will restore bimetallism, and then let England have bimetallism because the United States has it. If they dare to come out in the open field and defend the gold standard as a good thing, we will fight them to the uttermost. Having behind us the producing masses of this nation and the world, supported by the commercial interests, the laboring interests, and the toilers everywhere, we will answer their demand for a gold standard by saying to them: You shall not press down upon the brow of labor this crown of thorns, you shall not crucify mankind upon a cross of gold.

22

Social Engineers

The Populists may be seen as the last hurrah for the protection of agrarian interests and an agrarian way of life. During this period, cities were forging new definitions of life, liberty, and the pursuit of happiness. With these new changes, inconsistencies and illogical remnants of previous times and American traditional behaviors became silhouetted against the backdrop of the dawn of the 20th century. Attention turned toward positive and active steps to shape, craft, or even create a better America and Americans in the process.

In the swirls of reform and improvement, attention turned to women. Whether attention focused on Native American girls, women working in factories or seeking educational opportunities, or women attempting to exercise their skills and talents in partnering with the men of society in perfecting America, issues of gender became part of public discourse more than ever before.

As various people and groups tried to determine what was best for their compatriots, themselves, and the nation, the tendency to seek legislative relief and reform accelerated. A dizzying array of laws was passed in what has become known as the Progressive Era, all of which were designed to somehow contribute to the perfection of America. The creation of a Bureau of Corporations, the formalization of time zones in the country, and amendments to the Constitution which allowed taxation of the people to generate revenues to do other good things and which directly linked the public with the selection of the U.S. Senate, all suggested the law as an appropriate vehicle to achieve greater justice, equity, and even happiness for the nation.

Far distant from the urban reformism associated with the political movement known as Progressivism was another progressivism emanating from the energies of John Muir and like-minded conservationists who joined with him to create the Sierra Club. They sought to preserve what Muir once referred to as the "immortal truth and immortal beauty of Nature." Indeed, there were those who saw the beauty of nature and communing with nature as tonics and curatives for the ills that the modem hustle and bustle of industrial life were generating.

DOCUMENT 22.1

Education of Indian Girls in the West

Mary C. Todd

The social and business reconstruction which, in the past few years, has taken women from their homes all over the country and placed them in various public positions of honor and responsibility, positions requiring education, intelligence and good business judgment, has left untroubled but one class. With their patient faces, whose pathetic expression is but the shadow of the down-trodden life they lead, the Indian women have stood aside and have seen other women spreading into larger fields, and pluming their wings for larger flight. Wondering and ignorant, they have never thought that to them any good might come, or any release, from the debasement and servitude to which they have been born. Beasts of burden themselves, and accustomed to the slavish position which became theirs at their birth, they have looked for nothing better for their daughters. The rough camp life, the field labor, the uncleanly and demoralizing ties of "home" (if such it may be called), were accepted. Their sluggish minds looked for no help. But faithful teachers have gradually gathered into the government schools, the young girls; preferring indeed, if they can but get hold of them, children of two or three years of age, hoping that they may grow into civilized ways. Keeping these children, if their parents will permit, until eighteen years of age, there is but little danger that when released from school life, they will return to savage ways. Those who spend a few years in the schools look with loathing upon the early betrothals and marriages into which they are often forced upon their return to their homes. Many of these young girls beg to be allowed to stay always in the schools, and never to be obliged to go home. For this reason, upon our reservation of school land, a building is being prepared where such as wish may find a happy and civilized home when their school days are ended. In these government schools all the appliances of a thrifty and busy life are at hand. Kitchens and dormitories most beautifully kept; neat tables supplied with wholesome and well-cooked food, all the domestic work performed by these girls from all the western Indian tribes—this is the surprise which awaits those who will visit the government schools. Most delicate and beautiful needle work and well-fitting clothing are the products of the sewing rooms, where, under a skillful teacher, they learn the use of the sewing machine and spend happy days. This training of all kinds has one most excellent effect, and that is the overcoming the shyness and reticence by which their intercourse with white people is always marked, and the almost inaudible tone which they always use. They learn from this association with their teachers, to speak; their minds develop, their thoughts grow, and they learn to clothe them in language. Their affections are developed and they become fond of their teachers. The

Source: Mary C. Todd, "Education of Indian Girls in the West," in Mary Kavanaugh Oldham Eagle, ed., *The Congress of Women Held in the Women's Building, World Columbian Exposition, Chicago, U.S.A., 1893* (Chicago: W. B. Conkey Co., 1985), pp. 39–40.

writer witnessed an unexpected meeting of a class of girls of about fourteen years of age, with a teacher who had been absent over a year. While their manifested pleasure lacked the forwardness of many school girls, their pleasure at meeting her was unquestioned, as they followed her about, seeming unwilling to leave her, their conduct, reminding one of the silent and faithful affection of an animal.

The western schools established and supported by the government are most of them in Kansas, Oklahoma and the Indian Territory. These are mixed schools, and in every sense industrial schools. Shops for the carrying on of every kind of manual labor are provided for the boys, and the large grant of land which lies about every school is farmed by them.

The arrangement which the government has recently made with the various tribes for the opening up of their lands for settlement, will go far toward the civilization of the young people. For twenty-five years the government will extend to them its support. At the end of that time it is expected that, from their intercourse with white people, and their school education, they will have become self-supporting. It is hoped that at the end of a girl's school life she may go home to a house instead of a tent; to a permanent residence instead of a nomadic gypsy life; to a family clothed instead of blanketed; to a father and brothers who will serve her instead of exacting servitude. In the past, the years of study and training have been almost lost as the girl returns to the untidy tent upon the bleak and barren ground. What hope is there for her to maintain the tidy and systematic method which she has learned, when surrounded by the sights and sounds and blood-thirsty ways of an Otoe or a Ponca camp?

But surrounded by whites, and encouraged and taught by their teachers and native preachers, surely a bright future is before these poor Indian girls. Surely the dormant mind will awaken, and the sluggish energies quicken, when she sees around her the homes of intelligent white women. The education of the Indian girl means the uplifting of the tribes in every way, and yet it means also and soon, the losing of the races of red men from off the face of the earth.

DOCUMENT 22.2

Twenty Years at Hull-House

Jane Addams

We have in America a fast-growing number of cultivated young people who have no recognized outlet for their active faculties. They hear constantly of the great social maladjustment, but no way is provided for them to change it, and their uselessness hangs about them heavily. Huxley declares that the sense of uselessness is the severest shock which the human system can sustain, and that if persistently sustained, it results in atrophy of function. These young people

Source: From Jane Addams, *Twenty Years at Hull-House: With Autobiographical Notes* (New York: Macmillan Company, 1934), pp. 120–27.

have had advantages of college, of European travel, and of economic study, but they are sustaining this shock of inaction. They have pet phrases, and they tell you that the things that make us all alike are stronger than the things that make us different. They say that all men are united by needs and sympathies far more permanent and radical than anything that temporarily divides them and sets them in opposition to each other. If they affect art, they say that the decay in artistic expression is due to the decay in ethics, that art when shut away from the human interests and from the great mass of humanity is self-destructive. They tell their elders with all the bitterness of youth that if they expect success from them in business or politics or in whatever lines their ambition for them has run, they must let them consult all of humanity; that they must let them find out what the people want and how they want it. It is only the stronger young people, however, who formulate this. Many of them dissipate their energies in so-called enjoyment. Others not content with that, go on studying and go back to college for their second degrees; not that they are especially fond of study, but because they want something definite to do, and their powers have been trained in the direction of mental accumulation. Many are buried beneath this mental accumulation with lowered vitality and discontent. Walter Besant says they have had the vision that Peter had when he saw the great sheet let down from heaven, wherein was neither clean nor unclean. He calls it the sense of humanity. It is not philanthropy nor benevolence, but a thing fuller and wider than either of these.

This young life, so sincere in its emotion and good phrases and yet so undirected, seems to me as pitiful as the other great mass of destitute lives. One is supplementary to the other, and some method of communication can surely be devised. Mr. Barnett, who urged the first Settlement,—Toynbee Hall, in East London,—recognized this need of outlet for the young men of Oxford and Cambridge, and hoped that the Settlement would supply the communication. It is easy to see why the Settlement movement originated in England, where the years of education are more constrained and definite than they are here, where class distinctions are more rigid. The necessity of it was greater there, but we are fast feeling the pressure of the need and meeting the necessity for Settlements in America. Our young people feel nervously the need of putting theory into action, and respond quickly to the Settlement form of activity.

Other motives which I believe make toward the Settlement are the result of a certain renaissance going forward in Christianity. The impulse to share the lives of the poor, the desire to make social service, irrespective of propaganda, express the spirit of Christ, is as old as Christianity itself. We have no proof from the records themselves that the early Roman Christians, who strained their simple art to the point of grotesqueness in their eagerness to record a "good news" on the walls of the catacombs, considered this good news a religion. Jesus had no set of truths labeled Religious. On the contrary, his doctrine was that all truth is one, that the appropriation of it is freedom. His teaching had no dogma to mark it off from truth and action in general. He himself called it a revelation—a life. These early Roman Christians received the Gospel message, a command to love all men, with a certain joyous simplicity. The image of the Good Shepherd is blithe and gay beyond the gentlest shepherd of Greek mythology; the hart no longer pants, but rushes to the water brooks. The Christians looked for the continuous revelation, but believed what Jesus said, that this revelation, to be retained and made manifest, must be put into terms of action; that action is the only medium man has for receiving and appropriating truth; that the doctrine must be known through the will.

That Christianity has to be revealed and embodied in the line of social progress is a corollary to the simple proposition, that man's action is found in his social relationships in the way in which he connects with his fellows; that his motives for action are the zeal and affection with which he regards his fellows. By this simple process was created a deep enthusiasm for humanity, which regarded man as at once the organ and the object of revelation; and by this process came about the wonderful fellowship, the true democracy of the early Church, that so captivates the imagination. The early Christians were preëminently non-resistant. They believed in love as a cosmic force. There was no iconoclasm during the minor peace of the Church. They did not yet denounce nor tear down temples, nor preach the end of the world. They grew to a mighty number, but it never occurred to them, either in their weakness or in their strength, to regard other men for an instant as their foes or as aliens. The spectacle of the Christians loving all men was the most astounding Rome had ever seen. They were eager to sacrifice themselves for the weak, for children, and for the aged; they identified themselves with slaves and did not avoid the plague; they longed to share the common lot that they might receive the constant revelation. It was a new treasure which the early Christians added to the sum of all treasures, a joy hitherto unknown in the world—the joy of finding the Christ which lieth in each man, but which no man can unfold save in fellowship. A happiness ranging from the heroic to the pastoral enveloped them. They were to possess a revelation as long as life had new meaning to unfold, new action to propose.

I believe that there is a distinct turning among many young men and women toward this simple acceptance of Christ's message. They resent the assumption that Christianity is a set of ideas which belong to the religious consciousness, whatever that may be. They insist that it cannot be proclaimed and instituted apart from the social life of the community and that it must seek a simple and natural expression in the social organism itself. The Settlement movement is only one manifestation of that wider humanitarian movement which throughout Christendom, but preëminently in England, is endeavoring to embody itself, not in a sect, but in society itself.

I believe that this turning, this renaissance of the early Christian humanitarianism, is going on in America, in Chicago, if you please, without leaders who write or philosophize, without much speaking, but with a bent to express in social service and in terms of action the spirit of Christ. Certain it is that spiritual force is found in the Settlement movement, and it is also true that this force must be evoked and must be called into play before the success of any Settlement is assured. There must be the overmastering belief that all that is noblest in life is common to men as men, in order to accentuate the likenesses and ignore the differences which are found among the people whom the Settlement constantly brings into juxtaposition. It may be true, as the Positivists insist, that the very religious fervor of man can be turned into love for his race, and his desire for a future life into content to live in the echo of his deeds; Paul's formula of seeking for the Christ which lieth in each man and founding our likenesses on him, seems a simpler formula to many of us.

In a thousand voices singing the Hallelujah Chorus in Handel's "Messiah," it is possible to distinguish the leading voices, but the differences of training and cultivation between them and the voices of the chorus, are lost in the unity of purpose and in the fact that they are all human voices lifted by a high motive. This is a weak illustration of what a Settlement attempts to do. It aims, in a measure, to develop whatever of social life its neighborhood may afford, to focus and give form to that life, to bring to bear upon it the results of cultivation and training; but it receives in exchange for the music of isolated voices the volume and strength of the chorus. It is quite impossible for me to say in what proportion or degree the subjective necessity which led to the opening of Hull-House combined the three trends: first, the desire to interpret democracy in social terms; secondly, the impulse beating at the very source of our lives, urging us to aid in the race progress; and, thirdly, the Christian movement toward humanitarianism. It is difficult to analyze a living thing; the analysis is at best imperfect. Many more motives may blend with the three trends; possibly the desire for a new form of social success due to the nicety of imagination, which refuses worldly pleasures unmixed with the joys of self-sacrifice; possibly a love of approbation, so vast that it is not content with the treble clapping of delicate hands, but wishes also to hear the bass notes from toughened palms, may mingle with these.

The Settlement, then, is an experimental effort to aid in the solution of the social and industrial problems which are engendered by the modern conditions of life in a great city. It insists that these problems are not confined to any one portion of a city. It is an attempt to relieve, at the same time, the overaccumulation at one end of society and the destitution at the other; but it assumes that this overaccumulation and destitution is most sorely felt in the things that pertain to social and educational advantages. From its very nature it can stand for no political or social propaganda. It must, in a sense, give the warm welcome of an inn to all such propaganda, if perchance one of them be found an angel. The one thing to be dreaded in the Settlement is that it lose its flexibility, its power of quick adaptation, its readiness to change its methods as its environment may demand. It must be open to conviction and must have a deep and abiding sense of tolerance. It must be hospitable and ready for experiment. It should demand from its residents a scientific patience in the accumulation of facts and the steady holding of their sympathies as one of the best instruments for that accumulation. It must be grounded in a philosophy whose foundation is on the solidarity of the human race, a philosophy which will not waver when the race happens to be represented by a drunken woman or an idiot boy. Its residents must be emptied of all conceit of opinion and all self-assertion, and ready to arouse and interpret the public opinion of their neighborhood. They must be content to live quietly side by side with their neighbors, until they grow into a sense of relationship and mutual interests. Their neighbors are held apart by differences of race and language which the residents can more easily overcome. They are bound to see the needs of their neighborhood as a whole, to furnish data for legislation, and to use their influence to secure it. In short, residents are pledged to devote themselves to the duties of good citizenship and to the arousing of the social energies which too largely lie dormant in every neighborhood given over to industrialism. They are bound to regard the entire life of their city as organic, to make an effort to unify it, and to protest against its over-differentiation.

It is always easy to make all philosophy point one particular moral and all history adorn one particular tale; but I may be forgiven the reminder that the best speculative philosophy sets forth the solidarity of the human race; that the highest moralists have taught that without the advance and improvement of the whole, no man can hope for any lasting improvement in his own moral or material individual condition; and that the subjective necessity for Social Settlements is therefore identical with that necessity, which urges us on toward social and individual salvation.

DOCUMENT 22.3

Laws Affecting Women and Children in the Suffrage and Non-suffrage States

Alabama

Until 1915 Alabama was one of the most backward states in regard to protective legislation for women and children. A great advance was made in the child labor law passed in the session of 1915. The chief provisions of the Alabama laws are as follows:

No child under 13 shall be permitted to work in any gainful employment except domestic service or agriculture. (After Sept. 1, 1916, this age limit is raised to 14.) Provided, that boys over 12 may be employed out of school hours in offices or mercantile establishments in towns and cities of less than 25,000 population. No person under 18 shall be employed as messenger in any city of 25,000 or over in the distribution of goods or messages, between 9 P.M. and 5 A.M.; or in cities of less than 25,000 population between 10 P.M. and 5 A.M., and no person under 21 shall be employed in any place where intoxicating liquors are manufactured, packed, or sold.

No child under 16 shall be employed about dangerous machinery or on railroads or vessels, or among dangerous acids or poisonous dyes, or gases, nor on scaffolding, nor in building trades, nor in any tunnel or mine, coal breaker, coke oven, or quarry, nor in manufacturing or packing tobacco, nor in any concert hall, or theater stage, or other exhibition or show.

Source: From *Laws Affecting Women and Children in the Suffrage and Non-suffrage States*, 2nd ed. (New York: National Woman Suffrage Publishing Co., 1917).

No child under 16 shall be employed in any mill, factory, or manufacturing establishment for more than six days, or 60 hours a week, or 11 hours a day; nor between 6 P.M. and 6 A.M.

No child between 16 and 18 shall be detained in any mill, factory, or manufacturing establishment for more than eight hours in any one night. No woman, or boy under 16, shall be employed in or about any mine.

No child under 16 shall be employed in any factory, mill, or mercantile establishment, unless such child attend school eight weeks in each year of employment, six weeks of which shall be consecutive.

No child under 16 shall be employed unless he first present an employment certificate issued by the school authorities. Such certificates must contain proof of the age of the child and that he has attended school for at least 60 days in the preceding year. Schools must be provided in the vicinity of factories employing children.

Factories must be inspected without previous notice at least four times a year. No boy under 12, nor girl under 18, in any city of 25,000 or over, shall sell newspapers or engage in any street trade. Provided, that boys over 10 may distribute newspapers on routes. No boy under 16 shall engage in street trading between 8 P.M. and 5 A.M., nor unless he wear a badge issued by the school authorities.

Seats must be provided in every store or shop where girls or women are employed and their use permitted to such employees when not actively engaged in work.

After October 1, 1917, school attendance will be compulsory on all children between 8 and 15 for 80 days in each school year, unless the child shall have completed seven grades, or unless the services of the child are necessary for its own support or for the support of a widowed mother or disabled father.

DOCUMENT 22.4

The Bureau of Corporations

Section 6

That there shall be in the Department of Commerce and Labor a bureau to be called the Bureau of Corporations, and a Commissioner of Corporations who shall be the head of said bureau, to be appointed by the President, who shall receive a salary of five thousand dollars per annum. There shall also be in said bureau a deputy commissioner who shall receive a salary of three thousand five hundred dollars per annum, and who shall in the absence of the Commissioner act as, and perform the duties of, the Commissioner of Corporations, and who shall also perform such other duties as may be assigned to him by the Secretary of Commerce and Labor or by the said Commissioner. There shall also be in the said bureau a chief clerk and such special agents, clerks, and other employees as may be authorized by law.

Source: From "An Act to Establish the Department of Commerce and Labor," Fifty-seventh Congress, Session 2, Chap. 552, 1903, *U.S. Statutes at Large,* pp. 825–31.

The said Commissioner shall have power and authority to make, under the direction and control of the Secretary of Commerce and Labor, diligent investigation into the organization, conduct, and management of the business of any corporation, joint stock company or corporate combination engaged in commerce among the several States and with foreign nations excepting common carriers subject to "An Act to regulate commerce," approved February fourth, eighteen hundred and eighty-seven, and to gather such information and data as will enable the President of the United States to make recommendations to Congress for legislation for the regulation of such commerce, and to report such data to the President from time to time as he shall require; and the information so obtained or as much thereof as the President may direct shall be made public.

In order to accomplish the purposes declared in the foregoing part of this section, the said Commissioner shall have and exercise the same power and authority in respect to corporations, joint stock companies and combinations subject to the provisions hereof, as is conferred on the Interstate Commerce Commission in said "Act to regulate commerce" and the amendments thereto in respect to common carriers so far as the same may be applicable, including the right to subpœna and compel the attendance and testimony of witnesses and the production of documentary evidence and to administer oaths. All the requirements, obligations, liabilities, and immunities imposed or conferred by said "Act to regulate commerce" and by "An Act in relation to testimony before the Interstate Commerce Commission," and so forth, approved February eleventh, eighteen hundred and ninety-three, supplemental to said "Act to regulate commerce," shall also apply to all persons who may be subpœnaed to testify as witnesses or to produce documentary evidence in pursuance of the authority conferred by this section.

It shall also be the province and duty of said bureau, under the direction of the Secretary of Commerce and Labor, to gather, compile, publish, and supply useful information concerning corporations doing business within the limits of the United States as shall engage in interstate commerce or in commerce between the United States and any foreign country, including corporations engaged in insurance, and to attend to such other duties as may be hereafter provided by law.

DOCUMENT 22.5

Establishment of Standard Time

CHAP. 24. An Act To save daylight and to provide standard time for the United States.

Be it enacted by the Senate and House of Representatives of the United States of America in Congress assembled, That, for the purpose of establishing the standard time

Source: Sixty-fifth Congress, Session 2, Chap. 24, 1918, *U.S. Statutes at Large,* vol. 40, part 1 (Washington, DC: GPO, 1919), pp. 450–51.

of the United States, the territory of continental United States shall be divided into five zones in the manner hereinafter provided. The standard time of the first zone shall be based on the mean astronomical time of the seventy-fifth degree of longitude west from Greenwich; that of the second zone on the ninetieth degree; that of the third zone on the one hundred and fifth degree; that of the fourth zone on the one hundred and twentieth degree; and that of the fifth zone, which shall include only Alaska, on the one hundred and fiftieth degree. That the limits of each zone shall be defined by an order of the Interstate Commerce Commission, having regard for the convenience of commerce and the existing junction points and division points of common carriers engaged in commerce between the several States and with foreign nations, and such order may be modified from time to time.

Section 2

That within the respective zones created under the authority hereof the standard time of the zone shall govern the movement of all common carriers engaged in commerce between the several States or between a State and any of the Territories of the United States, or between a State or the Territory of Alaska and any of the insular possessions of the United States or any foreign country. In all statutes, orders, rules, and regulations relating to the time of performance of any act by any officer or department of the United States, whether in the legislative, executive, or judicial branches of the Government, or relating to the time within which any rights shall accrue or determine, or within which any act shall or shall not be performed by any person subject to the jurisdiction of the United States, it shall be understood and intended that the time shall be the United States standard time of the zone within which the act is to be performed.

Section 3

That at two o'clock antemeridian of the last Sunday in March of each year the standard time of each zone shall be advanced one hour, and at two o'clock antemeridian of the last Sunday in October in each year the standard time of each zone shall, by the retarding of one hour, be returned to the mean astronomical time of the degree of longitude governing said zone, so that between the last Sunday in March at two o'clock antemeridian and the last Sunday in October at two o'clock antemeridian in each year the standard time in each zone shall be one hour in advance of the mean astronomical time of the degree of longitude governing each zone, respectively.

Section 4

That the standard time of the first zone shall be known and designated as United States Standard Eastern Time; that of the second zone shall be known and designated as United States Standard Central Time; that of the third zone shall be known and designated as United States Standard Mountain Time; that of the fourth zone shall be known and designated as United States Standard

Pacific Time; and that of the fifth zone shall be known and designated as United States Standard Alaska Time.

Section 5

That all Acts and parts of Acts in conflict herewith are hereby repealed.
Approved, March 19, 1918.

DOCUMENT 22.6

Sixteenth Amendment

The Congress shall have power to lay and collect taxes on incomes, from whatever source derived, without apportionment among the several states, and without regard to any census or enumeration.

DOCUMENT 22.7

Seventeenth Amendment

The Senate of the United States shall be composed of two Senators from each state, elected by the people thereof, for six years; and each Senator shall have one vote. The electors in each state shall have the qualifications requisite for electors of the most numerous branch of the state legislatures.

When vacancies happen in the representation of any state in the Senate, the executive authority of such state shall issue writs of election to fill such vacancies: Provided, that the legislature of any state may empower the executive thereof to make temporary appointments until the people fill the vacancies by election as the legislature may direct.

This amendment shall not be so construed as to affect the election or term of any Senator chosen before it becomes valid as part of the Constitution.

DOCUMENT 22.8

The Endangered Valley--The Hetch Hetchy Valley in the Yosemite National Park

John Muir

From San Francisco and the Hetch Hetchy Reservoir: Hearing held before the committee on the Public Lands of the House of Representatives, December 16, 1908, on House Joint Resolution 184, part 8.

The fame of the Merced Yosemite has spread far and wide, while Hetch Hetchy, the Tuolumne Yosemite, has until recently remained comparatively unknown, notwithstanding it is a wonderfully exact counterpart of the famous valley. As the Merced flows in tranquil beauty through Yosemite, so does the Tuolumne through Hetch Hetchy. The floor of Yosemite is about 4,000 feet above the sea, and that of Hetch Hetchy about 3,700 while in both the walls are of gray granite, very high, and rise precipitously out of flowery gardens and groves. Furthermore the two wonderful valleys occupy the same relative positions on the flank of the Sierra, were formed by the same forces in the same kind of granite, and have similar waterfalls, sculpture, and vegetation. Hetch Hetchy lies in a northwesterly direction from Yosemite at a distance of about 18 miles, and is now easily accessible by a trail and wagon road from the Big Oak Flat road at Sequoia. . . .

Hetch Hetchy weather is delightful and invigorating all the year. Snow seldom lies long on the floor and is never very deep. On the sunny north wall many a sheltered nook may be found embraced by sun-warmed rock bosses in which flowers bloom every month of the year. Even on the shaded south side of the valley the frost is never severe.

A good many birds winter in the valley and fill the short days with merry chatter and song. A cheerier company never sang in snow. First and best of all is the water ouzel, a dainty, dusky little bird, about the size of a robin, that sings a sweet fluty song all winter as well as in summer, and haunts the wild rapids and falls with marvelous constancy through all sorts of weather. A few robins, belated on their way down from the upper mountain meadows, make out to spend the winter here in comparative comfort, feeding on mistletoe berries. The kingfisher also winters in the valley, the golden-winged woodpecker, and the species that stores acorns in the bark of the trees, as well as jays, wrens, sparrows, and flocks of bluebirds and snowbirds, which make lively pictures in their quest for food.

Toward the end of March the sprouting grasses make the meadows green, the aments of the alders are nearly ripe, the libocedrus is sowing its pollen, willows putting forth their catkins, and a multitude of swelling buds proclaim the promise of spring. Wild strawberries are ripe in May, the early flowers are in bloom, the birds are busy in the groves, and the frogs in pools.

In June and July summer is in prime, and the tide of happy, throbbing life is at its highest. August is the peaceful season of ripe nuts and berries—raspberries, blackberries, thimbleberries, gooseberries, shadberries, currants, puckery choke cherries, pine nuts, etc., offering royal feasts to Indians, squirrels, and birds of every feather. Then comes mellow, golden Indian summer, with its gorgeous colors and falling leaves, calm, thoughtful days, when everything, even the huge rocks, seems to be hushed and expectant, awaiting the coming of winter and rest.

Excepting only Yosemite, Hetch Hetchy is the most attractive and wonderful valley within the bounds of the great Yosemite National Park and the best of all the camp grounds. People are now flocking to it in ever-increasing numbers for health and recreation of body and mind. Though the walls are less sublime in height than those of Yosemite, its groves, gardens, and broad, spacious meadows are more beautiful and picturesque. It is many years since sheep and cattle were pastured in it, and the vegetation now shows scarce a trace of their ravages. Last year in October I visited the valley with Mr. William Keith, the artist. He wandered about from view to view, enchanted, made thirty-eight sketches, and enthusiastically declared that in varied picturesque beauty Hetch Hetchy greatly surpassed Yosemite. It is one of God's best gifts and ought to be faithfully guarded.

23

Unilateralism among Friends

The frenetic activity of the Progressive Era produced a mixed bag of reform legislation and regulations. It also coincided with the opening salvos of what many Europeans viewed as a fundamental clash of civilizations—World War I. For policy makers and people on both sides of the Atlantic, the United States loomed as a gargantuan enigma: too big, prosperous, and potentially power-ful to be ignored in global geo-political calculations but perhaps too self-absorbed with its internal perfection or reluctance as a world player to be anxious for a major role in the drama. It seemed to Americans themselves that the most prudent thing was a solid defense while the winds of war evaporated the fluids of life elsewhere. Eventually President Wilson, deeply desirous of re-forms in the international arena that would spread the benefits of democracy, determined that it was time for the United States to fight the forces of evil.

The implications of the U.S. decision directly affected life, liberty, and the pursuit of happiness for many. George Creel reveals the efforts by the govern-ment to use virtually every possible method and strategy to articulate to the American people the nation's purpose and goals in fighting and to achieve a powerful national solidarity that would sustain the war effort. Perhaps these efforts contributed to the excesses of overly zealous patriotic behavior, as German Americans, dissenters, and social critics regardless of their heritage and background were sometimes subjected to humiliation, attacks, and even death at the hands of loyal citizens. Miriam E. Tefft offers the perspective of a 15-year-old girl as she watched the application of wartime values to workers seeking to share some of the profits of wartime contracts in Bisbee, Arizona.

While battles were waged over worker's rights, the draft, the power and be-havior of the federal government, and the loyalty of citizens, American soldiers found themselves in deadly battles on the western front. A truly national effort produced national measures such as the draft that mustered a formidable army of American citizens from all walks of life. Mathew Chopan provides one vantage point, that of an average doughboy, while William Hayward in his letter to Emmett J. Scott explains how and why World War I was significant to African Americans. Finally, the First World War is frequently considered a watershed for the American suffrage movement and the aspirations of feminists. Ida Clyde Clarke adds the perspective of American women volunteering for or being "drafted" into the war effort as well.

DOCUMENT 23.1

The Council of National Defense

That the Council of National Defense shall nominate to the President, and the President shall appoint, an advisory commission, consisting of not more than seven persons, each of whom shall have special knowledge of some industry, public utility, or the development of some natural resource, or be otherwise specially qualified, in the opinion of the council, for the performance of the duties hereinafter provided. The members of the advisory commission shall serve without compensation, but shall be allowed actual expenses of travel and subsistence when attending meetings of the commission or engaged in investigations pertaining to its activities. The advisory commission shall hold such meetings as shall be called by the council or be provided by the rules and regulations adopted by the council for the conduct of its work.

That it shall be the duty of the Council of National Defense to supervise and direct investigations and make recommendations to the President and the heads of executive departments as to the location of railroads with reference to the frontier of the United States so as to render possible expeditious concentration of troops and supplies to points of defense; the coordination of military, industrial, and commercial purposes in the location of extensive highways and branch lines of railroad; the utilization of waterways; the mobilization of military and naval resources for defense; the increase of domestic production of articles and materials essential to the support of armies and of the people during the interruption of foreign commerce; the development of seagoing transportation; data as to amounts, location, method and means of production, and availability of military supplies; the giving of information to producers and manufacturers as to the class of supplies needed by the military and other services of the Government, the requirements relating thereto, and the creation of relations which will render possible in time of need the immediate concentration and utilization of the resources of the Nation.

That the Council of National Defense shall adopt rules and regulations for the conduct of its work, which rules and regulations shall be subject to the approval of the President, and shall provide for the work of the advisory commission to the end that the special knowledge of such commission may be developed by suitable investigation, research, and inquiry and made available in conference and report for the use of the council; and the council may organize

Source: Sixty-fourth Congress, Session 1, Chap. 418, 1916, *U.S. Statutes at Large*, pp. 649–50.

subordinate bodies for its assistance in special investigations, either by the employment of experts or by the creation of committees of specially qualified persons to serve without compensation, but to direct the investigations of experts so employed.

That the sum of $200,000, or so much thereof as may be necessary, is hereby appropriated, out of any money in the Treasury not otherwise appropriated, to be immediately available for experimental work and investigations undertaken by the council, by the advisory commission, or subordinate bodies, for the employment of a director, expert and clerical expenses and supplies, and for the necessary expenses of members of the advisory commission or subordinate bodies going to and attending meetings of the commission or subordinate bodies. Reports shall be submitted by all subordinate bodies and by the advisory commission to the council, and from time to time the council shall report to the President or to the heads of executive departments upon special inquiries or subjects appropriate thereto, and an annual report to the Congress shall be submitted through the President, including as full a statement of the activities of the council and the agencies subordinate to it as is consistent with the public interest, including an itemized account of the expenditures made by the council or authorized by it, in as full detail as the public interest will permit: *Provided, however,* That when deemed proper the President may authorize, in amounts stipulated by him, unvouchered expenditures and report the gross sums so authorized not itemized.

DOCUMENT 23.2

Woodrow Wilson's War Message

Gentlemen of the Congress:

I have called the Congress into extraordinary session because there are serious, very serious, choices of policy to be made, and made immediately, which it was neither right nor constitutionally permissible that I should assume the responsibility of making.

On the third of February last I officially laid before you the extraordinary announcement of the Imperial German Government that on and after the first day of February it was its purpose to put aside all restraints of law or of humanity and use its submarines to sink every vessel that sought to approach either the ports of Great Britain and Ireland or the western coasts of Europe or any of the ports controlled by the enemies of Germany within the Mediterranean. That had seemed to be the object of the German submarine warfare earlier in the war, but since April of last year the Imperial Government had somewhat restrained the commanders of its undersea craft in conformity with

Source: From Woodrow Wilson, "Address of the President of the United States: Delivered at a Joint Session of the Two Houses of Congress, April 2, 1917" (Washington: GPO, 1917; 65th Congress, 1st Session, *Senate Documents*, vol. 10).

its promise then given to us that passenger boats should not be sunk and that due warning would be given to all other vessels which its submarines might seek to destroy, when no resistance was offered or escape attempted, and care taken that their crews were given at least a fair chance to save their lives in their open boats. The precautions taken were meagre and haphazard enough, as was proved in distressing instance after instance in the progress of the cruel and unmanly business, but a certain degree of restraint was observed. The new policy has swept every restriction aside. Vessels of every kind, whatever their flag, their character, their cargo, their destination, their errand, have been ruthlessly sent to the bottom without warning and without thought of help or mercy for those on board, the vessels of friendly neutrals along with those of belligerents. Even hospital ships and ships carrying relief to the sorely bereaved and stricken people of Belgium, though the latter were provided with safe conduct through the proscribed areas by the German Government itself and were distinguished by unmistakable marks of identity, have been sunk with the same reckless lack of compassion or of principle.

I was for a little while unable to believe that such things would in fact be done by any government that had hitherto subscribed to the humane practices of civilized nations. International law had its origin in the attempt to set up some law which would be respected and observed upon the seas, where no nation had right of dominion and where lay the free highways of the world. By painful stage after stage has that law been built up, with meagre enough results, indeed, after all was accomplished that could be accomplished, but always with a clear view, at least, of what the heart and conscience of mankind demanded. This minimum of right the German Government has swept aside under the plea of retaliation and necessity and because it had no weapons which it could use at sea except these which it is impossible to employ as it is employing them without throwing to the winds all scruples of humanity or of respect for the understandings that were supposed to underlie the intercourse of the world. I am not now thinking of the loss of property involved, immense and serious as that is, but only of the wanton and wholesale destruction of the lives of non-combatants, men, women, and children, engaged in pursuits which have always, even in the darkest periods of modern history, been deemed innocent and legitimate. Property can be paid for; the lives of peaceful and innocent people cannot be. The present German submarine warfare against commerce is a warfare against mankind.

It is a war against all nations. American ships have been sunk, American lives taken, in ways which it has stirred us very deeply to learn of, but the ships and people of other neutral and friendly nations have been sunk and overwhelmed in the waters in the same way. There has been no discrimination. The challenge is to all mankind. Each nation must decide for itself how it will meet it. The choice we make for ourselves must be made with a moderation of counsel and a temperateness of judgment befitting our character and our motives as a nation. We must put excited feeling away. Our motive will not be revenge or the victorious assertion of the physical might of the nation, but only the vindication of right, of human right, of which we are only a single champion.

When I addressed the Congress on the twenty-sixth of February last I thought that it would suffice to assert our neutral rights with arms, our right to use the seas against unlawful interference, our right to keep our people safe against unlawful violence. But armed neutrality, it now appears, is impracticable. Because submarines are in effect outlaws when used as the German submarines have been used against merchant shipping, it is impossible to defend ships against their attacks as the law of nations has assumed that merchantment would defend themselves against privateers or cruisers, visible craft giving chase upon the open sea. It is common prudence in such circumstances, grim necessity indeed, to endeavour to destroy them before they have shown their own intention. They must be dealt with upon sight, if dealt with at all. The German Government denies the right of neutrals to use arms at all within the areas of the sea which it has proscribed, even in the defense of rights which no modern publicist has ever before questioned their right to defend. The intimation is conveyed that the armed guards which we have placed on our merchant ships will be treated as beyond the pale of law and subject to be dealt with as pirates would be. Armed neutrality is ineffectual enough at best; in such circumstances and in the face of such pretensions it is worse than ineffectual; it is likely only to produce what it was meant to prevent; it is practically certain to draw us into the war without either the rights or the effectiveness of belligerents. There is one choice we cannot make, we are incapable of making: we will not choose the path of submission and suffer the most sacred rights of our nation and our people to be ignored or violated. The wrongs against which we now array ourselves are no common wrongs; they cut to the very roots of human life.

With a profound sense of the solemn and even tragical character of the step I am taking and of the grave responsibilities which it involves, but in unhesitating obedience to what I deem my constitutional duty, I advise that the Congress declare the recent course of the Imperial German Government to be in fact nothing less than war against the government and people of the United States; that it formally accept the status of belligerent which has thus been thrust upon it; and that it take immediate steps not only to put the country in a more thorough state of defense but also to exert all its power and employ all its resources to bring the Government of the German Empire to terms and end the war.

What this will involve is clear. It will involve the utmost practicable cooperation in counsel and action with the governments now at war with Germany, and, as incident to that, the extension to those governments of the most liberal financial credits, in order that our resources may so far as possible be added to theirs. It will involve the organization and mobilization of all the material resources of the country to supply the materials of war and serve the incidental needs of the nation in the most abundant and yet the most economical and efficient way possible. It will involve the immediate full equipment of the navy in all respects but particularly in supplying it with the best means of dealing with the enemy's submarines. It will involve the immediate addition to the armed forces of the United States already provided for by law in case of war at least five hundred thousand men, who should, in my opinion, be chosen upon the principle of universal liability to service, and also the authorization of subsequent additional increments of equal force so soon as they may be needed and can be handled in training. It will involve also, of course, the granting of adequate credits to the Government, sustained, I hope, so far as they can equitably be sustained by the present generation, by well conceived taxation.

I say sustained so far as may be equitable by taxation because it seems to me that it would be most unwise to base the credits which will now be necessary entirely on money borrowed. It is our duty, I most respectfully urge, to protect our people so far as we may against the very serious hardships and evils which would be likely to arise out of the inflation which would be produced by vast loans.

In carrying out the measures by which these things are to be accomplished we should keep constantly in mind the wisdom of interfering as little as possible in our own preparation and in the equipment of our own military forces with the duty—for it will be a very practical duty—of supplying the nations already at war with Germany with the materials which they can obtain only from us or by our assistance. They are in the field and we should help them in every way to be effective there.

I shall take the liberty of suggesting, through the several executive departments of the Government, for the consideration of your committees, measures for the accomplishment of the several objects I have mentioned. I hope that it will be your pleasure to deal with them as having been framed after very careful thought by the branch of the Government upon which the responsibility of conducting the war and safeguarding the nation will most directly fall.

While we do these things, these deeply momentous things, let us be very clear, and make very clear to all the world what our motives and our objects are. My own thought has not been driven from its habitual and normal course by the unhappy events of the last two months, and I do not believe that the thought of the nation has been altered or clouded by them. I have exactly the same things in mind now that I had in mind when I addressed the Senate on the twenty-second of January last; the same that I had in mind when I addressed the Congress on the third of February and on the twenty-sixth of February. Our object now, as then, is to vindicate the principles of peace and justice in the life of the world as against selfish and autocratic power and to set up amongst the really free and self-governed peoples of the world such a concert of purpose and of action as will henceforth ensure the observance of those principles. Neutrality is no longer feasible or desirable where the peace of the world is involved and the freedom of its peoples, and the menace to that peace and freedom lies in the existence of autocratic governments backed by organized force which is controlled wholly by their will, not by the will of their people. We have seen the last of neutrality in such circumstances. We are at the beginning of an age in which it will be insisted that the same standards of conduct and of responsibility for wrong done shall be observed among nations and their governments that are observed among the individual citizens of civilized states.

We have no quarrel with the German people. We have no feeling towards them but one of sympathy and friendship. It was not upon their impulse that their government acted in entering this war. It was not with their previous knowledge or approval. It was a war determined upon as wars used to be determined upon in the old, unhappy days when peoples were nowhere consulted by their rulers and wars were provoked and waged in the interest of dynasties or of little groups of ambitious men who were accustomed to use their fellow men as pawns and tools. Self-governed nations do not fill their neighbour states with spies or set the course of intrigue to bring about some critical posture of affairs which will give them an opportunity to strike and make conquest. Such designs can be successfully worked out only under cover and where no one has the right to ask questions. Cunningly contrived plans of deception or aggression, carried, it may be, from generation to generation, can be worked out and kept from the light only within the privacy of courts or behind the carefully guarded confidences of a narrow and privileged class. They are happily impossible where public opinion commands and insists upon full information concerning all the nation's affairs.

A steadfast concert for peace can never be maintained except by a partnership of democratic nations. No autocratic government could be trusted to keep faith within it or observe its covenants. It must be a league of honour, a partnership of opinion. Intrigue would eat its vitals away; the plottings of inner circles who could plan what they would and render account to no one would be a corruption seated at its very heart. Only free peoples can hold their purpose and their honour steady to a common end and prefer the interests of mankind to any narrow interest of their own.

Does not every American feel that assurance has been added to our hope for the future peace of the world by the wonderful and heartening things that have been happening within the last few weeks in Russia? Russia was known by those who knew it best to have been always in fact democratic at heart, in all the vital habits of her thought, in all the intimate relationships of her people that spoke their natural instinct, their habitual attitude towards life. The autocracy that crowned the summit of her political structure, long as it had stood and terrible as was the reality of its power, was not in fact Russian in origin, character, or purpose; and now it has been shaken off and the great, generous Russian people have been added in all their naive majesty and might to the forces that are fighting for freedom in the world, for justice, and for peace. Here is a fit partner for a League of Honour.

DOCUMENT 23.3

How We Advertised America

George Creel

It was in this recognition of Public Opinion as a major force that the Great War differed most essentially from all previous conflicts. The trial of strength was not only between massed bodies of armed men, but between opposed ideals, and moral verdicts took on all the value of military decisions. Other wars went

Source: From George Creel, *How We Advertised America* (New York: Harper & Brothers, 1920), pp. 3–9.

no deeper than the physical aspects, but German *Kultur* raised issues that had to be fought out in the hearts and minds of people as well as on the actual firing-line. The approval of the world meant the steady flow of inspiration into the trenches; it meant the strengthened resolve and the renewed determination of the civilian population that is a nation's second line. The condemnation of the world meant the destruction of morale and the surrender of that conviction of justice which is the very heart of courage.

The Committee on Public Information was called into existence to make this fight for the "verdict of mankind," the voice created to plead the justice of America's cause before the jury of Public Opinion. The fantastic legend that associated gags and muzzles with its work may be likened only to those trees which are evolved out of the air by Hindu magicians and which rise, grow, and flourish in gay disregard of such usual necessities as roots, sap, and sustenance. *In no degree was the Committee an agency of censorship, a machinery of concealment or repression. Its emphasis throughout was on the open and the positive. At no point did it seek or exercise authorities under those war laws that limited the freedom of speech and press.* In all things, from first to last, without halt or change, it was a plain publicity proposition, a vast enterprise in salesmanship, the world's greatest adventure in advertising. . . .

Starting with the initial conviction that the war was not the war of an administration, but the war of one hundred million people, and believing that public support was a matter of public understanding, we opened up the activities of government to the inspection of the citizenship. A voluntary censorship agreement safeguarded military information of obvious value to the enemy, but in all else the rights of the press were recognized and furthered. Trained men, at the center of effort in every one of the war-making branches of government, reported on progress and achievement, and in no other belligerent nation was there such absolute frankness with respect to every detail of the national war endeavor.

As swiftly as might be, there were put into pamphlet form America's reasons for entering the war, the meaning of America, the nature of our free institutions, our war aims, likewise analyses of the Prussian system, the purposes of the imperial German government, and full exposure of the enemy's misrepresentations, aggressions, and barbarities. Written by the country's foremost publicists, scholars, and historians, and distinguished for their conciseness, accuracy, and simplicity, these pamphlets blew as a great wind against the clouds of confusion and misrepresentation. Money could not have purchased the volunteer aid that was given freely, the various universities lending their best men and the National Board of Historical Service placing its three thousand members at the complete disposal of the Committee. Some thirty-odd booklets, covering every phase of America's ideals, purposes, and aims, were printed in many languages other than English. Seventy-five millions reached the people of America, and other millions went to every corner of the world, carrying our defense and our attack.

The importance of the spoken word was not underestimated. A speaking division toured great groups like the Blue Devils, Pershing's Veterans, and the Belgians, arranged mass-meetings in the communities, conducted forty-five war conferences from coast to coast, co-ordinated the entire speaking activities of the nation, and assured consideration to the crossroads hamlet as well as to the city.

The Four Minute Men, an organization that will live in history by reason of its originality and effectiveness, commanded the volunteer services of 75,000 speakers, operating in 5,200 communities, and making a total of 755,190 speeches, every one having the carry of shrapnel.

With the aid of a volunteer staff of several hundred translators, the Committee kept in direct touch with the foreign-language press, supplying selected articles designed to combat ignorance and disaffection. It organized and directed twenty-three societies and leagues designed to appeal to certain classes and particular foreign-language groups, each body carrying a specific message of unity and enthusiasm to its section of America's adopted peoples. . . .

"Pershing's Crusaders," "America's Answer," and *"Under Four Flags"* were types of feature films by which we drove home America's resources and determinations, while other pictures, showing our social and industrial life, made our free institutions vivid to foreign peoples. From the domestic showings alone, under a fair plan of distribution, the sum of $878,215 was gained, which went to support the cost of the campaigns in foreign countries where the exhibitions were necessarily free. . . .

Unlike other countries, the United States had no subsidized press service with which to meet the emergency. As a matter of bitter fact, we had few direct news contacts of our own with the outside world, owing to a scheme of contracts that turned the foreign distribution of American news over to European agencies. The volume of information that went out from our shores was small, and, what was worse, it was concerned only with the violent and unusual in our national life. It was news of strikes and lynchings, riots, murder cases, graft prosecutions, sensational divorces, the bizarre extravagance of "sudden millionaires." Naturally enough, we were looked upon as a race of dollar-mad materialists, a land of cruel monopolists, our real rulers the corporations and our democracy a "fake."

DOCUMENT 23.4

Recollections As a 15-Year-Old Girl in Bisbee, Arizona

Miriam E. Tefft

Last of the Vigilantes

I was 15. I was there when the tragic hysteria which was World War I broke out in the copper mining camp of Bisbee, Arizona, where I lived, and the citizens took over the law. . . .

Source: Excerpted from Miriam E. Tefft's recollections as a 15-year-old girl in Bisbee. Dated 2 February 1982. Arizona Historical Society Library, Tefft Bio File. Copyright © 2000 Arizona Board of Regents, digital.library.arizona.edu/bisbee/docs2/rec_teff.php.

For the first time we heard the ideology of radicals. We gathered from what speakers said that the aim was to create a revolutionary industrial union to overthrow capitalism. They maintained that once all workers combined in one big strike they could launch a national strike that would displace capitalists from power and place workers in possession. The mines would belong to the people. Men yelled and cheered the speakers, women shrieked, songs were sung. We were introduced to Joe Hill and his songs for the people. The climax of the meeting, for us, was when there was an incitement to action which reduced us to giggling fits. A skinny, rough-haired old woman whom we knew as Sally Hapgood, raced up and down the aisle yelling, "Hallelujah. Hallelujah." And denouncing capitalists at the top of her lungs. . . .

There began to be violence in the mines. Old Mag was bombed. Miners on strike were harassed. Groups of men gathered on the streets and near mine entrances—Finns, Serbs, Welshmen, "Cousin Jacks," and Mexes, cursing, making violent gestures, shouting, having fist fights. We could see what a strike meant. We knew it was contended to be in protest over bad working conditions. Solid citizens of Bisbee saw it as unpatriotic and led by the IWWs (we called them "I Won't Work"). The IWW's had infiltrated the district. They were easy to spot; we knew the regular miners. These strangers were menacing. We'd never been afraid before. Our doors were never locked. The code we lived by was the open door and the pot of frijoles on the back of the stove.

Betty Clearly's father was the lawyer for these people, so we were not allowed to speak to her. "Whitely" was a suspect name. Milmay's father became very important. When the street car stopped at Johnson Addition, Florence McKenzie wasn't there to go to school; her mother had been assaulted by strikers because her husband remained loyal. Sadie Thomas gave us all a look that said "no compromise," her mouth was set in a straight line, and her hair was pulled back tighter than ever. Her father was an agitator. . . .

Our beautiful country club with its wide verandas and green lawns, our touch of richness and refinement in the drab sand and stones of the surrounding countryside, was mysteriously burned one night. No more elegant dances, no more summer parties for the children, no more hiking around the greens to look for lost golf balls. Only a charred rubble remained. There were rumors and counter-rumors, all of them ugly.

You could almost smell fear. Men didn't look at each other in the face. Everyone was under suspicion. Loyalties were divided. One could sense an undercurrent of outrage seething. Our fathers were often from home. They were closed mouthed when asked questions, so one did not ask too many questions. Something was brewing in this atmosphere of wild emotions.

Posse is the legal term for vigilantes. Vigilantes left an undying mark on the forming of Arizona. I remember the men who met weekly, practiced shooting and riding. In those early days when Arizona was a territory, vigilante justice was the major force bringing law and order. The general public did not know who these men were, but these were the men who made history: bookkeepers, auditors, clerks, paymasters, teachers—mostly friendly men, hard working and just. During the Mexican Revolution, these men protected the town before the U.S. troops were sent in by the government. Soft-spoken and gentle, for the main part, when called on to fight for justice they were single-minded, fearless, accurate shots. "One of the most flagrant acts of vigilantism in the history of the West" was the dramatic moment in Arizona history which took place on July 12, 1917.

The street lights flickered and went out one by one. A few cars went by. The sounds of horses were muted. Voices were low, words indistinguishable. Dad got up from his bed when a low tap on the front door tattooed a signal. He hushed our questions: "Stay indoors. Keep quiet. Don't build a fire." We could hear him dressing, and speaking to his hunting dog, "No, Rex. Stay here." He took his rifle down from the wall, the door opened, and he was gone. We heard Uncle Arthur's car and Mr. Bankherd's car. It seemed strange to be awake at this hour, to lie in the darkness and keep quiet.

It was so hot. The air vibrated with the shrill cicadas. We knew that Dad and the other men had been going to "meetings" every night that week, but the meetings were unexplained. We were eating a cold breakfast when the first signs of dawn appeared. We didn't leave the house. Mr. Hill and some of the miners from Black Knob View, who were not on strike, went past the house to the street car stop on the way to Lowell. Half an hour later we saw them return. This was ominous. Hortense and Carolyn White, I found out later, spent the night in their home in Jiggerville, crouching behind the piano which had been dragged across a corner of the room to form a triangle. Their father was out, they didn't know where. Jiggerville was a quiet, respectable settlement of homes, not a place which would harbor a nest of troublemakers, but the sound of shooting at a near neighbor's house made them realize that they, too, were in danger. (It was learned next day that two men had been killed, an IWW agitator and one of Sheriff Wheeler's men.)

The *Bisbee Review* was delivered about 10:00 on this morning of July 12. Headline: ALL WOMEN AND CHILDREN STAY OFF THE STREETS. We were putting out the flag as Dad had told us to, when we suddenly noticed a long double line extending from the direction of Bisbee toward the ball park in Warren.

Our house was a good vantage point, only a few blocks from the park, eight steps up to the porch on two sides. Mother brought out her favorite rocker and her crocheting. Other people began sitting on their porches and doing handwork like Mother. Children were sitting on fence railings and steps, but they didn't leave the yard.

We began to see that deputies and armed citizens were keeping the strikers in line as they were herded into the ball park behind the high board fence. The men had evidently been taken completely by surprise; some were still in their nightshirts, many in long underwear; some apparently hadn't been given time to put on their shoes. We could see snipers on the opposite hill overlooking the park. We recognized Mr. Greenway on his white horse, Dr. Bledsoe on his black, and saw that Captain Wheeler was directing maneuvers. A rather small man, he was an imposing figure on horseback.

This was too tame for me. I had to go where the action was. I slipped out the back door and joined Hazel and her brother Hoogie, and Claude and Bertha Berquist at the C and A office. They didn't know exactly where their fathers were any more than I did. We sat on the top steps where we could see what was going on. Ray Foster, whose father was detective for the Arizona Banker's Assoc., was sitting on some railroad ties near the tracks of the Southern Pacific Don Luis spur line where 25 box cars and cattle cars were standing.

A machine gun burst. Capt. Wheeler rode into the park. Through a megaphone he announced: the strikers were guilty of treason. If they wanted to go back to work there was a job for them, if not, out they would go. We could hear shouting, "Don't go. Don't go. Don't go." About half the men broke line and went out the gate. Some 1,200 strikers stayed in the park. These men were driven into the cars on the siding. No guns were fired. There were oaths, some lack of cooperation, but guns are a good persuader. Twenty-five deputies, all crack shots, mounted the tops of the cars. Every tactical movement was carried out with precision. The engine whistled, the train gathered speed. Last echoes from the train faded. Then a cheer went up from the hundreds who had been watching through this hot violent day. Justice had been done, they felt, the swift way it was always done in Arizona—no quibbling, but with authority and efficiency. Gun-toting citizens straggled home. No one remembered the machine guns.

"Where are they taking them?" we wanted to know. "That you will find out in a few days," was the only answer Dad would give us. "The IWW had plans to round up our men and get rid of them. We just beat them to it." Overnight, sheriff's deputies and armed citizens had made a sweep of Bisbee, from Chihuahua Hill to Bucky O'Neill, Brewery Gulch to School Hill, taking in Tintown, Jiggerville, Bakerville, Lowell, rounding up strikers and dissidents.

The next morning, and for a few days, everything moved in slow motion. Everyone acted completely depleted. Men shuffled, women burned dinners, children drooped around. No hopscotch, no kick the can, no baseball. But it was calm. The mines were working again. The threat we had lived under was gone. We breathed quietly.

Four days later we heard the cattle cars at the train stop on the Warren siding. The weary deputies had returned. The cars were empty. The loads of strikers had been shipped to New Mexico, where they were turned out into the desert near Columbus.

Greenway, Douglas, and a man named McDowell, whom we didn't know, were indicted. It was an anticlimax when President Wilson, breathing fire and brimstone, sent a commission to investigate. The commission was headed by Felix Frankfurter. They found the government was helpless to punish anyone. No law could be found against kidnapping people en masse and dumping them into another state.

DOCUMENT 23.5

Through the Valley of Death

*Chapter Fourteen: Advancing over the Top
and Carrying Wounded Comrade Under Shell-Fire*

Mathew Chopin
A.O.O. A.E.F. Middle Western 89th Division

In January of 1919—having yet to return home—my grandfather wrote his memories of the Great War. *L. McCauley*

At early dawn we continued advancing "over the top" through clouds of gas and smoke—under rain of machine gun bullets, shrapnel and steel. The Huns were shelling heavily the edge of the roadside. It was freezing cold; we were out of water and had just a small ration of salmon and hard-tack. Completely exhausted and thirsting for a drink, I remember grabbing a canteen from a passing artillery caison to soothe my parched lips, when the explosion of a shell sent over deadly gas, getting four of our men. We got down in a valley for awhile during a machine gun barrage and then up again, firing away at the enemy as fast as our automatics could work. For hours the fight continued, for hours the veterans of the 89th pushed forward.

A little farther ahead, in a ditch, my partner and I took turn about to rest, but our work had just begun. So many of our men were getting wounded and as the litter-bearer was killed while going out under fire for wounded, my sergeant sent me with another man to replace him. It was a dangerous situation going over grounds of Hell, as we had to go up and get them under machine gun and rifle fire. Now and then our men were hit while changing reliefs, our dead and wounded lay everywhere. We picked up our first man with a bullet in his stomach and started back one-third of a mile to the horse-drawn ambulance as fast as we could when an enemy shell exploded, throwing dirt all over us and sending shrapnel between the stretcher and me. I felt a cold chill run down my back, as it was a wonder it didn't get all three of us; yet I was not going to put down that stretcher with the poor fellow on it for the world! They followed us up a second time but could not get the exact range on us. The next day we moved up to Beauclair, another town which the Germans were shelling. We started back again to get other wounded, continuing our first aid and litter-bearer work. Our next trip was for two of our own boys. As I carried their wounded forms from off the battlefield of carnage and misery, I thought of their mothers, who were keeping the home fires burning, waiting for the return of these boys! On our way back again to the lines, we turned off abruptly, dodging two German "snipers" who gave us hell for a few moments before we got the best of them. We began picking up the wounded as fast as they came and bandaging those in need of first aid. It was a heart rending sight that weakened the strongest, for everywhere were wounded

Source: From Mathew Chopin, *Through the Valley of Death,* 1919. Available at www.geocities.com/louisiana_doughboy/index.htm.

and lifeless forms—some all torn to pieces, their limbs and heads entirely severed from their bodies! I remember making a trip about a mile under heavy gun fire to get a wounded stretcher-bearer whose partner had been killed. He was a game little Yank, yet a pitiful sight, with his side all ripped open by shrapnel. As I laid him gently on the stretcher, I still remember his last uttered words, "Oh God, if I could only live to die at home!"

DOCUMENT 23.6

Letter on Negro Soldiers

"Dear Scott:

"Am writing this from away up on the French front where the 'Fighting Fifteenth,' now the 369th U.S., is really fighting in a French Division. We are known to the French as 369 R.I.M.S. and our *Secteur Postal* is No. 54, France.

"I have two battalions in the trenches of the *first* line and the third in relief at rest just behind our trenches. The three rotate. Our boys have had their baptism of fire. They have patrolled No Man's Land. They have gone on raids and one of my lieutenants has been cited for a decoration. Of course, it is still in the experimental stage, but two questions of the gravest importance to our country and to your race have, in my opinion, been answered.

"First: How will American Negro soldiers, including commissioned officers (of whom I still have five), get along in service with French soldiers and officers—as for instance a Negro regiment of infantry serving in a French combat division?

"Second: Will the American Negro stand up under the terrible shell fire of this war as he has always stood under rifle fire and thus prove his superiority, spiritually and intellectually, to all the black men of Africa and Asia, who have failed under these conditions and whose use must be limited to attack or for shock troops?

"We have answered the first question in a most gratifying way. The French soldiers have not the slightest prejudice or feeling. The poilus and my boys are great chums, eat, dance, sing, march and fight together in absolute accord. The French officers have *little,* if any feeling about Negro officers. What little, if any, is not racial but from skepticism that a colored man (judging of course by those they have known) can have the technical education necessary to make an efficient officer. However, as I write these lines, Capt. Napoleon Bonaparte Marshall and Lieut. D. Lincoln Reed are living at the French Officers' Mess at our division *Infanterie* School, honored guests.

"The program I enclose gives you an idea of the way I've cultivated friendship between my boys and the poilus. You should have seen the 500 soldiers, French and mine, all mixed up together, cheering and laughing at the show arranged while the Boche shells (boxcar size) went screaming over our heads.

Source: From Emmett J. Scott, *Scott's Official History of the American Negro in the World War.* © 1919 by Emmett J. Scott.

"Now, on the second question, perhaps I am premature. But both my two battalions which have gone in have been under shell fire, serious and prolonged once, and the boys just laughed and cuddled into their shelter and read old newspapers. French company got shelled and it was getting very warm around the rolling kitchen. The cooks went along about their business in absolute unconcern until the alarmed French soldiers ran to them and told them to beat it. One of the cooks said, 'Oh, that's all right, boss. They ain't hurting us none.' They are positively the most stoical and mysterious men I've ever known. Nothing surprises them. And we now have expert opinion. The French officers say they are entirely different from their own African troops and the Indian troops of the British, who are so excitable under shell fire. Of course, I have explained that my boys are public school boys, wise in their day and generation, no caste prejudice, accustomed to the terrible noises of the subway, elevated and street traffic of New York City (which would drive any desert man or Himalaya mountaineer mad) and are all Christians. Also, that while the more ignorant ones might not like to have a black cat hanging around for fear it would turn into a fish or something, they have no delusions about the Boche shells coming from any Heathen Gods. They know the d—— child-killing Germans are firing at them with pyrocellulose and they know how the breech mechanism works.

"I am very proud of what we've done and are doing. I put the whole regiment through grenade (live grenade) practice. Nasty, dangerous business. They did it beautifully. I found one rank arrant coward, who refused to throw. Said he couldn't. Another threw prematurely after igniting the bomb. We asked him why he did not wait for the command to throw (barrage). He said, 'Kunnel, that old grenade, she begun to swell right in my hand.' The boys keep writing home that the 'war is not so bad if you just go at it right.' Well, a very wise command somewhere, I don't know where, has let us go at it right. You know I've always told these boys I'd never send them anywhere I would not go myself, so I went first to the trenches, prowled around, saw it all and came back to the regiment to take in the battalion which was to go in first. When they saw me covered with mud, but safe and sound they said, 'How is she, Kunnel?' 'She's all right,' I said. They all laughed and then the sick and the lame of that battalion began to get well miraculously and begged to go. Captain Clark called for twelve volunteers for a raid and the company fell in to the last man—all wanted to go, and he had to pick his twelve after all.

"Do you wonder that I love them, every one, good, bad and indifferent?

"Personally I am well, strong, and the happiest man in the world. I've learned more about the military game, at least the fighting of this war, since I have been here with the French than I learned in all the years as drummer boy, private; Sergeant, Captain, Major and Colonel Second Nebraska Infantry, Spanish War, Maneuvers, Officers' School, Gettysburg and Leavenworth problems, etc., etc., and all the time I spent with my present regiment in the New York National Guard.

"And another thing, I believe I know more about Negro soldiers and how to handle them, especially the problem of Negro and white officers, than any other man living today. Of course, the other regiment I commanded for three years was a white regiment, so I had a lot to learn, but I've learned it and I wouldn't trade back now.

"Suppose after I've held my sector up here by blood and iron two or three months, some National Guard Brigadier, who has just arrived in France, will come along and point out all the mistakes I've made and tell me just how to do it. Well, 'C'est la guerre,' as we French say.

"Brother Boche doesn't know who we are yet, as none of my men have been captured so far, and the boys wear a French blue uniform when they go on raids. I've been thinking if they capture one of my Porto Ricans (of whom I have a few) in the uniform of a Normandy French regiment and this black man tells them in Spanish that he is an American soldier in a New York National Guard regiment, it's going to give the German intelligence department a headache trying to figure it out.

"We are proud to think our boys were the first Negro American soldiers in the trenches. Jim Europe was certainly the first Negro officer in. You can imagine how important he feels! In addition to the personal gratification at having done well as a regiment I feel it has been a tremendously important experiment, when one considers the hosts of colored men who must come after us. I wish I had a brigade, yes, a division or a corps of them. We'd make history and plant the hob-nailed boots of the 'Heavy Ethiopian Foot' in the Kaiser's face all right.

"We were so disappointed that the Secretary didn't get up to see us. The town we were holding then had been named by me 'Bakerville' and it is so on our maps.

"Regards and good wishes to you.

"Sincerely,

"William Hayward."

DOCUMENT 23.7

American Women and the World War

Ida Clyde Clarke

... Addressing a company of women war workers in Washington in September, 1917, the Secretary of War said: "Never before in the history of any people has an army been assembled under conditions so wholesome, so clean, and so stimulating to the personal pride and to the national credit as the army we are now assembling in the United States. The old stories of soldiers' camps, with their perils, their disasters, their temptations, are in a large degree past, and because we are a civilized people, because our civilization is more than a matter of collars and cuffs, because we are a moral people, we have determined to surround our army, not with a system of prohibitions and restraints, but with a system of wholesome environments and stimulating inducements to self-improvement and high conduct, of such character that everybody who visits one of our camps

Source: Excerpted from Ida Clyde Clarke, *American Women and the World War* (New York: D. Appleton & Co., 1918). Available at www.lib.byu.edu/~rdh/wwi/comment/Clarke/Clarke00TC.htm.

will come away thrilled with the thought that at last this sort of business can be carried on in a manner highly creditable to a great nation." . . .

In every state where a camp of soldiers are in training, the Woman's Committee has been grappling with the grist of problems that they create. First, there is the problem of hospitality. What will be practical and acceptable for them to undertake? One worker divides the work into retail and wholesale hospitality. The former consists of inviting the boys into the homes, taking them on motor drives, and furnishing them healthful amusements and wholesome company. Wholesale hospitality is defined as that undertaken by the big organizations where soldiers and sailors are invited en masse to lectures, entertainments, or dinners.

As soon as the North Carolina Division of the Woman's Committee learned that there was to be a cantonment of some sixty thousand men near Charlotte, the women at once began to lay their plans to operate with the city authorities in making the camp what they would desire it to be. The State Chairman, Mrs. Eugene Reilly, said that the Committee on Health and Recreation was most active in arranging with all the women's organizations of the community to provide entertainment for the soldiers. They arranged that every organization in the town should adopt or stand sponsor for one company of men, furnishing them with amusements, magazines, and books, inviting them to church and to dinner, opening their club or society rooms to them, and in every way possible surrounding them with wholesome and friendly influences. The Committee Chairman said that the women were just as attentive to the soldiers who come to them as strangers from New England as they are to their own boys, "and," she adds, "we expect that strangers will do the same for our boys."

Certainly Massachusetts reciprocated this thoughtfulness. A special committee from the women's colleges provided club houses and homes outside the camp. Their purpose is to have as many of these homes as possible where soldiers will find recreation, friendly interest, and refined surroundings; the kind of homes from which the majority of them have come. Each home will be provided for by a separate college group, either alumnae, undergraduates, or both, and each will have a college "mother." The college mother will be permanent or as nearly so as possible, but the helpers may vary from week to week. A few will give their services in the home itself and others will provide the things needed to make it attractive—furnishings, games, books, pianos, victrolas. Such an undertaking is particularly practicable in the case of the reserve officer training camps made up largely of college men. With modifications to suit local needs, the plan could be worked out to advantage in connection with almost any camp.

A helpful camp service in which many of the State Divisions are preparing to cooperate, is that undertaken by the American Library Association. It is organizing committees to collect and distribute reading matter in the training camps and has even prepared to put up libraries in some of the camps. The Missouri Division took hold of this work with particular zest, giving the matter wide publicity and arranging for the collection of books at local libraries throughout the state. It has even furnished boxes of the proper dimensions in which to pack the books collected.

Several of the groups of women involved have reechoed the word laid down by the Library Association, that only worthwhile books are wanted. "Do not go up to the garret and pick up material that has been discarded because it is too dull to be kept on the library shelves—give the boys the best. They want good fiction. They are keen for scientific books and periodicals. They want everything you can give them about war, about sports, they want the news of the world. Because a thing has been printed and bound it does not follow that it will be useful to send to a cantonment." No woman, either, need have any doubt about her contributions being well taken care of. The American Library Association is directly responsible to the Government in this work.

Where soldiers are temporarily camped in a town, or where they are traveling, one much appreciated attention is supervising the food that the boys get. This seems to have been managed very well by the women of the Woman's Committee in Grand Rapids, Michigan. They responded immediately not only to the call of furnishing good wholesome amusements for the boys mobilized at their gates, but during the two weeks when the camp of eight hundred boys was at Grand Rapids they furnished their meals. The different days of the week were assigned to various organizations so that while hundreds of women were engaged in the feeding of the soldiers, no one group was in constant service. In the two weeks the women furnished thirteen hundred meals, including breakfasts, dinners and suppers. They did it so economically that from the allotment of twenty-five cents per head a meal, they had a surplus to go into the mess fund of the Grand Rapids Battalion, and the boys were satisfied, for when the camp broke up the praise came to the women from all sides for the catering they had done.

The greatest of all problems that confront the women in the vicinity of the camps is that of guarding the young girl. Where soldiers are stationed either temporarily or permanently, the problem of preventing girls from being misled by the glamour and romance of war and beguiling uniforms looms large. Maryland has proposed a Patriotic League of Honor which will inspire girls to adopt the highest standards of womanliness and loyalty to their country. From New York comes the suggestion that the teachers of girls may be invaluable in making girls realize the dangers. In clubs formed for war service, guidance could be given incidentally with instruction. Girls employed in the big industries are most in danger, but if some happy slogan should be found which would in itself constitute a sort of badge of courage and loyalty, it would be far better than depending on supervision. The number it is possible to chaperone carefully is necessarily limited.

24

The Tribal Twenties

The decade of the 1920s, more than most, fascinates students of American history. Perhaps it is the inability to easily generalize about it or the contradictions inherent in the prosperity in the urban, industrial sector at the same time rural America and the once rich Appalachian area of western Pennsylvania through the middle border states were slipping into depression. Socially and culturally the era was also replete with contradictions, from life styles associated with the new modernity and the conservative, even repressive reactions it produced in various retreats to orthodoxy. Even the patriotic crusade to carry the fruits of American progressivism to the rest of the world slipped quickly into provincialism when the Senate refused to ratify the Versailles Treaty, suggesting a lack of concern for international issues.

The selections in this chapter begin with the prosperity unleashed by business acumen, illustrated by Alfred P. Sloan's reflections on the automobile industry. Technological innovations, cars and radios to mention two, began to change American social life and cultural patterns, contributing to prosperity and lively times. Yet, here too, the institution of installment buying contained its own time bomb, as did an excessively bullish market with its own slow-burning fuse.

Though prosperity was shared unevenly and there was a strong conservative reaction to modernity—marked by a rise in the membership of the KKK and intellectual arm wrestling between the champions of religion and science— even minority groups were able to nibble at the national cornucopia of goods and services as they had never before done. Many people found themselves faced with new and in some cases seemingly "foreign" ideas. Native Americans were granted citizenship, while a resurgent nativism triggered efforts to racially restrict immigration to preserve the purity of the American bloodline. Looking at the table on immigration, one has to wonder how transparent were the objectives of those who engineered the quota legislation.

During this exciting "jazz" age and the height of the Harlem Renaissance, New York continued to play a major role as the laboratory in which American culture was mixed and refined. The cultural patterns that evolved in Greenwich Village certainly helped recast traditional understandings of life, liberty, and the pursuit of happiness.

DOCUMENT 24.1

My Years with General Motors

Alfred P. Sloan, Jr.

As the economy, led by the automobile industry, rose to a new high level in the twenties, a complex of new elements came into existence to transform the market once again and create the watershed which divides the present from the past.

. . . Installment selling, the used-car trade-in, the closed body, and the annual model. . . . So imbedded are these elements in the nature of the [automotive] industry today that to conceive of the market without them is almost impossible. Before 1920 and for a while thereafter the typical car buyer was in the situation of buying his first car; he would buy it for cash or with some special loan arrangement; and the car would be a roadster or touring car, most likely of a model which was the same as last year's and could be expected to be the same as next year's. This situation was not to change for some years and the change would not be sudden except at its climax. For each of the new elements of change had a separate beginning and rate of development before they all interacted to cause complete transformation.

Installment selling of automobiles in regularized form first appeared in a small way shortly before World War I. This form of borrowing, or inverse saving, when placed on a routine basis, enabled large numbers of consumers to buy an object as expensive as an automobile. The statistics of installment selling in those days were very poor, but it is clear that it grew from some very low level in 1915 to around 65 per cent for new cars in 1925. We believed that with rising incomes and the expectation of a continuance of that rise, it was reasonable to assume that consumers would lift their sights to higher levels of quality. Installment selling, we thought, would stimulate this trend.

As the first car buyers came back for the second round and brought their old cars as down payments, the custom of trading was established. That the industry was engaged in a trading business had revolutionary significance not only for dealer arrangements but for manufacturing and the whole character of production, since dealers usually had to sell to a man who already had a car with mileage left in it.

The statistics for used-car trade-ins before 1925 are as poor as those for installment selling. It stands to reason, however, that there was some kind of upward curve in used cars traded from World War I on, if only because there were

Source: From Alfred P. Sloan, Jr., *My Years with General Motors* (New York: Macfadden-Bartell Corp., 1963), pp.150–52.

relatively few cars in existence before that time. Until some unknown date in the early 1920s, the majority of car buyers were buying their first car. The total number of passenger cars in operation in the United States from 1919 through 1929 rose by years in millions approximately as follows: 6, 7.3, 8.3, 9.6, 11.9, 13.7, 15.7, 16.8, 17.5, 18.7, 19.7. The industry, on the other hand, produced in those years passenger cars for domestic and export markets in approximate millions as follows: 1.7, 1.9, 1.5, 2.3, 3.6, 3.2, 3.7, 3.7, 2.9, 3.8, 4.5. This production was enough to cover both the growth in numbers and the scrappage. The used car was traded perhaps two or three times on the way to the scrap heap. So I assume there must have been a rising curve of used-car trade-ins.

The closed body was a specialty and mainly a custom-job affair before World War I. In the years 1919 through 1927, in round numbers by years, the industry sold closed cars in the following uninterruptedly rising percentages: 10, 17, 22, 30, 34, 43, 56, 72, and 85.

Of the annual model I shall say more later; suffice it to say here that in the early twenties it was not a formal concept as we know it today, except as it was negatively expressed in Ford's concept of a static model.

We were not unconscious of the unfolding of these four elements when the administration of General Motors changed in 1921. We started GMAC in the installment financing field in 1919. We had an interest in Fisher Body, which made closed bodies. As large sellers of medium- and high-price cars, we met the used-car trade-in early. And we tried to make our models more attractive each year. Yet we did not see the movement—especially the interaction—of these elements in the whole automobile market as I can see it today looking back. We saw them then as uncertainties, unknowns, and trends, in the form of figures to study at a desk. However, the plan of campaign laid down in the product program of 1921 logically fitted better and better the unfolding situation.

DOCUMENT 24.2

Middletown

Robert S. Lynd and Helen Merrell Lynd

The first real automobile appeared in Middletown in 1900. About 1906 it was estimated that "there are probably 200 in the city and county." At the close of 1923 there were 6,221 passenger cars in the city, one for every 6.1 persons, or roughly two for every three families. Of these 6,221 cars, 41 per cent were Fords; 54 per cent of the total were cars of models of 1920 or later, and 17 per cent models earlier than 1917. These cars average a bit over 5,000 miles a year. For some of the workers and some of the business class, use of the automobile is a seasonal matter, but the increase in surfaced roads and in closed cars is rapidly making the car a year-round tool for leisure-time as well as getting-a-living activities. As, at

Source: From Robert S. Lynd and Helen Merrell Lynd, *Middletown: A Study in Contemporary American Culture* (Harcourt, Brace & Co., 1929), pp. 253–71.

the turn of the century, business class people began to feel apologetic if they did not have a telephone, so ownership of an automobile has now reached the point of being an accepted essential of normal living.

Into the equilibrium of habits which constitutes for each individual some integration in living has come this new habit, upsetting old adjustments, and blasting its way through such accustomed and unquestioned dicta as "Rain or shine, I never miss a Sunday morning at church"; "A high school boy does not need much spending money"; "I don't need exercise, walking to the office keeps me fit"; "I wouldn't think of moving out of town and being so far from my friends"; "Parents ought always to know where their children are." The newcomer is most quickly and amicably incorporated into those regions of behavior in which men are engaged in doing impersonal, matter-of-fact things; much more contested is its advent where emotionally charged sanctions and taboos are concerned. No one questions the use of the auto for transporting groceries, getting to one's place of work or to the golf course, or in place of the porch for "cooling off after supper" on a hot summer evening; however much the activities concerned with getting a living may be altered by the fact that a factory can draw from workmen within a radius of forty-five miles, or however much old labor union men resent the intrusion of this new alternate way of spending an evening, these things are hardly major issues. But when auto riding tends to replace the traditional call in the family parlor as a way of approach between the unmarried, "the home is endangered," and all-day Sunday motor trips are a "threat against the church"; it is in the activities concerned with the home and religion that the automobile occasions the greatest emotional conflicts. . . .

The automobile has apparently unsettled the habit of careful saving for some families. "Part of the money we spend on the car would go to the bank, I suppose," said more than one working class wife. A business man explained his recent inviting of social oblivion by selling his car by saying: "My car, counting depreciation and everything, was costing mighty nearly $100.00 a month, and my wife and I sat down together the other night and just figured that we're getting along, and if we're to have anything later on, we've just got to begin to save." The "moral" aspect of the competition between the automobile and certain accepted expenditures appears in the remark of another business man, "An automobile is a luxury, and no one has a right to one if he can't afford it. I haven't the slightest sympathy for any one who is out of work if he owns a car."

Men in the clothing industry are convinced that automobiles are bought at the expense of clothing,[1] and the statements of a number of the working class wives bear this out: "We'd rather do without clothes than give up the car," said one mother of nine children. "We used to go to his sister's to visit, but by the

---

[1]"The *National Retail Clothier* has been devoting space to trying to find out what is the matter with the clothing industry and has been inclined to blame it on the automobile. In one city, to quote an example cited in the articles, a store 'put on a campaign that usually resulted in a business of 150 suits and overcoats on a Saturday afternoon. This season the campaign netted seventeen sales, while an automobile agency across the street sold twenty-five cars on the weekly payment plan.' In another, 'retail clothiers are unanimous in blaming the automobile for the admitted slump in the retail clothing trade.'" (*Chicago Evening Post*, December 28, 1923)

time we'd get the children shoed and dressed there wasn't any money left for carfare. Now no matter how they look, we just poke 'em in the car and take 'em along." "We don't have no fancy clothes when we have the car to pay for," said another. "The car is the only pleasure we have." Even food may suffer: "I'll go without food before I'll see us give up the car," said one woman emphatically, and several who were out of work were apparently making precisely this adjustment.

Twenty-one of the twenty-six families owning a car for whom data on bathroom facilities happened to be secured live in homes without bathtubs. Here we obviously have a new habit cutting in ahead of an older one and slowing down the diffusion of the latter.[2]

Meanwhile, advertisements pound away at Middletown people with the tempting advice to spend money for automobiles for the sake of their homes and families: "Hit the trail to better times!" says one such advertisement.

Another depicts a gray-haired banker lending a young couple the money to buy a car and proffering the friendly advice: "Before you can save money, you first must make money. And to make it you must have health, contentment, and full command of all your resources. . . . I have often advised customers of mine to buy cars, as I felt that the increased stimulation and opportunity of observation would enable them to earn amounts equal to the cost of their cars."

Many families feel that an automobile is justified as an agency holding the family group together. "I never feel as close to my family as when we are all together in the car," said one business class mother, and one or two spoke of giving up Country Club membership or other recreations to get a car for this reason. "We don't spend anything on recreation except for the car. We save every place we can and put the money into the car. It keeps the family together," was an opinion voiced more than once. Sixty-one per cent of 337 boys and 60 per cent of 423 girls in the three upper years of the high school say that they motor more often with their parents than without them.[3]

---

[2]This low percentage of bathtubs would not hold for the entire car-owning group. The interviewers asked about bathtubs in these twenty-six cases out of curiosity, prompted by the run-down appearance of the homes.

While inroads upon savings and the re-allocation of items of home expenditure were the readjustments most often mentioned in connection with the financing of the family automobile, others also occur: "It's prohibition that's done it," according to an officer in the Middletown Trades Council; "drink money is going into cars." The same officer, in answering the question as to what he thought most of the men he comes in contact with are working for, guessed: "Twenty-five per cent are fighting to keep their heads above water; 10 per cent want to own their own homes; 65 per cent are working to pay for cars." "All business is suffering," says a Middletown candy manufacturer and dealer. "The candy business is poor now to what it was before the war. There is no money in it any more. People just aren't buying candy so much now. How can they? Even laboring-men put all their money into cars, and every other branch of business feels it."

[3]As over against these answers regarding the automobile, 21 per cent of the boys and 33 per cent of the girls said that they go to the movies more often with their parents than without them, 25 per cent and 22 per cent respectively answered similarly as regards "listening to the radio," and 31 per cent and 48 per cent as regards "singing or playing a musical instrument." On the basis of these answers it would appear that the automobile is at present operating as a more active agency drawing Middletown families together than any of these other agencies.

But this centralizing tendency of the automobile may be only a passing phase; sets in the other direction are almost equally prominent. "Our daughters [eighteen and fifteen] don't use our car much because they are always with somebody else in their car when we go out motoring," lamented one business class mother. And another said, "The two older children [eighteen and sixteen] never go out when the family motors. They always have something else on." "In the nineties we were all much more together," said another wife. "People brought chairs and cushions out of the house and sat on the lawn evenings. We rolled out a strip of carpet and put cushions on the porch step to take care of the unlimited overflow of neighbors that dropped by. We'd sit out so all evening. The younger couples perhaps would wander off for half an hour to get a soda but come back to join in the informal singing or listen while somebody strummed a mandolin or guitar." "What on earth *do* you want me to do? Just sit around home all evening!" retorted a popular high school girl of today when her father discouraged her going out motoring for the evening with a young blade in a rakish car waiting at the curb. The fact that 348 boys and 382 girls in the three upper years of the high school placed "use of the automobile" fifth and fourth respectively in a list of twelve possible sources of disagreement between them and their parents suggests that this may be an increasing decentralizing agent.

An earnest teacher in a Sunday School class of working class boys and girls in their late teens was winding up the lesson on the temptations of Jesus: "These three temptations summarize all the temptations we encounter today: physical comfort, fame, and wealth. Can you think of any temptation we have today that Jesus didn't have?" "Speed!" rejoined one boy. The unwanted interruption was quickly passed over. But the boy had mentioned a tendency underlying one of the four chief infringements of group laws in Middletown today, and the manifestations of Speed are not confined to "speeding." "Auto Polo next Sunday!!" shouts the display advertisement of an amusement park near the city. "It's motor insanity—too fast for the movies!" The boys who have cars "step on the gas," and those who haven't cars sometimes steal them: "The desire of youth to step on the gas when it has no machine of its own," said the local press, "is considered responsible for the theft of the greater part of the [154] automobiles stolen from [Middletown] during the past year."

The threat which the automobile presents to some anxious parents is suggested by the fact that of thirty girls brought before the juvenile court in the twelve months preceding September 1, 1924, charged with "sex crimes," for whom the place where the offense occurred was given in the records, nineteen were listed as having committed the offense in an automobile. Here again the automobile appears to some as an "enemy" of the home and society.

Sharp, also, is the resentment aroused by this elbowing new device when it interferes with old-established religious habits. The minister trying to change people's behavior in desired directions through the spoken word must compete against the strong pull of the open road strengthened by endless printed "copy" inciting to travel. Preaching to 200 people on a hot, sunny Sunday in midsummer on "The Supreme Need of Today," a leading Middletown minister denounced "automobilitis—the thing those people have who go off motoring on Sunday instead of going to church. If you want to use your car on Sunday, take it out Sunday morning and bring some shut-ins to church and Sunday School; then in the afternoon, if you choose, go out and worship God in the beauty of nature—but don't neglect to worship Him indoors too." This same month there appeared in the *Saturday Evening Post*, reaching approximately one family in six in Middletown, a two-page spread on the automobile as an "enricher of life," quoting "a bank president in a Mid-Western city" as saying, "A man who works six days a week and spends the seventh on his own doorstep certainly will not pick up the extra dimes in the great thoroughfares of life." "Some sunny Sunday very soon," said another two-page spread in the *Post*, "just drive an Overland up to your door—tell the family to hurry the packing and get aboard—and be off with smiles down the nearest road—free, loose, and happy—bound for green wonderlands." Another such advertisement urged Middletown to "Increase Your Week-End Touring Radius." If we except the concentrated group pressure of war time, never perhaps since the days of the camp-meeting have the citizens of this community been subjected to such a powerfully focused stream of habit diffusion. To get the full force of this appeal, one must remember that the nearest lakes or hills are one hundred miles from Middletown in either direction and that an afternoon's motoring brings only mile upon mile of level stretches like Middletown itself. . . .

Though less widely diffused as yet than automobile owning or movie attendance, the radio nevertheless is rapidly crowding its way in among the necessities in the family standard of living. Not the least remarkable feature of this new invention is its accessibility. Here skill and ingenuity can in part offset money as an open sesame to swift sharing of the enjoyments of the wealthy. With but little equipment one can call the life of the rest of the world from the air, and this equipment can be purchased piecemeal at the ten-cent store. Far from being simply one more means of passive enjoyment, the radio has given rise to much ingenious manipulative activity. In a count of representative sections of Middletown, it was found that, of 303 homes in twenty-eight blocks in the "best section" of town, inhabited almost entirely by the business class, 12 per cent had radios; of 518 workers' homes in sixty-four blocks, 6 per cent had radios.[4]

As this new tool is rolling back the horizons of Middletown for the bank clerk or the mechanic sitting at home and listening to a Philharmonic concert or a sermon by Dr. Fosdick, or to President Coolidge bidding his father good night on the eve of election,[5] and as it is wedging its way with the movie, the

[4]Both percentages have undoubtedly increased notably since 1924, when the counts were made.

[5]In 1890 the local press spoke of an occasional citizen's visiting "Paris, France," and London, England," and even in 1924 a note in one of the papers recording the accident of some Middletown people finding themselves in a box at a New York theater with a group of Englishmen was captioned "Lucky they weren't Chinese!" The rest of the world is still a long way from Middletown, but movies and radio are doing much to break down this isolation: "I've got 120 stations on my radio," gleefully announced a local working man. Meanwhile, the president of the Radio Corporation of America proclaims an era at hand when "the oldest and newest civilizations will throb together at the same intellectual appeal, and to the same artistic emotions."

automobile, and other new tools into the twisted mass of habits that are living for the 38,000 people of Middletown, readjustments necessarily occur. Such comments as the following suggest their nature:

> *"I use time evenings listening in that I used to spend in reading."*

> *"The radio is hurting movie going, especially Sunday evening."* (From a leading movie exhibitor.)

> *"I don't use my car so much any more. The heavy traffic makes it less fun. But I spend seven nights a week on my radio. We hear fine music from Boston."* (From a shabby man of fifty.)

> *"Sundays I take the boy to Sunday School and come straight home and tune in. I get first an eastern service, then a Cincinnati one. Then there's nothing doing till about two-thirty, when I pick up an eastern service again and follow 'em across the country till I wind up with California about ten-thirty. Last night I heard a ripping sermon from Westminster Church somewhere in California. We've no preachers here that can compare with any of them."*

> *"One of the bad features of radio,"* according to a teacher, *"is that children stay up late at night and are not fit for school next day."*

> *"We've spent close on to $100 on our radio, and we built it ourselves at that,"* commented one of the worker's wives. *"Where'd we get the money? Oh, out of our savings, like everybody else."*

In the flux of competing habits that are oscillating the members of the family now towards and now away from the home, radio occupies an intermediate position. Twenty-five per cent of 337 high school boys and 22 per cent of 423 high school girls said that they listen more often to the radio with their parents than without them, and, as pointed out above, 20 per cent of 274 boys in the three upper years of the high school answered "radio" to the question, "In what thing that you are doing at home this fall are you most interested?"—more than gave any other answer.[6] More than one mother said that her family used to scatter in the evening—"but now we all sit around and listen to the radio."

Likewise the place of the radio in relation to Middletown's other leisure habits is not wholly clear. As it becomes more perfected, cheaper, and a more accepted part of life, it may cease to call forth so much active, constructive ingenuity and become one more form of passive enjoyment. Doubtless it will continue to play a mighty rôle in lifting Middletown out of the humdrum of every day; it is beginning to take over that function of the great political rallies or the trips by the trainload to the state capital to hear a noted speaker or to see a monument dedicated that a generation ago helped to set the average man in a wide place. But it seems not unlikely that, while furnishing a new means of diversified

---

[6]Less than 1 per cent of the 341 girls answered "radio."

enjoyment, it will at the same time operate, with national advertising, syndicated newspapers, and other means of large-scale diffusion, as yet another means of standardizing many of Middletown's habits. Indeed, at no point is one brought up more sharply against the impossibility of studying Middletown as a self-contained, self-starting community than when one watches these space-binding leisure-time inventions imported from without—automobile, motion picture, and radio—reshaping the city.

DOCUMENT 24.3

Extension Work among Negroes
Conducted by Negro Agents, 1923

J. A. Evans

Extension work among negroes in many sections of the South has been conducted under trying conditions for the past few years. The practical failure of the cotton crop in some sections for two or three successive years, owing to bad seasons and boll weevils, and the general depression in the price of other farm products resulted in many thousands of negro farmers being reduced to a state of extreme poverty. Farms were abandoned, and the migration to the industrial centers of the North and East, where employment and good wages could be obtained, assumed startling proportions in 1922 and continued through 1923.

The northward exodus of negro farmers embraced all classes—farm owners, tenants, and share croppers. Many landowners sold their farms at a sacrifice before going. Others simply moved off and left them. The movement of negro farmers and farm tenants was heaviest from sections in which there was most suffering due to crop disasters. But thousands who had no compelling economic reasons for seeking new fields and employment caught the fever to go North and either sacrificed their holdings and moved at once or began making plans to go, and so lost interest in local affairs. Tenants, frequently between suns, abandoned their growing crops and joined the exodus. All this of course, adversely affected all forms of extension work with both adults and juniors. The State agent for Alabama reported as follows: "The problem as affecting our work is not alone created by those who actually go out, but by the mental attitude of those who are still at work on their farms. Agents are more and more confronted with interference in the execution of constructive programs on the part of farmers who are well-meaning but who have become victims of the epidemic of unrest that is invading the South."

Source: From J. A. Evans, "Extension Work among Negroes Conducted by Negro Agents, 1923," U.S. Dept. of Agriculture, Dept. Circular 355 (Washington, D.C.: September 1925), pp. 6–7.

There are no dependable statistics showing the number of negro farmers who have left the farms and gone North, or to the cities in the South, in the past two or three years; but there is little doubt that it would total close to 100,000, or approximately 10 per cent of the entire number of negro farm operators in the South, as shown by the census of 1920. The States of South Carolina, Georgia, Alabama, and Mississippi suffered by far the heaviest loss of negro farmers because of successive disasters to the cotton crop, but all the Southern States were more or less affected.

The demoralizing tendency of this situation, as it affected extension work among negroes during the past year, was at least partially offset by the increased support and cooperation of the press, the church, civic organizations, and the public generally. It seemed to be generally considered that extension work offered the best means of overcoming the poverty, dissatisfaction, and unrest prevailing among negro farmers, and of thus checking the migration from the rural sections. Many leading city papers of the South called editorial attention to the work of negro agents and the possibilities of their effective influence in allaying the unrest among colored people, and urged greater cooperation and support for them. The county papers and the agricultural press, as well as city journals, carried frequent news stories of the success of negro demonstration work. Liberal premiums were given at community, county, and State fairs to inspire rivalry and encourage negro farmers and club members.

DOCUMENT 24.4

The Indian Citizenship Act

An Act To authorize the Secretary of the Interior to issue certificates of citizenship to Indians.

Be it enacted by the Senate and House of Representatives of the United States of America in Congress assembled, That all non-citizen Indians born within the territorial limits of the United States be, and they are hereby, declared to be citizens of the United States: *Provided,* That the granting of such citizenship shall not in any manner impair or otherwise affect the right of any Indian to tribal or other property.

Approved, June 2, 1924.

Source: H.R. 6355, Public, No. 175. Sixty-Eighth Congress. SesslCHS.233.1924. Available at www.angelfire.com/tn2/senaa/annamae/IndianCitizenshipAct1924.htm.

DOCUMENT 24.5

Immigration by the Numbers

TABLE 1. Foreign-Born Population in the United States from
          Selected Countries, 1880–1920

	CENSUS YEAR				
	1880	1890	1900	1910	1920
Total U.S. Population	43,475,840	62,622,250	76,303,387	91,972,266	105,710,620
Total Foreign-Born in U.S.	6,679,943	9,249,547	10,460,085	13,515,886	13,920,629
Country Group A					
England	662,676	908,141	843,491	877,719	813,853
France	106,971	113,174	104,534	117,418	153,072
Holland	58,090	81,828	105,098	120,063	131,766
Norway	181,729	322,665	338,426	403,877	363,863
Wales	83,302	100,079	93,744	82,488	67,066
Country Group B					
Hungary	11,526	62,435	145,815	496,605	397,283
Ireland	1,854,571	1,871,509	1,619,469	1,352,251	1,037,234
Italy	44,230	182,580	484,703	1,343,125	1,610,113
Mexico	68,399	77,853	103,445	221,915	486,418
Turkey	1,205	1,839	9,949	61,959	16,303

TABLE 2. Percentage of U.S. Foreign-Born Population from
          Selected Countries, 1880–1920

	CENSUS YEAR				
	1880	1890	1900	1910	1920
Total Foreign-Born in U.S.	15.400%	14.800%	13.700%	14.700%	13.200%
Country Group A					
England	1.524	1.450	1.105	0.954	0.770
France	0.246	0.181	0.137	0.128	0.145
Holland	0.134	0.131	0.138	0.131	0.125
Norway	0.418	0.515	0.444	0.439	0.344
Wales	0.192	0.160	0.123	0.090	0.063
Country Group B					
Hungary	0.027	0.100	0.191	0.539	0.376
Ireland	4.266	2.989	2.122	1.470	0.981
Italy	0.102	0.292	0.635	1.460	1.523
Mexico	0.157	0.124	0.136	0.241	0.460
Turkey	0.003	0.003	0.013	0.067	0.015

TABLE 3. Percentage Increase in Selected Foreign-Born Populations in the United States, 1880–1920

	CENSUS YEAR				
	1880–1890	1890–1900	1900–1910	1910–1920	1880–1920
Total U.S. Population	44.0%	21.8%	20.5%	14.9%	143.1%
Total Foreign-Born in U.S.	38.5	13.1	29.2	3.0	1.0
Country Group A					
England	37.0	−7.1	4.1	−7.3	22.8
France	5.8	−7.6	12.3	30.4	43.1
Holland	40.9	28.4	14.2	9.7	126.8
Norway	77.6	4.9	19.3	−9.9	100.2
Wales	20.1	−6.3	−12.0	−18.7	−19.5
Country Group B					
Hungary	441.7	133.5	239.9	−19.8	3346.8
Ireland	0.9	−13.5	−16.5	−23.3	−44.1
Italy	312.8	165.5	177.1	19.9	3540.3
Mexico	13.8	32.9	114.5	119.2	611.1
Turkey	52.6	441.0	522.8	−73.7	1252.9

Source: 1880 Population Figures: U.S. Department of the Interior, Bureau of the Census, *Population of the United States at the Tenth Census: 1880* (Washington, DC: Government Printing Office, 1883), xxxix. 1890 Population Figures: U.S. Department of the Interior, Census Office, Report of the Population of the United States at the Eleventh Census: 1890. Part I. (Washington, DC: Government Printing Office, 1895), 395, 606–609. 1900 Population Figures: U.S. Department of the Interior, Census Office, Report of the Population of the United States at the Twelfth Census: 1900. Vol. 1. (Washington, DC: Government Printing Office, 1903), xviii, 732–735. 1910 Population Figures: U.S. Department of the Interior, Census Office, The Thirteenth Census of the United States taken in the year 1910. Vol. 1: Population. (Washington, DC: Government Printing Office, 1913), 834–835. 1920 Population Figures: U.S. Department of the Interior, Census Office, The Fourteenth Census of the United States taken in the year 1920. Vol. II: Population (Washington, DC: Government Printing Office, 1922), 629; 693.

Immigration Act of 1921

An Act to limit the immigration of aliens into the United States. (U.S. Statutes at Large, 42:5–7) May 19, 1921

 . . . Sec. 2. (a) . . . the number of aliens of any nationality who may be admitted under the immigration laws of the United States in any fiscal year shall be limited to 3 per centum of the number of foreign-born persons of such nationality resident in the United States as determined by the United States census of 1910.

Immigration Act of 1924

An Act to limit the immigration of aliens into the United States, and for other purposes. (U.S. Statutes at Large, 43:153–169.

. . . Numerical Limitations

Sec. 11. (a) The annual quota of any nationality shall be 2 per centum of the number of foreign-born individuals of such nationality resident in continental United States as determined by the United States Census of 1890, but the minimum quota shall be 100.

(b) The annual quota of any nationality for the fiscal year beginning July 1, 1927, and for each fiscal year thereafter, shall be a number which bears the same ratio to 150,000 as the number of inhabitants in continental United States in 1920 having that national origin . . . but the minimum quota of any nationality shall be 100.

DOCUMENT 24.6

Exile's Return: A Narrative of Ideas

Malcolm Cowley

Greenwich Village was not only a place, a mood, a way of life: like all Bohemias, it was also a doctrine. Since the days of Gautier and Murger, this doctrine had remained the same in spirit, but it had changed in several details. By 1920, it had become a system of ideas that could roughly be summarized as follows:

1. The idea of salvation by the child.—Each of us at birth has special potentialities which are slowly crushed and destroyed by a standardized society and mechanical methods of teaching. If a new educational system can be introduced, one by which children are encouraged to develop their own personalities, to blossom freely like flowers, then the world will be saved by this new, free generation.

2. The idea of self-expression.—Each man's, each woman's, purpose in life is to express himself, to realize his full individuality through creative work and beautiful living in beautiful surroundings.

3. The idea of paganism.—The body is a temple in which there is nothing unclean, a shrine to be adorned for the ritual of love.

4. The idea of living for the moment.—It is stupid to pile up treasures that we can enjoy only in old age, when we have lost the capacity for enjoyment. Better to seize the moment as it comes, to dwell in it intensely, even at the cost of future suffering. Better to live extravagantly, gather June rosebuds, "burn our candle at both ends."

5. The idea of liberty.—Every law, convention or rule of art that prevents self-expression or the full enjoyment of the moment should be shattered and abolished. Puritanism is the great enemy. The crusade against Puritanism is the only crusade with which free individuals are justified in allying themselves.

6. The idea of female equality.—Women should be the economic and moral equals of men. They should have the same pay, the same working conditions, the same opportunity for drinking, smoking, taking or dismissing lovers.

Source: From Malcolm Cowley, *Exile's Return: A Narrative of Ideas* (New York: W.W. Norton, 1934), pp. 69–76.

7. The idea of psychological adjustment.—We are unhappy because we are maladjusted, and maladjusted because we are repressed. If our individual repressions can be removed—by confessing them to a Freudian psychologist—then we can adjust ourselves to any situation, and be happy in it. (But Freudianism is only one method of adjustment. What is wrong with us may be our glands, and by a slight operation, or merely by taking a daily dose of thyroid, we may alter our whole personalities. Again, we may adjust ourselves by some such psycho-physical discipline as is taught by Gurdjieff. The implication of all these methods is the same—that the environment itself need not be altered. This explains why most radicals who became converted to psychoanalysis or glands or Gurdjieff gradually abandoned their political radicalism.)

8. The idea of changing place.—"They do things better in Europe." England and Germany have the wisdom of old cultures; the Latin peoples have admirably preserved their pagan heritage. By expatriating himself, by living in Paris, Capri or the South of France, the artist can break the Puritan shackles, drink, live freely and be wholly creative.

All these, from the standpoint of the business-Christian ethic then represented by the *Saturday Evening Post,* were corrupt ideas. This older ethic is familiar to most people, but one feature of it has not been sufficiently emphasized. Substantially, it was a *production* ethic. The great virtues it taught were industry, foresight, thrift and personal initiative. The workman should be industrious in order to produce more for his employer; he should look ahead to the future; he should save money in order to become a capitalist himself; then he should exercise personal initiative and found new factories where other workmen would toil industriously, and save, and become capitalists in their turn.

During the process many people would suffer privations: most workers would live meagerly and wrack their bodies with labor; even the employers would deny themselves luxuries that they could easily purchase, choosing instead to put back the money into their business; but after all, our bodies were not to be pampered; they were temporary dwelling places, and we should be rewarded in Heaven for our self-denial. On earth, our duty was to accumulate more wealth and produce more goods, the ultimate use of which was no subject for worry. They would somehow be absorbed, by new markets opened in the West, or overseas in new countries, or by the increased purchasing power of workmen who had saved and bettered their position.

This was the ethic of a young capitalism, and it worked admirably, so long as the territory and population of the country were expanding faster than its industrial plant. But after the War, the situation changed. Our industries had grown enormously to satisfy a demand that suddenly ceased. To keep the factory wheels turning, a new domestic market had to be created. Industry and thrift were no longer adequate. There must be a new ethic that encouraged people to buy, a *consumption* ethic.

It happened that many of the Greenwich Village ideas proved useful in the altered situation. Thus, *self-expression* and *paganism* encouraged a demand for all sorts of products, modern furniture, beach pajamas, cosmetics, colored bathrooms with toilet paper to match. *Living for the moment* meant buying an automobile, radio or house, using it now and paying for it tomorrow. *Female equality* was capable of doubling the consumption of products formerly used by men alone. Even *changing place* would help to stimulate business in the country from which the artist was being expatriated. The exiles of art were also trade missionaries: involuntarily they increased the foreign demand for fountain pens, silk stockings, grapefruit and portable typewriters. They drew after them an invading army of tourists, thus swelling the profits of steamship lines and travel agencies. Everything fitted into the business picture.

I don't mean to say that Greenwich Village was the source of the revolution in morals that affected all our lives in the decade after the War, and neither do I mean that big business deliberately plotted to render the nation extravagant, pleasure worshiping and reckless of tomorrow.

The new moral standards arose from conditions that had nothing to do with the Village. They were, as a matter of fact, not really new. Always, even in the great age of the Puritans, there had been currents of licentiousness that were favored by the immoderate American climate and held in check only by hellfire preaching and the hardships of settling a new country. Old Boston, Providence, rural Connecticut, all had their underworlds. The reason why Puritanism became so strong in America was perhaps that it had to be strong in order to checkmate its enemies. But it was already weakening as the country grew richer in the twenty years before the War; and the War itself was the Puritan crisis and defeat.

All standards were relaxed in the stormy-sultry wartime atmosphere. It wasn't only the boys of my age, those serving in the army, who were transformed by events: their sisters and younger brothers were affected in a different fashion. With their fathers away, perhaps, and their mothers making bandages or tea-dancing with lonely officers, it was possible for boys and girls to do what they pleased. For the first time they could go to dances unchaperoned, drive the family car and park it by the roadside while they made love, and come home after midnight a little tipsy with nobody to reproach them in the hallway. They took advantage of these stolen liberties—indeed, one might say that the revolution in morals began as a middle-class children's revolt.

But everything conspired to further it. Prohibition came and surrounded the new customs with illicit glamor; prosperity made it possible to practise them; Freudian psychology provided a philosophical justification and made it unfashionable to be repressed; still later the sex magazines and the movies, even the pulpit, would advertise a revolution that had taken place silently and triumphed without a struggle. In all this Greenwich Village had no part. The revolution would have occurred if the Village had never existed, but—the point is important—it could not have followed the same course. The Village, older in revolt, gave form to the movement, created its fashions, and supplied the writers and illustrators who would render them popular. As for American business, though it laid no plots in advance, it was quick enough to use the situation, to exploit the new markets for cigarettes and cosmetics, and to realize that, in advertising pages and movie palaces, sex appeal was now the surest appeal.

The Greenwich Village standards, with the help of business, had spread through the country. Young women east and west had bobbed their hair, let it grow and bobbed it again; they had passed through the period when corsets were checked in the cloakroom at dances and the period when corsets were not worn. They were not very self-conscious when they talked about taking a lover; and the conversations ran from mother fixations to birth control while they smoked cigarettes between the courses of luncheons eaten in black-and-orange tea shops just like those in the Village. People of forty had been affected by the younger generation: they spent too much money, drank too much gin, made love to one another's wives and talked about their neuroses. Houses were furnished to look like studios. Stenographers went on parties, following the example of the boss and his girl friend and her husband. The "party," conceived as a gathering together of men and women to drink gin cocktails, flirt, dance to the phonograph or radio and gossip about their absent friends, had in fact become one of the most popular American institutions; nobody stopped to think how short its history had been in this country. It developed out of the "orgies" celebrated by the French 1830 Romantics, but it was introduced into this country by Greenwich Villagers—before being adopted by salesmen from Kokomo and the younger country-club set in Kansas City.

Wherever one turned the Greenwich Village ideas were making their way: even the *Saturday Evening Post* was feeling their influence. Long before Repeal, it began to wobble on Prohibition. It allowed drinking, petting and unfaithfulness to be mentioned in the stories it published; its illustrations showed women smoking. Its advertising columns admitted one after another of the strictly pagan products—cosmetics, toilet tissues, cigarettes—yet still it continued to thunder against Greenwich Village and bohemian immorality. It even nourished the illusion that its long campaign had been successful. On more than one occasion it announced that the Village was dead and buried: "The sad truth is," it said in the autumn of 1931, "that the Village was a flop." Perhaps it was true that the Village was moribund—of this we can't be sure, for creeds and ways of life among artists are hard to kill. If, however, the Village was really dying, it was dying of success. It was dying because it became so popular that too many people insisted on living there. It was dying because women smoked cigarettes on the streets of the Bronx, drank gin cocktails in Omaha and had perfectly swell parties in Seattle and Middletown—in other words, because American business and the whole of middle-class America had been going Greenwich Village.

25

Restoring the Temple

To everything there is a season, and the prosperity of the 1920s was built upon thin and brittle foundations. Did anyone see the warning signs of what was just over the economic horizon? It is unclear why Calvin Coolidge decided against a bid for reelection, but Herbert Hoover was undaunted. In his inaugural address, Hoover outlined his policies toward the "important" issues of the day—one of which was the enforcement of prohibition. Within only a few months, such concerns seemed trivial, if not irrelevant, in the face of the nation's crushing economic depression. By 1932 the time seemed right for overhauling the American political process and certainly that of the presidency. President Roosevelt, for his part, saw a greater need for reform of American institutions in general and of the traditional relationship between Americans and their government.

As poverty swamped the lives of ordinary Americans, letters poured in to the White House chronicling threatened lives, endangered liberties, and unhappiness. Walker Evans and others captured on film the characters in the dramas of those days, and Woody Guthrie memorialized real folks in his folk songs as they struggled against poverty and powerlessness. Perhaps the widespread experience ordinary citizens gained with poverty and hard times created an empathetic and political base of support for the substantial growth of the role of the federal government and its changed relations with the American people.

To be sure, the foundations of the American system were being shaken, and some thought America was ripe for revolution as Russia had been in 1917. For some this offered hope, but for many others the struggle was survival and little else. With nerves rubbed raw, race relations took a turn for the worse despite the attentions and efforts of people in high places.

DOCUMENT 25.1

Herbert Hoover's Inaugural Address

If we survey the situation of our Nation both at home and abroad, we find many satisfactions; we find some causes for concern. We have emerged from the losses of the Great War and the reconstruction following it with increased virility and strength. From this strength we have contributed to the recovery and progress of the world. What America has done has given renewed hope and courage to all who have faith in government by the people. In the large view, we have reached a higher degree of comfort and security than ever existed before in the history of the world. Through liberation from widespread poverty we have reached a higher degree of individual freedom than ever before. The devotion to and concern for our institutions are deep and sincere. We are steadily building a new race—a new civilization great in its own attainments. The influence and high purposes of our Nation are respected among the peoples of the world. We aspire to distinction in the world, but to a distinction based upon confidence in our sense of justice as well as our accomplishments within our own borders and in our own lives. For wise guidance in this great period of recovery the Nation is deeply indebted to Calvin Coolidge. . . .

It appears to me that the more important further mandates from the recent election were the maintenance of the integrity of the Constitution; the vigorous enforcement of the laws; the continuance of economy in public expenditure; the continued regulation of business to prevent domination in the community; the denial of ownership or operation of business by the Government in competition with its citizens; the avoidance of policies which would involve us in the controversies of foreign nations; the more effective reorganization of the departments of the Federal Government; the expansion of public works; and the promotion of welfare activities affecting education and the home.

These were the more tangible determinations of the election, but beyond them was the confidence and belief of the people that we would not neglect the support of the embedded ideals and aspirations of America. These ideals and aspirations are the touchstones upon which the day-to-day administration and legislative acts of government must be tested. More than this, the Government must, so far as lies within its proper powers, give leadership to the realization of these ideals and to the fruition of these aspirations. No one can adequately reduce these things of the spirit to phrases or to a catalogue of definitions. We do know what the attainments of these ideals should be: The preservation of self-government and its full foundations in local government; the perfection of justice whether in economic or in social fields; the maintenance of ordered liberty; the denial of domination by any group or class; the building up and preservation of equality of opportunity; the stimulation of initiative and individuality; absolute integrity in public affairs; the choice of officials for fitness to office; the

Source: "Inaugural Addresses of the Presidents of the United States," 1989, www.bartleby.com/124/ pres48.html.

direction of economic progress toward prosperity for the further lessening of poverty; the freedom of public opinion; the sustaining of education and of the advancement of knowledge; the growth of religious spirit and the tolerance of all faiths; the strengthening of the home; the advancement of peace.

There is no short road to the realization of these aspirations. Ours is a progressive people, but with a determination that progress must be based upon the foundation of experience. Ill-considered remedies for our faults bring only penalties after them. But if we hold the faith of the men in our mighty past who created these ideals, we shall leave them heightened and strengthened for our children.

This is not the time and place for extended discussion. The questions before our country are problems of progress to higher standards; they are not the problems of degeneration. They demand thought and they serve to quicken the conscience and enlist our sense of responsibility for their settlement. And that responsibility rests upon you, my countrymen, as much as upon those of us who have been selected for office.

Ours is a land rich in resources; stimulating in its glorious beauty; filled with millions of happy homes; blessed with comfort and opportunity. In no nation are the institutions of progress more advanced. In no nation are the fruits of accomplishment more secure. In no nation is the government more worthy of respect. No country is more loved by its people. I have an abiding faith in their capacity, integrity and high purpose. I have no fears for the future of our country. It is bright with hope.

DOCUMENT 25.2

Radio Address of President Franklin D. Roosevelt, May 7, 1933

On a Sunday night a week after my Inauguration I used the radio to tell you about the banking crisis and the measures we were taking to meet it. I think that in that way I made clear to the country various facts that might otherwise have been misunderstood and in general provided a means of understanding which did much to restore confidence.

Tonight, eight weeks later, I come for the second time to give you my report—in the same spirit and by the same means to tell you about what we have been doing and what we are planning to do.

Two months ago we were facing serious problems. The country was dying by inches. It was dying because trade and commerce had declined to dangerously low levels; prices for basic commodities were such as to destroy the value of the assets of national institutions such as banks, savings banks, insurance companies, and others. These institutions, because of their great needs, were foreclosing mortgages, calling loans, refusing credit. Thus there was actually in process of destruction the property of millions of people who had borrowed money on that property in terms of dollars which had had an entirely different

Source: Available at www.fdrlibrary.marist.edu/05073.html.

value from the level of March, 1933. That situation in that crisis did not call for any complicated consideration of economic panaceas or fancy plans. We were faced by a condition and not a theory.

There were just two alternatives: The first was to allow the foreclosures to continue, credit to be withheld and money to go into hiding, and thus forcing liquidation and bankruptcy of banks, railroads and insurance companies and a recapitalizing of all business and all property on a lower level. This alternative meant a continuation of what is loosely called "deflation," the net result of which would have been extraordinary hardship on all property owners and, incidentally, extraordinary hardships on all persons working for wages through an increase in unemployment and a further reduction of the wage scale.

It is easy to see that the result of this course would have had not only economic effects of a very serious nature but social results that might bring incalculable harm. Even before I was inaugurated I came to the conclusion that such a policy was too much to ask the American people to bear. It involved not only a further loss of homes, farms, savings and wages but also a loss of spiritual values—the loss of that sense of security for the present and the future so necessary to the peace and contentment of the individual and of his family. When you destroy these things you will find it difficult to establish confidence of any sort in the future. It was clear that mere appeals from Washington for confidence and the mere lending of more money to shaky institutions could not stop this downward course. A prompt program applied as quickly as possible seemed to me not only justified but imperative to our national security. The Congress, and when I say Congress I mean the members of both political parties, fully understood this and gave me generous and intelligent support. The members of Congress realized that the methods of normal times had to be replaced in the emergency by measures which were suited to the serious and pressing requirements of the moment. There was no actual surrender of power, Congress still retained its constitutional authority and no one has the slightest desire to change the balance of these powers. The function of Congress is to decide what has to be done and to select the appropriate agency to carry out its will. This policy it has strictly adhered to. The only thing that has been happening has been to designate the President as the agency to carry out certain of the purposes of the Congress. This was constitutional and in keeping with the past American tradition.

The legislation which has been passed or in the process of enactment can properly be considered as part of a well-grounded plan.

First, we are giving opportunity of employment to one-quarter of a million of the unemployed, especially the young men who have dependents, to go into the forestry and flood prevention work. This is a big task because it means feeding, clothing and caring for nearly twice as many men as we have in the regular army itself. In creating this Civilian Conservation Corps we are killing two birds with one stone. We are clearly enhancing the value of our natural resources and, second, we are relieving an appreciable amount of actual distress. This great group of men have entered upon their work on a purely voluntary basis, no military training is involved, and we are conserving not only our natural resources but our human resources. One of the great values to this work is the fact that it is direct and requires the intervention of very little machinery. Second, I have requested the Congress and have secured action upon a proposal to put the great properties owned by our government at Muscle Shoals to work after long years of wasteful inaction, and with this a broad plan for the improvement of a vast area in the Tennessee Valley. It will add to the comfort and happiness of hundreds of thousands of people and the incident benefits will reach the entire nation.

Next, the Congress is about to pass legislation that will greatly ease the mortgage distress among the farmers and the home owners of the nation, by providing for the easing of the burden of debt now bearing so heavily upon millions of our people.

Our next step in seeking immediate relief is a grant of half a billion dollars to help the states, counties and municipalities in their duty to care for those who need direct and immediate relief.

The Congress also passed legislation authorizing the sale of beer in such states as desired. This has already resulted in considerable reemployment and, incidentally, has provided much needed tax revenue.

We are planning to ask the Congress for legislation to enable the government to undertake public works, thus stimulating directly and indirectly the employment of many others in well-considered projects.

Further legislation has been taken up which goes much more fundamentally into our economic problems. The Farm Relief Bill seeks by the use of several methods, alone or together, to bring about an increased return to farmers for their major farm products, seeking at the same time to prevent in the days to come disastrous over-production which so often in the past has kept farm commodity prices far below a reasonable return. This measure provides wide powers for emergencies. The extent of its use will depend entirely upon what the future has in store. . . .

We are working toward a definite goal, which is to prevent the return of conditions which came very close to destroying what we call modern civilization. The actual accomplishment of our purpose cannot be attained in a day. Our policies are wholly within purposes for which our American constitutional government was established 150 years ago.

DOCUMENT 25.3

Letters from the "Forgotten Man"

Lawndale, California,
Feb. 1—34.

Most Honorable President:
I am writing you this morning in all faiths, that if I can get word to you of our horrible plight you will not pass it by unnoticed.

Source: From Robert S. McElvaine, *Down and Out in the Great Depression: Letters from the "Forgotten Man"* (Chapel Hill: University of North Carolina Press, l983), pp. 57–58, 117, 162, 179–80).

I am a mother of seven children, and utterly heart broken, in that they are hungry, have only 65¢ in money. The father is in L.A. trying to find something to do,—provisions all gone—at this writing—no meat, milk—sugar—in fact, about enough flour for bread two meals—and thats all, I have two children in High School—and our pride isn't all gone, our story is this—and if we have a chance we can care for ourselves and be happy.

We have a boy 17 yrs. old who is capable of holding a good position as a musician, is an excellent French Horn player, I have been told by good musicians he is a professional now. There is a job he could have had a while ago in the C.W.A. program of music that would help us out. but this being handled thru county we could not take advantage of it, having not been here a year. . . . O, President, my heart is breaking, as I see him go from home with half enough to eat, and go all day with out a bite of lunch, to be sure he could beg his lunch but he's to proud to beg as long as he can help it, and I have spent the day yesterday praying God to help me bear this, and as I tried to prepare their very scarce breakfast, [illegible] that came if only the President could know he would help you to help your selves, and on this impulse I try to tell you. . . . O, what a burden and how helpless I am, how proud I am of my children, and how dark a future under this condition.

Their father is 62 yrs, old—a preacher a good carpenter—a saw-filer—but Industry won't hire a man This age, scarcely, even if they are strong in body, and he has no church to preach in—so—

O, surely there's a place for us in the world. . . .

I humbly pray God's Divine blessing on you, for you have tried every way to help the people.

Very Sincerely,
Mrs. I. H.

[February, 1936]

Mr. and Mrs. Roosevelt.
Wash. D.C.

Dear Mr. President:

I'm a boy of 12 years. I want to tell you about my family   My father hasn't worked for 5 months   He went plenty times to relief, he filled out application. They won't give us anything. I don't know why. Please you do something. We haven't paid 4 months rent, Everyday the landlord rings the door bell, we don't open the door for him. We are afraid that will be put out, been put out before, and don't want to happen again. We haven't paid the gas bill, and the electric bill, haven't paid grocery bill for 3 months. My brother goes to Lane Tech. High School. he's eighteen years old, hasn't gone to school for 2 weeks because he got no carfare. I have a sister she's twenty years, she can't find work. My father he staying home. All the time he's crying because he can't find work. I told him why are you crying daddy, and daddy said why shouldn't I cry when there is nothing in the house. I feel sorry for him. That night I couldn't sleep. The next morning I wrote this letter to you. in my room. Were American citizens and were born in Chicago, Ill. and I don't know why they don't help us   Please answer right away because we need it. will starve   Thank you.

God bless you.

[Anonymous]
Chicago, Ill.

[New York, N.Y.
March 1936]

Dear President,

why is it that it is the work-man that is always kicked when things go wrong with the officials   my Husband has worke on W.P.A. for some time a carpenter @ 85 dols per month + this morning he was reduced to timberman @ 60 per month   I know there was a mistake as he is a good carpenter. I am sorry to trouble you but please Dear President I need that 25 dols he is cut   Do you know what it is to have money then find yourself broke, next children, + finally live in a cold water Dump get up to two children at night and find them nearly frozen from lack of clothing well I do, + struggled along although I very often thought of suicide as the best way out. I am not a coward but good Lord it is awful to stand helpless when you need things.

When that letter came from Project Labor officer Frank C. Hunt W.P.A. N.Y.C. this morning informing him that he was reduced to 60 per month. well I hate to think of what will happen. Please, get him replaced as carpenter again his tag number is "123986" + he works at 125 St. N.Y.C. I am sorry I cannot give you my name as I do not want publicity though I see no way of avoiding it if things do not pick up. Thanking you for favours + forgive scribbling as am all nerves.

[Anonymous]

Sept. 21, 1935.

Mr. Hopkins, Relief Administrator,
Washington, D.C.

Dear Sir:—

Why are the Relief Projects being help up in St. Louis? The Projects that have already been started and are being help up for no one knows why, but you and I do not think you know. They could be continued and at least put some of our men to work right away and not wait until all the rest are ready, for if that is done and you fool around and pass the buck like you have none will be started at all.

We are not getting the allowances we did and our children are suffering for lack of food. And some have no clothes where with to attend school. Now is that right? And we will soon need coal and will not receive the funds for it, then what about that?

Of course, you are getting yours, and never have suffered like our people have, therefore you do not care. You have never been hungry and without all the luxuries of life, let alone the bare necessitities. It is not the fault of our people that this condition exzists here, for they have tried and worked at anything at all to make a few pennies, but there is not the work to be had here.

Now there is work waiting here for some of our men and you are responsible for them not getting it. How can you answer to these people for that. They demand some consideration. And I am afraid they will soon tire of this delay and take some action themselves. They have been held down long enough through your petty Political Playing. That is all it is. The red tape could have been cut long ago. But that is your excuse. We know it is not true. Petty Politics is the answer. You will never get yours later by such actions.

Your plate at the table is full. Your family can enjoy life from the peoples money, and not have a care where this and that is coming from.

a distracted Mother.

DOCUMENT 25.4

Photograph from *Let Us Now Praise Famous Men*

Walker Evans

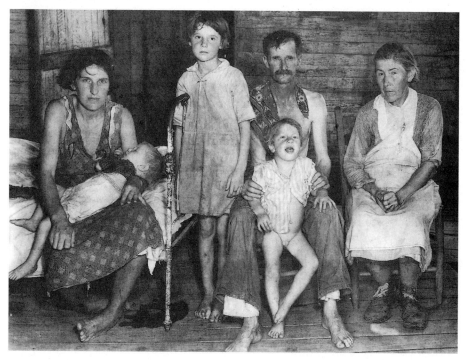

Source: Walker Evans, image 19, *Let Us Now Praise Famous Men,* by James Agee and Walker Evans (Boston: Houghton Mifflin, 1941).

DOCUMENT 25.5

Tom Joad

Woody Guthrie

Source: Words and Music by Woody Guthrie (Melody based on a traditional theme) TRO–© Copyright 1960 and 1963 Ludlow Music, Inc., New York, N.Y. International copyright secured. All rights reserved including public performance for profit.

*Not the key of F major, but a transposed Mixolydian mode on C. In other words, a C major scale with a flatted 7th, C D E F G A Bb C.

3. That truck rolled away in a cloud of dust,
   Tommy turned his face toward home,
   He met Preacher Casey and they had a little drink,
   But they found that his family they was gone,
   He found that his family they was gone.

4. He found his mother's old-fashioned shoe,
   Found his daddy's hat,
   And he found little Muley and Muley said:
   "They've been tractored out by the cats.
   They've been tractored out by the cats."

5. Tom Joad walked down to the neighbor's farm,
   Found his family.
   They took Preacher Casey and loaded in a car
   And his mother said: "We've got to git away."
   His mother said: "We've got to git away."

6. Now the twelve of the Joads made a mighty heavy load,
   But Grandpa Joad did cry.
   He picked up a handful of land in his hand,
   Said: "I'm stayin' with the farm till I die.
   Yes, I'm stayin' with my farm till I die."

7. They fed him short ribs and coffee and soothing syrup
   And Grandpa Joad did die.
   They buried Grandpa Joad by the side of the road,
   Grandma on the California side.
   They buried Grandma on the California side.

8. They stood on a mountain and they looked to the West,
   And it looked like the promised land,
   That bright green valley with a river running through,
   There was work for every single hand, they thought.
   There was work for every single hand.

9. The Joads rode away to jungle camp,
   There they cooked a stew,
   And the hungry little kids of the jungle camp
   Said: "We'd like to have some too."
   Said: "We'd like to have some too."

10. Now a deputy sheriff fired loose at a man,
    Shot a woman in the back.
    Before he could take his aim again
    Preacher Casey dropped him in his tracks.
    Preacher Casey dropped him in his tracks.

11. They handcuffed Casey and they took him to jail,
    And then he got away.
    And he met Tom Joad on the old river bridge,
    And these few words he did say, poor boy,
    These few words he did say:

12. "I preached for the Lord a mighty long time,
    Preached about the rich and the poor.
    Us workin' folks is all get together
    'Cause we ain't got a chance anymore,
    We ain't got a chance anymore."

13. Now the deputies come and Tom and Casey run
    To the bridge where the water run down.
    But the vigilante thugs hit Casey with a club,
    They laid Preacher Casey on the ground, poor Casey,
    They laid Preacher Casey on the ground.

14. Tom Joad he grabbed that deputy's club,
    Hit him over the head.
    Tom Joad took flight in the dark, rainy night,
    And a deputy and a preacher lying dead, two men,
    A deputy and a preacher lying dead.

15. Tom run back where his mother was asleep,
    He woke her up out of bed.
    Then he kissed goodbye to the mother that he loved.
    Said what Preacher Casey said, Tom Joad,
    He said what Preacher Casey said.

16. "Ev'rybody might be just one big soul,
    Well it looks that-a way to me.
    Everywhere that you look in the day or night
    That's where I'm gonna be, Ma,
    That's where I'm gonna be."

17. "Wherever little children are hungry and cry,
    Wherever people ain't free,
    Wherever men are fightin' for their rights,
    That's where I'm gonna be, Ma,
    That's where I'm gonna be."

I wrote this song one night in New York. It was the night that I saw the moving picture, *The Grapes of Wrath* by John Steinbeck. If I could only think of the name of the friend that lived in that apartment I would sure like to say thank you. You are friendly and wine is good. And this is on a Victor Record.

DOCUMENT 25.6

A Battle in San Francisco

San Francisco is a busy city of 600,000, its heart the waterfront, the chief source of its life. And yet the men who kept the city alive, who did its most important work, the longshoremen who loaded and unloaded the vessels that made the city prosperous with trade, the seamen who manned the ships, received in 1933 little more than $10 a week. To be precise, the average weekly wage of longshoremen was $10.45 while able seamen received $53 a month and ordinary seamen $36. . . .

And yet even more important was the fact that the maritime workers were voiceless serfs in an industrial autocracy, powerless employees of the shipping industry which received millions on millions of dollars, according to the Black Senatorial Investigation [Sen. Hugo Black], in subsidies from the federal government. A few seamen belonged to a corrupt, sell-out organization, the International Seamen's Union and still fewer to the militant Marine Workers Industrial Union (TUUL), but to all practical purposes they were unorganized. The longshoremen since 1919 had been dragooned into a creature of the shipping industry known as the Blue Book Union, an employers' organization, controlled by gangsters who forced the underpaid longshoremen to bribe them for jobs.

In 1933, under the impetus of NIRA and Section 7(a) as well as the spur of intolerable conditions, longshoremen in San Francisco and up and down the Pacific coast began flocking into the International Longshoremen's Association, AFL. Knowing something of Joseph P. Ryan, its president, they were determined on rank and file control. One of their leaders was a sharp-featured, sharp-witted longshoreman by the name of Harry Bridges. A tough and rugged character, his assets were an impregnable honesty and a stout belief in the ability and right of the rank and file to govern themselves.

Although federal law made it mandatory that the shipping magnates negotiate in collective bargaining with any union that their employees chose, they unhesitatingly broke the law by refusing to so negotiate. Instead, in September, 1933, they discharged four rank and file leaders of the union. When the regional labor board ordered their reinstatement, the longshoremen surged into the ILA. . . .

After the employers had refused to negotiate or recognize the union over a period of months 12,000 longshoremen went on strike at 8 p.m. on May 9, 1934, in San Francisco, Seattle, Tacoma, Portland, San Pedro, San Diego, Stockton, Bellingham, Aberdeen, Grays Harbor, Astoria and all other Pacific coast ports. The Marine Workers Industrial Union followed suit and by May 23 eight maritime unions and 35,000 workers were out on strike up and down the coast.

It was primarily unprecedented police brutality that turned the seamen's strike into a general strike of 127,900 San Francisco workers that in an instant

Source: From Philip Bart, ed., *Highlights of a Fighting History: 60 Years of the Communist Party, USA* (New York: International Publishers, 1979), pp. 114–15.

transformed the city into a ghost town in which there was no movement. The police took their line from the Industrial Association, the combination of San Francisco's most powerful tycoons, organized in 1919 as a Law and Order Committee to break a waterfront strike and developing until it was the real ruler of San Francisco. . . .

The longshoremen had drawn up a list of demands, pay of $1 an hour, a six-hour day, a thirty-hour week, a union hiring hall, but officials of the Industrial Association declared there was no issue at stake but the suppression of a Red Revolt. Press, pulpit and radio combined with tireless unanimity to whip up hysteria against workers striving to better their lives. Not unusual was the first-page story of the [San Francisco] *Chronicle*, "Red Army Marching on City." The story read in part: "The reports stated the communist army planned the destruction of railroad and highway facilities to paralyze transportation and later, communication, while San Francisco and the Bay Area were made a focal point in a red struggle for control of government. . . . "

Bumbling Joseph P. Ryan, president of the International Longshoremen's Association, but in league with the gangsters of New York, was rushed from New York to quiet the strikers. Long known as an ardent fighter against Communism, he did his part as expected when unable to sell out the maritime workers. . . .

"A deafening roar went up from the pickets. Standing on the running board of a patrol car at the head of the caravan, Police Captain Thomas M. Hoertkorn flourished a revolver and shouted, 'The port is open.'

"With single accord the great mass of pickets surged forward. The Embarcadero became a vast tangle of fighting men. Bricks flew and clubs battered skulls. The police opened fire with revolvers and riot guns. Clouds of tear gas swept the picket lines and sent the men choking in defeat. Mounted police were dragged from their saddles and beaten to the pavement.

"The cobblestones of the Embarcadero were littered with fallen men; bright puddles of blood colored the gray expanse.

DOCUMENT 25.7

A Letter on Lynching

Eleanor Roosevelt

PERSONAL AND CONFIDENTIAL.

THE WHITE HOUSE
WASHINGTON

March 19, 1936

Rec'd W.W. 3-21-36

My dear Mr. White:

      Before I received your letter today I had been in to the President, talking to him about your letter enclosing that of the Attorney General. I told him that it seemed rather terrible that one could get nothing done and that I did not blame you in the least for feeling there was no interest in this very serious question. I asked him if there were any possibility of getting even one step taken, and he said the difficulty is that it is unconstitutional apparently for the Federal Government to step in in the lynching situation. The Government has only been allowed to do anything about kidnapping because of its interstate aspect, and even that has not as yet been appealed so they are not sure that it will be declared constitutional.

      The President feels that lynching is a question of education in the states, rallying good citizens, and creating public opinion so that the localities themselves will wipe it out. However, if it were done by a Northerner, it will have an antagonistic effect. I will talk to him again about the Van Nuys resolution and will try to talk also to Senator Byrnes and get his point of view. I am deeply troubled about the whole situation as it seems to be a terrible thing to stand by and let it continue and feel that one cannot speak out as to his feeling. I think your next step would be to talk to the more prominent members of the Senate.

      Very sincerely yours,

Source: Letter, Eleanor Roosevelt to Walter White, detailing the First Lady's lobbying efforts for federal action against lynchings, March 19, 1936. (National Association for the Advancement of Colored People Records.) From the American Memory Project of the Library of Congress (www.memory.loc.gov).

26

American Money, American Guns, and Russian Blood

For the second time in roughly a generation, the leadership of the United States, after first attempting to avoid entanglement in world affairs, became full-fledged belligerents in a vast global conflict. The immediate circumstances of American involvement were different for World War II than for World War I. For many, World War II seemed nothing less than a Manichean struggle that would determine the fate of civilization itself. To make America's participation and sacrifices logical and palatable to the American people, President Roosevelt sought to outline our purpose in the Atlantic Charter. But despite the nobility of the cause, again, and in far more substantial ways, the perceived needs of national security and the rights to life, liberty, and pursuit of happiness of those who might assault that security came into conflict. In February 1942, President Roosevelt issued Executive Order 9006, which set in motion the imprisonment of over 100,000 Japanese residents and Japanese American citizens without due process of law or any criminal activity on their part. Their sole crime was their ethnic heritage. Perhaps the lingering echo of the fearful cries of Japanese American children as they were hustled off to places and a future unknown will put E. B. White's moving essay into a different context.

The Second World War was a patently racist war. The leadership in many countries held ideologies that hinged on concepts of racial superiority. Propaganda emanating from those charged with motivating their nations to fight was frequently filled with racist stereotypes and derogatory imagery. Simultaneously, African Americans again answered the call to serve their nation and to suffer and die to attain freedoms in other parts of the world that were not granted them in their own hometowns. William Manchester experienced the war on the ground and in the thick of more than one battle. The memories he lived with the rest of his life were not pleasant ones, and he admits to spending significant effort trying to suppress them. But like ghosts they would come back to him and he would have to reassess concepts of heroism and gallantry.

Individuals and governments have been wrestling with their degree of respon-sibility for victory and defeat—and the only actual deployment of nuclear weapons yet in the history of humanity. The two poems from Toge Sankichi suggest that nations and individuals flirt with disaster if they attempt to "play God."

DOCUMENT 26.1

The Atlantic Charter

The President of the United States of America and the Prime Minister, Mr. Churchill, representing His Majesty's Government in the United Kingdom, being met together, deem it right to make known certain common principles in the national policies of their respective countries on which they base their hopes for a better future for the world.

First,

their countries seek no aggrandizement, territorial or other;

Second,

they desire to see no territorial changes that do not accord with the freely expressed wishes of the peoples concerned;

Third,

they respect the right of all peoples to choose the form of government under which they will live; and they wish to see sovereign rights and self-government restored to those who have been forcibly deprived of them;

Fourth,

they will endeavor, with due respect for their existing obligations, to further the enjoyment by all States, great or small, victor or vanquished, of access, on equal terms, to the trade and to the raw materials of the world which are needed for their economic prosperity;

Fifth,

they desire to bring about the fullest collaboration between all nations in the economic field with the object of securing, for all, improved labor standards, economic adjustment and social security;

Sixth,

after the final destruction of the Nazi tyranny, they hope to see established a peace which will afford to all nations the means of dwelling in safety within their own boundaries, and which will afford assurance that all the men in all the lands may live out their lives in freedom from fear and want;

Source: Franklin D. Roosevelt, *Public Papers and Addresses of Franklin D. Roosevelt,* compiled by Samuel Rosenman, 13 vols. (New York: Russell & Russell, 1969), 10:314.

Seventh,

such a peace should enable all men to traverse the high seas and oceans without hindrance;

Eighth,

they believe that all of the nations of the world, for realistic as well as spiritual reasons, must come to the abandonment of the use of force. Since no future peace can be maintained if land, sea or air armaments continue to be employed by nations which threaten, or may threaten, aggression outside of their frontiers, they believe, pending the establishment of a wider and permanent system of general security, that the disarmament of such nations is essential. They will likewise aid and encourage all other practicable measures which will lighten for peace-loving peoples the crushing burden of armaments.

Franklin D. Roosevelt
Winston S. Churchill

DOCUMENT 26.2

Executive Order No. 9066

[Internment]

The President

Executive Order Authorizing the Secretary of War to Prescribe Military Areas

Whereas the successful prosecution of the war requires every possible protection against espionage and against sabotage to national-defense material, national-defense premises, and national-defense utilities as defined in Section 4, Act of April 20, 1918, 40 Stat. 533, as amended by the Act of November 30, 1940, 54 Stat. 1220, and the Act of August 21, 1941, 55 Stat. 655 (U.S.C., Title 50, Sec. 104);

Now, Therefore, by virtue of the authority vested in me as President of the United States, and Commander in Chief of the Army and Navy, I hereby authorize and direct the Secretary of War, and the Military Commanders whom he may from time to time designate, whenever he or any designated Commander deems such action necessary or desirable, to prescribe military areas in such places and of such extent as he or the appropriate Military Commander may determine, from which any or all persons may be excluded, and with respect to which, the right of any person to enter, remain in, or leave shall be subject to whatever restrictions the Secretary of War or the appropriate Military Commander may impose in his discretion. The Secretary of War is hereby authorized to provide for residents of any such area who are excluded therefrom, such transportation, food, shelter, and other accommodations as may be necessary, in the judgment of the Secretary of War or the said Military Commander,

Source: February 19, 1942, 1 [No. 9066] [F. R. Doc. 421563; Filed, February 21, 1942; 12:51 p.m.] Federal Register, Vol. 7, No. 38, p. 1407 (Feb. 25, 1942).

and until other arrangements are made, to accomplish the purpose of this order. The designation of military areas in any region or locality shall supersede designations of prohibited and restricted areas by the Attorney General under the Proclamations of December 7 and 8, 1941, and shall supersede the responsibility and authority of the Attorney General under the said Proclamations in respect of such prohibited and restricted areas.

I hereby further authorize and direct the Secretary of War and the said Military Commanders to take such other steps as he or the appropriate Military Commander may deem advisable to enforce compliance with the restrictions applicable to each Military area hereinabove authorized to be designated, including the use of Federal troops and other Federal Agencies, with authority to accept assistance of state and local agencies.

I hereby further authorize and direct all Executive Departments, independent establishments and other Federal Agencies, to assist the Secretary of War or the said Military Commanders in carrying out this Executive Order, including the furnishing of medical aid, hospitalization, food, clothing, transportation, use of land, shelter, and other supplies, equipment, utilities, facilities, and services.

This order shall not be construed as modifying or limiting in any way the authority heretofore granted under Executive Order No. 8972, dated December 12, 1941, nor shall it be construed as limiting or modifying the duty and responsibility of the Federal Bureau of Investigation, with respect to the investigation of alleged acts of sabotage or the duty and responsibility of the Attorney General and the Department of Justice under the Proclamations of December 7 and 8, 1941, prescribing regulations for the conduct and control of alien enemies, except as such duty and responsibility is superseded by the designation of military areas hereunder.

Franklin D. Roosevelt
The White House,
February 19, 1942

DOCUMENT 26.3

Democracy

E. B. White

July 3, 1943

We received a letter from the Writer's War Board the other day asking for a statement on "The Meaning of Democracy." It presumably is our duty to comply with such a request, and it is certainly our pleasure. Surely the Board knows what democracy is. It is the line that forms on the right. It is the don't in don't

Source: E. B. White, "Democracy," in Mary Lou Colin, ed., *Patterns Plus: A Short Prose Reader with Argumentation*, 2nd ed. (Boston: Houghton Mifflin, 1987), p. 103.

shove. It is the hole in the stuffed shirt through which the sawdust slowly trickles; it is the dent in the high hat.

Democracy is the recurrent suspicion that more than half of the people are right more than half of the time. It is the feeling of privacy in the voting booths, the feeling of communion in the libraries, the feeling of vitality everywhere. Democracy is a letter to the editor. Democracy is the score at the beginning of the ninth. It is an idea that hasn't been disproved yet, a song the words of which have not gone bad. It is the mustard on the hot dog and the cream in the rationed coffee. Democracy is a request from a War Board, in the middle of the morning in the middle of a war, wanting to know what democracy is.

DOCUMENT 26.4

A Tuskegee Airman Remembers

World War Two was not a pleasant experience. It's anti everything I stand for. It was a frustrating and revealing time of my life.

I was born and raised in Los Angeles. I'd never been south. I had not too much experience with discrimination. I went to integrated schools. And the first time I reached manhood, things were frustrating. When I left school to sign up for the air force, I found out I could not go into the service with my friends. I was the only black on the basketball team. We had decided among ourselves that we would all go into the air force. The others did. When I went down to sign up, they didn't know what to do with me. Just told me they couldn't send me to the air force. Ten months later I was finally called. That's when they decided what they could do with me. I was sent to Tuskegee, an all-segregated base, deep in the heart of Alabama. . . .

The summer of '42 is when I went through the training phase, graduated. I had various brushes with Alabama bigotry, such as my wife trying to buy a hat. They'd tell her, "If you put it on, you have bought it." You couldn't try on anything. You had to eat in separate quarters, of course. And live in separate places.

Ran into it again when I went overseas. I could understand the white American soldiers' antagonism to black soldiers who dated white girls. Then one day I was assigned temporary duty in North Africa. The white soldiers there were antagonistic to black soldiers dating black girls. This got kinda fuzzy. This I couldn't understand.

During the war, we took short terms of rest and rehabilitation from the rigors of flyin' combat missions. Maybe for a week. The Isle of Capri, the rest camp for the area, was off-limits to black pilots. We had a few confrontations at the local USO. Now this was in the theater of war. Somebody got us a private, completely equipped segregated rest camp in Naples. The 332nd Fighter Group with that combat record. These things all mount up, one on top of another. This

Source: From Studs Terkel, *The Good War: An Oral History of World War Two* (New York: Pantheon Books, 1984), pp. 343–44.

is why World War Two doesn't read popular things in my mind. They were fighting fascism and letting racism run rampant.

DOCUMENT 26.5

Goodbye, Darkness

Blood That Never Dried

William Manchester

I have another drink, and then I learn, for the hundredth time, that you can't drown your troubles, not the real ones, because if they are real they can swim. One of my worst recollections, one I had buried in my deepest memory bank long ago, comes back with a clarity so blinding that I surge forward against the seat belt, appalled by it, filled with remorse and shame. . . .

The situation was as clear as the deduction from a euclidean theorem, but my psychological state was extremely complicated. S. L. A. Marshall once observed that the typical fighting man is often at a disadvantage because he "comes from a civilization in which aggression, connected with the taking of life, is prohibited and unacceptable." This was especially true of me, whose horror of violence had been so deep-seated that I had been unable to trade punches with other boys. But since then life had become cheaper to me. "Two thousand pounds of education drops to a ten rupee," wrote Kipling of the fighting on India's North-West Frontier. My plight was not unlike that described by the famous sign in the Paris zoo: "Warning: this animal is vicious; when attacked, it defends itself." I was responding to a basic biological principle first set down by the German zoologist Heini Hediger in his *Skizzen zu einer Tierpsychologie um und im Zirkus.* Hediger noted that beyond a certain distance, which varies from one species to another, an animal will retreat, while within it, it will attack. He called these "flight distance" and "critical distance." Obviously I was within critical distance of the hut. It was time to bar the bridge, stick a finger in the dike—to do *something.* I could be quick or I could be dead.

My choices were limited. Moving inland was inconvenient; the enemy was there, too. I was on the extreme left of our perimeter, and somehow I couldn't quite see myself turning my back on the shack and fleeing through the rest of the battalion screaming, like Chicken Little, "A Jap's after me! A Jap's after me!" Of course, I could order one of my people to take out the sniper; but I played the role of the NCO in Kipling's poem who always looks after the black sheep, and if I ducked this one, they would never let me forget it. Also, I couldn't be certain that the order would be obeyed. I was a gangling, long-boned youth, wholly lacking in what the Marine Corps called "command presence"—charisma—and I led nineteen highly insubordinate men. I couldn't even be sure that Barney would budge. It is war, not politics, that makes strange bedfellows. The fact that I outranked Barney was in itself odd. He was a great blond buffalo of a youth,

Source: From William Manchester, *Goodbye, Darkness* (New York: Little, Brown & Co., 1979), pp. 3–7.

with stubby hair, a scraggly mustache, and a powerful build. Before the war he had swum breaststroke for Brown, and had left me far behind in two inter-collegiate meets. I valued his respect for me, which cowardice would have wiped out. So I asked him if he had any grenades. He didn't; nobody in the section did. The grenade shortage was chronic. That sterile exchange bought a little time, but every moment lengthened my odds against the Nip sharp-shooter. Finally, sweating with the greatest fear I had known till then, I took a deep breath, told Barney, "Cover me," and took off for the hut at Mach 2 speed in little bounds, zigzagging and dropping every dozen steps, remembering to roll as I dropped. I was nearly there, arrowing in, when I realized that I wasn't wearing my steel helmet. The only cover on my head was my cloth Raider cap. That was a violation of orders. I was out of uniform. I remember hoping, idioti-cally, that nobody would report me.

Utterly terrified, I jolted to a stop on the threshold of the shack. I could feel a twitching in my jaw, coming and going like a winky light signaling some dis-order. Various valves were opening and closing in my stomach. My mouth was dry, my legs quaking, and my eyes out of focus. Then my vision cleared. I unlocked the safety of my Colt, kicked the door with my right foot, and leapt inside. My horror returned. I was in an empty room. There was another door opposite the one I had unhinged, which meant another room, which meant the sniper was in there—and had been warned by the crash of the outer door. But I had committed myself. Flight was impossible now. So I smashed into the other room and saw him as a blur to my right. I wheeled that way, crouched, gripped the pistol butt in both hands, and fired.

Not only was he the first Japanese soldier I had ever shot at; he was the only one I had seen at close quarters. He was a robin-fat, moon-faced, roly-poly little man with his thick, stubby, trunklike legs sheathed in faded khaki puttees and the rest of him squeezed into a uniform that was much too tight. Unlike me, he was wearing a tin hat, dressed to kill. But I was quite safe from him. His Arisaka rifle was strapped on in a sniper's harness, and though he had heard me, and was trying to turn toward me, the harness sling had him trapped. He couldn't disentangle himself from it. His eyes were rolling in panic. Realizing that he couldn't extricate his arms and defend himself, he was backing toward a corner with a curious, crablike motion.

My first shot had missed him, embedding itself in the straw wall, but the second caught him dead-on in the femoral artery. His left thigh blossomed, swiftly turning to mush. A wave of blood gushed from the wound; then another boiled out, sheeting across his legs, pooling on the earthen floor. Mutely he looked down at it. He dipped a hand in it and listlessly smeared his cheek red. His shoulders gave a little spasmodic jerk, as though someone had whacked him on the back; then he emitted a tremendous, raspy fart, slumped down, and died. I kept firing, wasting government property.

Already I thought I detected the dark brown effluvium of the freshly slain, a sour, pervasive emanation which is different from anything else you have known. Yet seeing death at that range, like smelling it, requires no previous ex-perience. You instantly recognize the spastic convulsion and the rattle, which in his case was not loud, but deprecating and conciliatory, like the manners of civilian Japanese. He continued to sink until he reached the earthen floor. His eyes glazed over. Almost immediately a fly landed on his left eyeball. It was joined by another. I don't know how long I stood there staring. I knew from previous combat what lay ahead for the corpse. It would swell, then bloat, bursting out of the uniform. Then the face would turn from yellow to red, to purple, to green, to black. My father's account of the Argonne had omitted certain vital facts. A feeling of disgust and self-hatred clotted darkly in my throat, gagging me.

Jerking my head to shake off the stupor, I slipped a new, fully loaded magazine into the butt of my .45. Then I began to tremble, and next to shake, all over. I sobbed, in a voice still grainy with fear: "I'm sorry." Then I threw up all over myself. I recognized the half-digested C-ration beans dribbling down my front, smelled the vomit above the cordite. At the same time I noticed another odor; I had urinated in my skivvies. I pondered fleetingly why our excretions become so loathsome the instant they leave the body. Then Barney burst in on me, his carbine at the ready, his face gray, as though he, not I, had just become a partner in the firm of death. He ran over to the Nip's body, grabbed its stacking swivel—its neck—and let go, satisfied that it was a cadaver. I marveled at his courage; I couldn't have taken a step toward that corner. He approached me and then backed away, in revulsion, from my foul stench. He said: "Slim, you stink." I said nothing. I knew I had become a thing of tears and twitchings and dirtied pants. I remember wondering dumbly: *Is this what they mean by "conspicuous gallantry"?*

DOCUMENT 26.6

Poems about Hiroshima

August 6
Tōge Sankichi

> That brilliant flash—who can forget it?
> In a split second, 30,000 in the streets vanished;
> the screams of 50,000 pinned under in pitch black
> died away.
>
> The churning yellow smoke thinned to reveal Hiroshima:
> buildings split, bridges fallen,
> packed streetcars burned,
> an endless heap of rubble and embers.
> Soon a procession of the naked, crying, walking in bunches,
> trampling on brain matter:

Source: Tōge Sankichi, "August 6" and "Flames," in Richard H. Minear, ed. and trans., *Hiroshima: Three Witnesses* (Princeton, NJ: Princeton University Press, 1990), pp. 306-7, 311-12.

charred clothes about waists,
skin hanging like rags
from arms raised to breasts.

Corpses at the Parade Ground, scattered about like stone statues;
at the river's edge, too, fallen in a heap, a group that had crawled
      toward a tethered raft,
turning gradually, under the burning rays of the sun, into corpses;
in the glare of the flames piercing the night sky,
the area where Mother and Brother were pinned under alive—
it too went up in flames.

In the feces and urine on the floor of the arsenal
a group of schoolgirls who had fled lay fallen;
bellies swollen like drums, blinded in one eye,
      skin half-gone, hairless, impossible to tell
      one from the other—
by the time the rays of the morning sun picked them out,
they had all stopped moving;
amid the stagnant stench, the only sound:
flies buzzing about metal washbasins.

The stillness that reigned over the city of 300,000:
who can forget it?
In that hush
the white eyes of dead women and children
sent us
a soul-rending appeal:
who can forget it?

Flames
Tōge Sankichi

Pushing up through smoke
from a world half-darkened
by overhanging cloud—
the shroud that mushroomed out
and struck the dome of the sky,
the angry flames—
black, red, blue—
dance into the air,
merge,
scatter glittering sparks,
already tower
over the whole city.

Quivering like seaweed,
the mass of flames spurts forward.
Cattle bound for the slaughterhouse
avalanche down the riverbank;
wings drawn in, a single ash-colored pigeon

lies on its side atop the bridge.
Popping up in the dense smoke,
crawling out
wreathed in fire:
countless human beings
on all fours.
In a heap of embers that erupt and subside,
hair rent,
rigid in death,
there smolders a curse.

After that concentrated moment
of the explosion,
pure incandescent hatred
spreads out, boundless.
Blank silence
piles up into the air.

The hot rays of uranium
that shouldered the sun aside
burn onto a girl's back
the flowered pattern of thin silk,
set instantaneously ablaze
the black garb of the priest—
August 6, 1945:
that midday midnight
man burned the gods
at the stake.
Hiroshima's
night of fire
casts its glow over sleeping humanity;
before long
history will set an ambush
for all who would play God.

27

Organizational Men and Governments

With the war over, the United States once again faced the challenges of reconversion to civilian life; for the rest of the world the challenge was the reconstruction of their nations and societies. Perhaps one of the most significant pieces of legislation ever passed by the United States Congress was the Serviceman's Readjustment Act of 1944. It showered upon America's veterans the gratitude of a nation. The GI benefits incorporated in that act would become a lynchpin to a contemporary "post industrial" economy and society. Chief among those rights and benefits were the educational benefits that made an advanced education—including a college degree—possible for hundreds of thousands of people who had never before thought they could or even should dream of getting a college degree.

But it was not just American warriors who won the war. Indeed, an argument can be made that it was the weight of America's industrial capacity and material that overwhelmed the Axis powers. American industries produced munitions and matériel at a mind-boggling pace and rate. In order to unleash a heretofore unimagined productivity, American businesses were allowed to profit from the war—in some estimations they were generously compensated for their efforts. The wealth and prosperity resulting from acquiring a government contract seemed to confuse some Americans—especially some American warriors disturbed by the thought that they fought and many had died so that others might get rich.

Others were not even close to dealing with the problems of wealth—they just wanted to get their foot in the door to a decent life. If President Roosevelt fumbled constitutional issues with Executive Order 9066, he drove an early stake into the heart of racism in America with Executive Order 8802, which established the Committee on Fair Employment Practices, a place to which African Americans could turn if they experienced discrimination or racism in defense work during the war. Roosevelt was pushed in this direction by A. Philip Randolph and other leaders of the African American community who *wanted to secure some tangible and immediate benefits from volunteering their blood and sweat fighting racism and fascism. Though the behavior of the federal government was inconsistent after the war, various states saw the value and the logic of beginning to secure equal rights and opportunities for their citizens regardless of their race, color, or creed. There were those, however, who were disturbed by the signs of acceptance of a new perspective on race and the role of government in securing individual liberties and who sought to turn back the clock to a time when their particular definition of "American" ways and values was in vogue.*

If there was concern after the war about African Americans breaking out of the constraints that had limited and channeled their lives, there were others worried about the role and position of women in society. The Second World War had been another wrecking ball hammering away at traditionalist assumptions about what women could and should do. Even more than during the First World War, the national government maintained a steady stream of propaganda about the positive contributions women were making to the war effort—particularly in that industrial complex where victory was being forged. Under the guise of seeking solutions to the problems women and society were facing after the war, many people suggested that women, for their own well-being, ought to resign from the competitive world of work and career and return to their "natural" place in the home.

As veterans, African Americans, women, and society in general tried to sort out America's new position of primacy in world affairs, President Truman received notification of the commencement of hostilities in Korea. It did not take long for the troubled and unclear international situation, combined with the uncertainties of new social behaviors domestically, to create an anxiety that sought explanations, excuses, and perhaps even scapegoats for how the United States seemingly won World War II but lost the peace.

DOCUMENT 27.1

The Servicemen's Readjustment Act of 1944

The G.I. Bill

Section 100

The Veterans' Administration is hereby declared to be an essential war agency and entitled, second only to the War and Navy Departments, to priorities in personnel, equipment, supplies, and material under any laws, Executive orders, and regulations pertaining to priorities, and in appointments of personnel from civil-service registers the Administrator of Veterans' Affairs is hereby granted the same authority and discretion as the War and Navy Departments and the

Source: Excerpted from the *Servicemen's Readjustment Act of 1944* [G.I. Bill of Rights], *U.S. Statutes at Large* 58, approved June 22, 1944.

United States Public Health Service: *Provided,* That the provisions of this section as to priorities for materials shall apply to any State institution to be built for the care or hospitalization of veterans.

*   *   *

"1. Any person who served in the active military or naval service on or after September 16, 1940, and prior to the termination of the present war, and who shall have been discharged or released therefrom under conditions other than dishonorable, and whose education or training was impeded, delayed, interrupted, or interfered with by reason of his entrance into the service, or who desires a refresher or retraining course, and who either shall have served ninety days or more, exclusive of any period he was assigned for a course of education or training under the Army specialized training program or the Navy college training program, which course was a continuation of his civilian course and was pursued to completion, or as a cadet or midshipman at one of the service academies, or shall have been discharged or released from active service by reason of an actual service-incurred injury or disability, shall be eligible for and entitled to receive education or training under this part: *Provided,* That such course shall be initiated not later than two years after either the date of his discharge or the termination of the present war, whichever is the later: *Provided further,* That no such education or training shall be afforded beyond seven years after the termination of the present war: *And provided further,* That any such person who was not over 25 years of age at the time he entered the service shall be deemed to have had his education or training impeded, delayed, interrupted, or interfered with.

"2. Any such eligible person shall be entitled to education or training, or a refresher or retraining course, at an approved educational or training institution, for a period of one year (or the equivalent thereof in continuous part-time study), or for such lesser time as may be required for the course of instruction chosen by him. Upon satisfactory completion of such course of education or training, according to the regularly prescribed standards and practices of the institutions, except a refresher or retraining course, such person shall be entitled to an additional period or periods of education or training, not to exceed the time such person was in the active service on or after September 16, 1940, and before the termination of the war, exclusive of any period he was assigned for a course of education or training under the Army specialized training program or the Navy college training program, which course was a continuation of his civilian course and was pursued to completion, or as a cadet or midshipman at one of the service academies, but in no event shall the total period of education or training exceed four years: *Provided,* That his work continues to be satisfactory throughout the period, according to the regularly prescribed standards and practices of the institution: *Provided, however,* That wherever the additional period of instruction ends during a quarter or semester and after a major part of such quarter or semester has expired, such period of instruction shall be extended to the termination of such unexpired quarter or semester.

DOCUMENT 27.2

All My Sons

Arthur Miller

From Act Three

ANN: Larry is dead, Kate,

MOTHER [*she stops*]: Don't speak to me.

ANN: I said he's dead. I know! He crashed off the coast of China November twenty-fifth! His engine didn't fail him. But he died. I know . . .

MOTHER: How did he die? You're lying to me. If you know, how did he die?

ANN: I loved him. You know I loved him. Would I have looked at anyone else if I wasn't sure? That's enough for you.

MOTHER [*moving on her*]: What's enough for me? What're you talking about? [*She grasps* ANN'S *wrists.*]

ANN: You're hurting my wrists.

MOTHER: What are you talking about! [*Pause. She stares at* ANN *a moment, then turns and goes to* KELLER.]

ANN: Joe, go in the house . . .

KELLER: Why should I . . .

ANN: Please go.

KELLER: Lemme know when he comes. [KELLER *goes into house.*]

MOTHER [*she sees Ann take a letter from her pocket*]: What's that?

ANN: Sit down . . . [MOTHER *moves L. to chair, but does not sit.*] First you've got to understand. When I came, I didn't have any idea that Joe . . . I had nothing against him or you. I came to get married. I hoped . . . So I didn't bring this to hurt you. I thought I'd show it to you only if there was no other way to settle Larry in your mind.

MOTHER: Larry? {*Snatches letter from* Ann's *hand.*]

ANN: He wrote it to me just before he—[MOTHER *opens and begins to read letter.*] I'm not trying to hurt you, Kate. You're making me do this, now remember you're—Remember. I've been so lonely, Kate . . . I can't leave here alone again. [*A long, low moan comes from* MOTHER'S *throat as she reads.*] You made me show it to you. You wouldn't believe me. I told you a hundred times, why wouldn't you believe me!

MOTHER: Oh, my God . . .

ANN: [*with pity and fear*]: Kate, please, please . . .

MOTHER: My God, my God . . .

ANN: Kate, dear, I'm so sorry . . . I'm so sorry. [CHRIS *enters from driveway. He seems exhausted.*]

CHRIS: What's the matter . . . ?

ANN: Where were you? . . . you're all perspired. [MOTHER *doesn't move.*] Where were you?

CHRIS: Just drove around a little. I thought you'd be gone.

Source: From Arthur Miller, *All My Sons* (New York: Penguin, 2000).

ANN: Where do I go? I have nowhere to go.

CHRIS [*to* MOTHER]: Where's Dad?

ANN: Inside lying down.

CHRIS: Sit down, both of you. I'll say what there is to say.

MOTHER: I didn't hear the car . . .

CHRIS: I left it in the garage.

MOTHER: Jim is out looking for you.

CHRIS: Mother . . . I'm going away. There are a couple of firms in Cleveland, I think I can get a place. I mean, I'm going away for good. [*To* ANN *alone*] I know what you're thinking, Annie. It's true. I'm yellow. I was made yellow in this house because I suspected my father and I did nothing about it, but if I knew that night when I came home what I know now, he'd be in the district attorney's office by this time, and I'd have brought him there. Now if I look at him, all I'm able to do is cry.

MOTHER: What are you talking about? What else can you do?

CHRIS: I could jail him! I could jail him, if I were human any more. But I'm like everybody else now. I'm practical now. You made me practical.

MOTHER: But you have to be.

CHRIS: The cats in that alley are practical, the bums who ran away when we were fighting were practical. Only the dead ones weren't practical. But now I'm practical, and I spit on myself. I'm going away. I'm going now.

ANN [*goes up to stop him*]: I'm coming with you. . . .

CHRIS: No, Ann

ANN: Chris, I don't ask you to do anything about Joe.

CHRIS: You do, you do . . .

ANN: I swear I never will.

CHRIS: In your heart you always will.

ANN: Then do what you have to do!

CHRIS: Do what? What is there to do? I've looked all night for a reason to make him suffer.

ANN: There's reason, there's reason!

CHRIS: What? Do I raise the dead when I put him behind bars? Then what'll I do it for? We used to shoot a man who acted like a dog, but honor was real there, you were protecting something. But here? This is the land of the great big dogs, you don't love a man here, you eat him! That's the principle; the only one we live by—it just happened to kill a few people this time, that's all. The world's that way, how can I take it out on him? What sense does that make? This is a zoo, a zoo!

ANN [*to* MOTHER]: You know what he's got to do! Tell him!

MOTHER: Let him go.

ANN: I won't let him go. You'll tell him what he's got to do . . .

MOTHER: Annie!

ANN: Then I will! [KELLER *enters from house.* CHRIS *sees him, goes down* R. *near arbor.*]

KELLER: What's the matter with you? I want to talk to you.

CHRIS: I've got nothing to say to you.

KELLER [*taking his arm*]: I want to talk to you!

CHRIS [*pulling violently away from him*]: Don't do that, Dad. I'm going to hurt you if you do that. There's nothing to say, so say it quick.

KELLER: Exactly what's the matter? What's the matter? You got too much money? Is that what bothers you?

CHRIS [*with an edge of sarcasm*]: It bothers me.

KELLER: If you can't get used to it, then throw it away. You hear me? Take every cent and give it to charity, throw it in the sewer. Does that settle it? In the sewer, that's all. You think I'm kidding? I'm tellin' you what to do, if it's dirty then burn it. It's your money, that's not my money. I'm a dead man, I'm an old dead man, nothing's mine. Well, talk to me!—what do you want to do!

CHRIS: It's not what I want to do. It's what you want to do.

KELLER: What should I want to do? [*CHRIS is silent.*] Jail? You want me to go to jail? If you want me to go, say so! Is that where I belong?—then tell me so! [*Slight pause*] What's the matter, why can't you tell me? [*Furiously*] You say everything else to me, say that! [*Slight pause*] I'll tell you why you can't say it. Because you know I don't belong there. Because you know! [*With growing emphasis and passion, and a persistent tone of desperation*] Who worked for nothin' in that war? When they work for nothin', I'll work for nothin'. Did they ship a gun or a truck outa Detroit before they got their price? Is that clean? It's dollars and cents, nickels and dimes; war and peace, it's nickels and dimes, what's clean? Half the Goddam country is gotta go if I go! That's why you can't tell me.

CHRIS: That's exactly why.

KELLER: Then . . . why am *I* bad?

CHRIS: *I* know you're no worse than most men but I thought you were better. I never saw you as a man. I saw you as my father. [*Almost breaking*] I can't look at you this way, I can't look at myself! [*He turns away unable to face* KELLER. ANN *goes quickly to* MOTHER, *takes letter from her and starts for* CHRIS. MOTHER *instantly rushes to intercept her.*]

MOTHER: Give me that!

ANN: He's going to read it! [*She thrusts letter into* CHRIS'S *hand.*] Larry. He wrote it to me the day he died. . . .

KELLER: Larry!?

MOTHER: Chris, it's not for you. [*He starts to read.*] Joe . . . go away . . .

KELLER [*mystified, frightened*]: Why'd she say, Larry, what . . . ?

MOTHER [*she desperately pushes him toward alley, glancing at* CHRIS]: Go to the street, Joe, go to the street! [*She comes down beside* KELLER.] Don't Chris . . . [*Pleading from her whole soul*] Don't tell him . . .

CHRIS [*quietly*]: Three and one half years . . . talking, talking. Now you tell me what you must do. . . . This is how he died, now tell me where you belong.

KELLER [*pleading*]: Chris, a man can't be a Jesus in this world!

CHRIS: I know all about the world. I know the whole crap story. Now listen to this, and tell me what a man's got to be! [*Reads*] "My dear Ann: . . . " You listening? He wrote this the day he died. Listen, don't cry . . . listen! "My dear Ann: It is impossible to put down the things I feel. But I've got to tell you something. Yesterday they flew in a load of papers from the States and I read about Dad and your father being convicted. I can't express myself. I can't tell you how

I feel—I can't bear to live any more. Last night I circled the base for twenty minutes before I could bring myself in. How could he have done that? Every day three or four men never come back and he sits back there doing business. . . . I don't know how to tell you what I feel . . . I can't face anybody . . . I'm going out on a mission in a few minutes. They'll probably report me missing. If they do, I want you to know that you mustn't wait for me. I tell you, Ann, if I had him here now I could kill him—" [KELLER *grabs letter from* CHRIS'S *hand and reads it.*] [*After a long pause*] Now blame the world. Do you understand that letter?

KELLER [*he speaks almost inaudibly*]: I think I do. Get the car, I'll put on my jacket. [*He turns and starts slowly for the house.* MOTHER *rushes to intercept him.*]

MOTHER: Why are you going? You'll sleep, why are you going?

KELLER: I can't sleep here. I'll feel better if I go.

MOTHER: You're so foolish. Larry was your son too, wasn't he? You know he'd never tell you to do this.

KELLER [*looking at letter in his hand*]: Then what is this if it isn't telling me? Sure, he was my son. But I think to him they were all my sons. And I guess they were, I guess they were. I'll be right down. [*Exits into house.*]

MOTHER [*to* CHRIS, *with determination*]: You're not going to take him!

CHRIS: I'm taking him.

MOTHER: It's up to you, if you tell him to stay he'll stay. Go and tell him!

CHRIS: Nobody could stop him now.

MOTHER: You'll stop him! How long will he live in prison?—are you trying to kill him?

CHRIS [*holding out letter*]: I thought you read this!

MOTHER [*of Larry, the letter*]: The war is over! Didn't you hear?—it's over!

CHRIS: Then what was Larry to you? A stone that fell into the water? It's not enough for him to be sorry. Larry didn't kill himself to make you and Dad sorry.

MOTHER: What more can we be!

CHRIS: You can be better! Once and for all you can know there's a universe of people outside and you're responsible to it, and unless you know that you threw away your son because that's why he died.

DOCUMENT 27.3

New York State Anti-Discrimination Act

March 12, 1945

§ 125

Purposes of article. This article shall be known as the "Law Against Discrimination." It shall be deemed an exercise of the police power of the state for the

Source: Henry Steel Commager, ed., *Documents of American History,* vol. 2, *Since 1898,* 9th ed. (New York: Appleton-Century-Crofts, 1973).

protection of the public welfare, health and peace of the people of this state, and in fulfillment of the provisions of the constitution of this state concerning civil rights; and the legislature hereby finds and declares that practices of discrimination against any of its inhabitants because of race, creed, color or national origin are a matter of state concern, that such discrimination threatens not only the rights and proper privileges of its inhabitants but menaces the institutions and foundation of a free democratic state. A state agency is hereby created with power to eliminate and prevent discrimination in employment because of race, creed, color or national origin, either by employers, labor organizations, employment agencies or other persons, and to take other actions against discrimination because of race, creed, color or national origin, as herein provided; and the commission established hereunder is hereby given general jurisdiction and power for such purposes.

§ 126

Opportunity for employment without discrimination a civil right. The opportunity to obtain employment without discrimination because of race, creed, color or national origin is hereby recognized as and declared to be a civil right.

*   *   *

§ 131

Unlawful employment practices. It shall be an unlawful employment practice:
1. For an employer, because of the race, creed, color or national origin of any individual, to refuse to hire or employ or to bar or to discharge from employment such individual or to discriminate against such individual in compensation or in terms, conditions or privileges of employment.
2. For a labor organization, because of the race, creed, color or national origin of any individual, to exclude or to expel from its membership such individual or to discriminate in any way against any of its members or against any employer or any individual employed by an employer.
3. For any employer or employment agency to print or circulate or cause to be printed or circulated any statement, advertisement or publication, or to use any form of application for employment or to make any inquiry in connection with prospective employment, which expresses, directly or indirectly, any limitation, specification or discrimination as to race, creed, color or national origin, or any intent to make any such limitation, specification or discrimination, unless based upon a bona fide occupational qualification.
4. For any employer, labor organization or employment agency to discharge, expel or otherwise discriminate against any person because he has opposed any practices forbidden under this article or because he has filed a complaint, testified or assisted in any proceeding under this article.
5. For any person, whether an employer or an employee or not, to aid, abet, incite, compel or coerce the doing of any of the acts forbidden under this article, or to attempt to do so.

DOCUMENT 27.4

Alien Minorities and Mongrelization

Marilyn R. Allen

We have swung to such a dangerous extreme today in our national life that one who stands up for genuine Constitutional Christian Americanism (as founded by our Country's Fathers) is PERSECUTED by ALIEN MINORITY GROUPS and pro-Russian radicals: many of these adept persecutors being foreign-born enemy nationals. If we did not have at least a FEW staunch AMERICAN Americans, who value our ideals, institutions, and freedom, above their own personal security, above financial considerations and political preferment, then even NOW our country would have been delivered up to the enemies within our gates. As it is, instead of the Administration subsidizing and supporting these PATRIOTS (rather than squandering BILLIONS abroad to "stop Communism"), every effort is made to SILENCE them, persecute them, imprison them—while pusillanimous Harry Truman cries "Red Herring." Some of our "Liberal" scientists have complained of "unsubstantiated evidence" against those summoned to appear before the Committee on UN-American Activities. Well, how CAN this most excellent Committee SUBSTANTIATE its claims against SUSPICIOUS characters (against whom the FBI has collected evidence) when the Truman Administration absolutely REFUSES to give to this Congressional Investigating Committee either cooperation or necessary evidence, which it has in its possession? Let's put the BLAME on Mr. Truman—where it belongs—rather than on this truly *American* Committee, which is valiantly *fighting Communism* with all its limited resources. These scientists would not be so jittery, if their skirts were as clean as they pretend they are. Incidentally, Dr. Edward U. Condon was one of those royally entertained by the Russian Embassy when they celebrated the Russian (Bolshevik) revolution recently. NO loyal, honorable, informed *American* finds any cause for *celebration*, in this event.—A recent Gallup poll showed that the American people are OVERWHELMINGLY IN FAVOR OF EXPOSING AND PUNISHING SUBVERSIVE TRAITORS IN THIS COUNTRY, and in our Administration—as this Committee has been endeavoring to do. The House of Representatives recently voted 353 to 29 to give its Committee on UN-American Activities a fund of $200,000 to carry on its work in 1949. . . .

Let "Harried Harry" Truman and Mongrelizer Henry A. Wallace (two peas in the same pod) represent organized minorities of Negroes, Jews, Communists, hybrids and malcontents: SOMEBODY (such as the Southern Dixiecrats) should represent the UN-organized MAJORITY WHITE CHRISTIAN AMERICANS. It is time to call a halt on this "Minority Rule." It is always the militant MINORITIES in Russia, Europe, Asia, that destroy, divide, conquer, and dictate. *By this Minority rule, every country inexorably disappears into the quicksands of*

Source: Excerpted from Marilyn R. Allen, *Alien Minorities and Mongrelization* (Boston: Meador Publishing, 1949), pp. 28–44.

COMMUNISM. Will America LEARN anything by having observed this experience of other nations?

It is the purpose of Federal Buckley Bill 2848 (formerly Patterson HR 6897): of all State or Federal Fair Employment Practice (FEPC) laws: of the "Civil Rights" program, to SILENCE CRITICISM of Minorities, to give THEM more than EQUAL rights, and to set up a Federal and State-wide bureaucratic snooping gestapo (just as exists in the police state of Russia) to SPY UPON THE PEOPLE, and to ENFORCE these discriminatory proposed laws AGAINST the *majority* WHITE CHRISTIAN AMERICANS, *in favor of Alien Minorities.* Under such laws, the FIRST thing the Communists do is to LIQUIDATE White Christians—as is being done today in Czechoslovakia, Hungary, Bulgaria and all the other Iron Curtain countries. Stalin's regime itself has liquidated approximately 30 MILLION WHITE CHRISTIANS in Russia. . . .

The MONGRELIZING (mixing of the races) of America is THE No. 1 plank of the Communist Party. There has been no activity so INIMICAL to White America's interests since Reconstruction Days after the Civil War. It has as its purpose the lowering and degrading of the White Race, and making of our people a hybrid nondescript mixture, who can then the more readily be taken over by Communism (or Marxism). . . .

There is now NO easy, simple, solution of the Mongrelization problem in sight. In view of the White man's slothful, dilatory, cowardly sidestepping of this vital problem ever since Reconstruction Days: and in view of the present aggressive, militant, uncompromising stand of the organized Coloreds (backed and incited by the Jew), there appears to be NO man-made solution on the horizon. It is the writer's opinion that probably Divine Providence will step in and take a hand, since IT will not permit the destruction of the White Race through forbidden MONGRELIZATION. In olden times, whole cities were blotted from the face of the earth because of MISCEGENATION—mixing of the races and "going after strange flesh." The Arm of GOD is not shortened (Stalin, Wallace, or Truman to the contrary notwithstanding): HE STILL RULES HIS UNIVERSE!

DOCUMENT 27.5

Modern Woman: The Lost Sex

Ferdinand Lundberg and Marynia F. Farnham

Women . . . have moved more deeply into a blind alley, dragging all society with them through their tremendous influence on their children. This is as true of women consciously seeking a way out of their difficulties as of those proceeding more unconsciously.

Naturally, we do not say that every woman, without exception, is engulfed in psychic or psychosomatic difficulties. Just how many are leading a life that is,

Source: Excerpted From Ferdinand Lundberg and Marynia Farnham, *Modern Woman: The Lost Sex* (New York: Harper & Brothers, 1947), 201–2, 236–41.

on the whole, satisfactory to themselves and their associates we do not know. We are fairly certain, however, that they do not constitute a clear majority. And we are even more certain that the more modern they are, the fewer they are— that is, the more urban as opposed to rural; the more formally educated as op- posed to informally educated (such as farm women, whose practical knowledge is often vast); the more involved in careers; the more idle; the more childless; the mere fashionably dressed, more elaborately coiffed, heavily perfumed and po- maded, etc.

The further one penetrates behind the brave façade of modernity, the less impressive do surface values become and the more impressive the psychic dis- order. With the less modern woman, however, the sub-surface findings are more apt to point to distinct individuality and balanced character. In such women there is not so pretentious a façade because there is less need of ego de- fense and less libidinal deprivation.

The reason modern women find themselves inwardly stranded along the road of modern "progress" is not that insufficient intelligence has been brought to bear on their problems but that intelligence has been armed with insufficient insight. This insufficiency is reflected in the failure of objectively thinking women—that is, those who believe they think objectively—to develop adequate working concepts. Without the proper intellectual tools, approaches to the prob- lem of woman have not led to tension-easing solutions but, on the contrary, to a heightening of tensions. . . .

As the rivals of men, women must, and insensibly do, develop the charac- teristics of aggression, dominance, independence and power. These are qualities which insure success as co-equals in the world of business, industry and the professions. The distortion of character under pressure of modern attitudes and upbringing is driving women steadily deeper into personal conflict soluble only by psychotherapy. For their need to achieve and accomplish doesn't lessen, in any way, their deeper need to find satisfactions profoundly feminine. Much as they consciously seek those gratifications of love, sensual release and even motherhood, they are becoming progressively less able unconsciously to accept or achieve them. . . .

Many women can find no solution to their dilemma and are defeated in at- tempts at adaptation. These constitute the array of the sick, unhappy, neurotic, wholly or partly incapable of dealing with life. In a veritable army of women, the tensions and anxieties make their way to the surface in physical guise. They have always been known and dimly recognized for what they are—the miser- able, the half-satisfied, the frustrated, the angered. Unable to cope with the dis- appointments that they have met in their emotional lives, they become ill. Their illnesses take varied forms, attack any part of the body and are often disabling. Where formerly the connection was only suspected and assumed between these multifarious physical disorders and disturbing feeling states, we are now com- ing to the point of really understanding their sources in the child-based emo- tional disorders that give rise to them. Whether it be "sick headaches," pains of indeterminate nature in the back and limbs, gastric disorders, constipation, hy- pertension, or the enormous collections of disorders of the reproductive system, it is all one and all arises from an inability to master unconscious feelings constantly aroused by disappointment and frustration.

Such women are constant visitors to doctors or patrons of patent medicines. They are never cured and never comfortable. They suffer as authentically as those whose complaints rest upon physically determined pathology. They are just as sick and most emphatically their illnesses are not "imaginary." They can be helped permanently only by understanding obtained through psychological insight, therefore, through psychiatry. Many of them today are beginning to find their way to such help but many, many more are not. These remain the complaining army who keep their families, friends and physicians constantly at their beck and call by their sufferings.

Other women, more obviously in need of psychiatry for a solution of their troubles, do not show their difficulties in physical symptoms but present them more directly in the form of disturbances recognizably emotional. These are the "nervous," the sleepless, the depressed, the anxious, the driven, the sexually maladjusted, those who complain directly of misery and discontent.

These women are the overtly neurotic. They may have recurrent depressions which are either mild enough to be of only limited and passing concern or so severe as to require hospitalization. Whichever form they take, they are disabling for their duration and a constant threat when not actually present. A very large group of these women describe themselves as "nervous." They are often sleepless, hyper-irritable and extremely demanding of husbands and children, whom they unconsciously seek to punish for their own disabilities. There are many others with more obvious and easily categorized neurotic disorders some of whom complain of intense anxiety which renders them more or less helpless. The anxiety is often related to fear of some impending catastrophe for which they have no immediate evidence. Nevertheless, they constantly feel they are about to suffer from some physical disorder such as cancer or heart disease for which no relief will be found.

The relatively large number of women who complain of immediate sexual and marital difficulties stands out among the neurotic. Their complaints usually revolve about the sexual act and its insufficiency or unsatisfactory nature. Often, however, the general marital relationship is under attack, the woman not being able directly to place her problem as sexual. The husband is criticized for a thousand reasons as inconsiderate, selfish, harsh, or thoughtless, which he may not in fact be. These women range all the way from the frankly and completely frigid to those who complain of neglect and indifference on the part of their husbands and the feelings of loneliness and uselessness that arise from it. Many of them have the prospect of divorce prominently in mind, in hope either of finding satisfaction through removal of the irritating circumstance or, more remotely, of discovering gratification through another marriage.

A certain number of these women of inner masculine tendency are making a reasonable and satisfying adjustment. They have found, through an uneasy balance between work and home, a way of compromise that offers sufficient satisfaction in both spheres to provide happiness and completion. No doubt careful examination might discover defects in this adaptation, but it must be remembered that all adaptations are products of compromise and that where there is real satisfaction there is little reason to be captious. The difficulty lies not in the small group of women who have managed the difficult compromise, but in the much larger group who have not and who suffer from resulting frustrations.

It is not only the masculine woman who has met with an unhappy fate in the present situation. There are still many women who succeed in achieving adult life with largely unimpaired feminine strivings, for which home, a husband's love and children are to them the entirely adequate answers. It is their misfortune that they must enter a society in which such attitudes are little appreciated and are attended by many concrete, external penalties. Such women cannot fail to be affected by finding that their traditional activities are held in low esteem and that the woman who voluntarily undertakes them is often deprecated by her more aggressive contemporaries. She may come to believe that her situation is difficult, entailing serious deprivations, as against the more glamorous and exciting life other women seemingly enjoy. She may be set away from the main stream of life, very much in a backwater and fearful lest she lose her ability and talents through disuse and lack of stimulation. She may become sorry for herself and somewhat angered by her situation, gradually developing feelings of discontent and pressure. As her children grow older and require less of her immediate attention, the feelings of loss increase.

Unless she busies herself extensively with the poorly organized and generally unrewarding voluntary civic or cultural activities, she may find herself with much idle time and much frustration on her hands. Her home alone, unless it is a rural one, cannot occupy her whole time and attention because so much in it is now completely prefabricated and automatic. For amusement she is forced to resort either to the radio "soap opera," or to some other equally unrewarding use of leisure such as game playing, movie-going or aimless shopping. She is deprived of her husband's companionship during the long hours of the day when he is away from home and often the evening finds him preoccupied and disinterested in the affairs that concern her. Consequently she must construct her life out of artificial undertakings with no organic functional connection with the realities of her relationships or her interests. In this way she may easily and quickly develop attitudes of discontent and anger injurious to her life adjustment. She may begin to malfunction sexually, her libidinal depths shaken by her ego frustrations.

So it is that society today makes it difficult for a woman to avoid the path leading to discontent and frustration and resultant hostility and destructiveness. Such destructiveness is, unfortunately, not confined in its effects to the woman alone. It reaches into all her relationships and all her functions. As a wife she is not only often ungratified but ungratifying and has, as we have noted, a profoundly disturbing effect upon her husband. Not only does he find himself without the satisfactions of a home directed and cared for by a woman happy in providing affection and devotion, but he is often confronted by circumstances of even more serious import for his own emotional integrity. His wife may be his covert rival, striving to match him in every aspect of their joint undertaking. Instead of supporting and encouraging his manliness and wishes for domination and power, she may thus impose upon him feelings of insufficiency and weakness. Still worse is the effect upon his sexual satisfactions. Where the woman is unable to admit and accept dependence upon her husband as the source of gratification and must carry her rivalry even into the act of love, she will seriously damage his sexual capacity. To be unable to gratify in the sexual act is for a man an intensely humiliating experience; here it is that mastery and domination, the central capacity of the man's sexual nature, must meet acceptance or fail. So it is that by their own character disturbances these women succeed ultimately in depriving themselves of the devotion and power of their husbands and become the instruments of bringing about their own psychic catastrophe.

DOCUMENT 27.6

Harry S. Truman Remembers the Beginning of the Korean War

On Saturday, June 24, 1950, I was in Independence, Missouri, to spend the weekend with my family and to attend to some personal family business.

It was a little after ten in the evening, and we were sitting in the library of our home on North Delaware Street when the telephone rang. It was the Secretary of State calling from his home in Maryland.

"Mr. President," said Dean Acheson, "I have very serious news. The North Koreans have invaded South Korea."

My first reaction was that I must get back to the capital, and I told Acheson so. He explained, however, that details were not yet available and that he thought I need not rush back until he called me again with further information. In the meantime, he suggested to me that we should ask the United Nations Security Council to hold a meeting at once and declare that an act of aggression had been committed against the Republic of Korea. I told him that I agreed and asked him to request immediately a special meeting of the Security Council, and he said he would call me to report again the following morning, or sooner if there was more information on the events in Korea.

Acheson's next call came through around eleven-thirty Sunday morning, just as we were getting ready to sit down to an early Sunday dinner. Acheson reported that the U.N. Security Council had been called into emergency session. Additional reports had been received from Korea, and there was no doubt that an all-out invasion was under way there. The Security Council, Acheson said, would probably call for a cease-fire, but in view of the complete disregard the North Koreans and their big allies had shown for the U.N. in the past, we had to expect that the U.N. order would be ignored. Some decision would have to

Source: From Harry S. Truman, *Memoirs*, vol. 2, *Years of Trial and Hope* (Garden City, NY: Doubleday, 1956), pp. 331–33.

be made at once as to the degree of aid or encouragement which our government was willing to extend to the Republic of Korea. . . .

The plane left the Kansas City Municipal Airport at two o'clock, and it took just a little over three hours to make the trip to Washington. I had time to think aboard the plane. In my generation, this was not the first occasion when the strong had attacked the weak. I recalled some earlier instances: Manchuria, Ethiopia, Austria. I remembered how each time that the democracies failed to act it had encouraged the aggressors to keep going ahead. Communism was acting in Korea just as Hitler, Mussolini, and the Japanese had acted ten, fifteen, and twenty years earlier. I felt certain that if South Korea was allowed to fall Communist leaders would be emboldened to override nations closer to our own shores. If the Communists were permitted to force their way into the Republic of Korea without opposition from the free world, no small nation would have the courage to resist threats and aggression by stronger Communist neighbors. If this was allowed to go unchallenged it would mean a third world war, just as similar incidents had brought on the second world war. It was also clear to me that the foundations and the principles of the United Nations were at stake unless this unprovoked attack on Korea could be stopped.

DOCUMENT 27.7

Joseph McCarthy's Speech at Wheeling, West Virginia, 1950

Five years after a world war has been won, men's hearts should anticipate a long peace, and men's minds should be free from the heavy weight that comes with war. But this is not such a period—for this is not a period of peace. This is a time of the "cold war." This is a time when all the world is split into two vast, increasingly hostile armed camps—a time of a great armaments race. . . .

Today we are engaged in a final, all-out battle between communistic atheism and Christianity. The modern champions of communism have selected this as the time. And, ladies and gentlemen, the chips are down—they are truly down. . . .

Six years ago, at the time of the first conference to map out the peace—Dumbarton Oaks—there was within the Soviet orbit 180,000,000 people. Lined up on the anti-totalitarian side there were in the world at that time roughly 1,625,000,000 people. Today, only 6 years later, there are 800,000,000 people under the absolute domination of Soviet Russia—an increase of over 400 percent. On our side, the figure has shrunk to around 500,000,000. In other words, in less than 6 years the odds have changed from 9 to 1 in our favor to 8 to 5 against us. This indicates the swiftness of the tempo of Communist victories and American defeats in the cold war. As one of our outstanding historical figures once said,

Source: Excerpted from Joseph McCarthy, speech at Wheeling, West Virginia, 1950, *Congressional Record,* 81st Congress, 2nd session, 1954–57.

"When a great democracy is destroyed, it will not be because of enemies from without, but rather because of enemies from within." . . .

The reason why we find ourselves in a position of impotency is not because our only powerful potential enemy has sent men to invade our shores, but rather because of the traitorous actions of those who have been treated so well by this Nation. It has not been the less fortunate or members of minority groups who have been selling this Nation out, but rather those who have had all the benefits that the wealthiest nation on earth has had to offer—the finest homes, the finest college education, and the finest jobs in Government we can give.

This is glaringly true in the State Department. There the bright young men who are born with silver spoons in their mouths are the ones who have been the worst. . . . In my opinion the State Department, which is one of the most important government departments, is thoroughly infested with Communists.

I have in my hand 57 cases of individuals who would appear to be either card carrying members or certainly loyal to the Communist Party, but who nevertheless are still helping to shape our foreign policy. . . .

I know that you are saying to yourself, "Well, why doesn't the Congress do something about it?" Actually, ladies and gentlemen, one of the important reasons for the graft, the corruption, the dishonesty, the disloyalty, the treason in high Government positions—one of the most important reasons why this continues is a lack of moral uprising on the part of the 140,000,000 American people. In the light of history, however, this is not hard to explain.

It is the result of an emotional hang-over and a temporary moral lapse which follows every war. It is the apathy to evil which people who have been subjected to the tremendous evils of war feel. As the people of the world see mass murder, the destruction of defenseless and innocent people, and all of the crime and lack of morals which go with war, they become numb and apathetic. It has always been thus after war.

However, the morals of our people have not been destroyed. They still exist. This cloak of numbness and apathy has only needed a spark to rekindle them. Happily, this spark has finally been supplied.

As you know, very recently the Secretary of State proclaimed his loyalty to a man guilty of what has always been considered as the most abominable of all crimes—of being a traitor to the people who gave him a position of great trust. The Secretary of State in attempting to justify his continued devotion to the man who sold out the Christian world to the atheistic world, referred to Christ's Sermon on the Mount as a justification and reason therefore, and the reaction of the American people to this would have made the heart of Abraham Lincoln happy.

When this pompous diplomat in striped pants, with a phony British accent, proclaimed to the American people that Christ on the Mount endorsed communism, high treason, and betrayal of a sacred trust, the blasphemy was so great that it awakened the dormant indignation of the American people.

He has lighted the spark which is resulting in a moral uprising and will end only when the whole sorry mess of twisted, warped thinkers are swept from the national scene so that we may have a new birth of national honesty and decency in government.

28

Redeeming Promissory Notes

Winning a different peace was what was on the minds of African Americans from the cessation of World War II up through the 1960s and beyond. Not a few African American veterans returned to the United States and successfully cashed in on some of the opportunities and promises contained in the G.I. Bill of Rights. After such a shockingly racist war, the maintenance of racist systems became more problematic. For those who had served with General Patton and helped liberate survivors of the death camps, the horrendous results of racism were inescapable. Certainly there were those also who had not seen active duty who respected the veterans who had bravely served and suffered. Yet many of these found themselves caught on the horns of a dilemma of loyalties as they faced an African American decorated veteran who sought to register to vote. With each crack in the wall of the exclusive racist system, the wall weakened.

Recognizing that, African Americans began to rise up from their isolation and degradation and demand a fair and equal share of American life, liberty, and happiness. But the burgeoning Civil Rights movement was not a parade, as the testimony of Myrlie Evers suggests. Nor was the desire of people to rights and respect confined to any one group, as the "Declaration of Indian Purpose" attests.

The direct involvement of the federal government in Civil Rights issues in the 1960s brings us around one loop in American history. It was the involvement of the federal government in the 1860s that had given birth to both the freedom and the first round of hopes for equal access to life, liberty, and happiness. It was the departure of the federal government from the Civil Rights field after Reconstruction that had enabled racist systems to arise, Phoenix-like, from the ashes of the Civil War. Through years of neglect and quiet and not-so-quiet acquiescence, the federal government had become a partner to the Jim Crow system and the problems the federal government sought to correct in the 1960s. But in the 1960s the nation, seeing its own image in the press and on television, found itself, if not inspired, at least cajoled into doing better and began to produce such pieces of legislation as the Voting Rights Act of 1965. But in the crusade to right old wrongs and achieve justice, there was no clear roadmap to indicate where the nation was going and when it might know it got there. Muriel Hamilton, an African American graduate of Oberlin College, joined VISTA in 1965 and tried her best to steer Americans and America toward equality. Still, questions remained as to which road or roads might be the best paths toward justice: the exercise of voting rights or equal access to education achieved for children in South Boston by loading them onto buses to achieve racial balance in school districts?

Through all of this, Mamie Mobley attests to a reality that hatred can have permanent consequences. It was ordinary and thoroughly American to want to grow up and have a family of one's own. From that would quite naturally flow grandchildren, perhaps even a good boy who would help an aging grandmother shovel the snow. But such was not to be for Emmett Till's mother. On January 7, 2003, Mamie Mobley died and was set free from such concerns and nearly fifty years of missing her son, Emmett.

DOCUMENT 28.1

Myrlie Evers Remembers

We came to realize, in those last few days, last few months, that our time was short. It was simply in the air. You knew that something was going to happen, and the logical person for it to happen to was Medgar. It certainly brought us closer during that time. As a matter of fact, we didn't talk, we didn't have to. We communicated without words. It was a touch, it was a look, it was holding each other, it was music playing. And I used to try to reassure him and tell him, Nothing's going to happen to you, the FBI is here—laugh—everybody knows you, you're in the press, they wouldn't dare do anything to you.

When he left that morning of June 11, 1963, and went out of the door, he told the children how much he loved them, turned to me, and said, "I'm so tired. I don't know if I can go on, but I have to." And I remember rushing to him and holding him, and he kissed me and said, "I love you," and he walked out of the door. I told him how much I loved him, too, and that it was going to be all right. And we clung to each other and he walked out of the door and he came back in and said, "I love you. I'll call you." During that day, he called two or three times, which was a little unusual with all of the activity that was going on. And each time he said, "I love you. I want you to know how much I love you." And I told him the same thing. And he said, "I'll see you tonight." I said, "Fine." . . .

Source: From Henry Hampton and Steve Fayer, *Voices of Freedom: An Oral History of the Civil Rights Movement from the 1950s through the 1980s* (New York: Bantam Books, 1990), 153–55.

Late that night, he came home. The children were still up, I was asleep across the bed, and we heard the motor of the car coming in and pulling into the driveway. We heard him get out of the car and the car door slam, and in that same instant, we heard the loud gunfire. The children fell to the floor, as he had taught them to do. I made a run for the front door, turned on the light, and there he was. The bullet had pushed him forward, as I understand, and the strong man that he was, he had his keys in his hand and had pulled his body around the rest of the way, to the door. There he lay. And I screamed, and people came out. Our next-door neighbor fired a gun, as he said, to try to frighten anyone away, and I knew then that that was it.

When Medgar was felled by that shot, and I rushed out and saw him lying there, and people from the neighborhood began to gather, there were also some whose color happened to be white. I don't think I have ever hated as much in my life as I did at that particular moment anyone who had white skin. I screamed at the neighbors, and when the police finally got there, I told them that they had killed Medgar. And I can recall wanting so much to have a machine gun or something in my hands, and to stand there and mow them all down. I can't explain the depth of my hatred at that point. And it's interesting how Medgar's influence has directed me in terms of dealing with that hate, then and over the years. He told me, as well as his children, that hate was not a healthy thing.

DOCUMENT 28.2

Declaration of Indian Purpose

We, the Indian People, must be governed by principles in a democratic manner with a right to choose our way of life. Since our Indian culture is threatened by presumption of being absorbed by the American society, we believe we have the responsibility of preserving our precious heritage. . . .

WE BELIEVE in the inherent right of all people to retain spiritual and cultural values, and that the free exercise of these values is necessary to the normal development of any people. . . .

WE BELIEVE that the history and development of America show that the Indian has been subjected to duress, undue influence, unwarranted pressures, and policies which have produced uncertainty, frustration, and despair. . . .

What we ask of America is not charity, not paternalism, even when benevolent. We ask only that the nature of our situation be recognized and made the basis of policy and action.

Source: Excerpted from *Declaration of Indian Purpose: The Voice of the American Indian,* American Indian Chicago Conference, University of Chicago, June 13–20, 1961, pp. 4, 5, 20.

DOCUMENT 28.3

The Voting Rights Act of 1965

. . . (e) (1) Congress hereby declares that to secure the rights under the fourteenth amendment of persons educated in American-flag schools in which the predominant classroom language was other than English, it is necessary to prohibit the States from conditioning the right to vote of such persons on ability to read, write, understand, or interpret any matter in the English language.

(2) No person who demonstrates that he has successfully completed the sixth primary grade in a public school in, or a private school accredited by, any State or territory, the District of Columbia, or the Commonwealth of Puerto Rico in which the predominant classroom language was other than English, shall be denied the right to vote in any Federal, State, or local election because of his inability to read, write, understand, or interpret any matter in the English language, except that in States in which State law provides that a different level of education is presumptive of literacy, he shall demonstrate that he has successfully completed an equivalent level of education in a public school in, or a private school accredited by, any State or territory, the District of Columbia, or the Commonwealth of Puerto Rico in which the predominant classroom language was other than English.

*   *   *

Section 8

Whenever an examiner is serving under this Act in any political subdivision, the Civil Service Commission may assign, at the request of the Attorney General, one or more persons, who may be officers of the United States, (1) to enter and attend at any place for holding an election in such subdivision for the purpose of observing whether persons who are entitled to vote are being permitted to vote, and (2) to enter and attend at any place for tabulating the votes cast at any election held in such subdivision for the purpose of observing whether votes cast by persons entitled to vote are being properly tabulated. Such persons so assigned shall report to an examiner appointed for such political subdivision, to the Attorney General, and if the appointment of examiners has been authorized pursuant to section 3(a), to the court.

*   *   *

Section 11

(a) No person acting under color of law shall fail or refuse to permit any person to vote who is entitled to vote under any provision of this Act or is otherwise qualified to vote, or willfully fail or refuse to tabulate, count, and report such person's vote.

Source: Excerpted from the *Voting Rights Act of 1965*, in United States Commission on Civil Rights, *The Voting Rights Act Summary And Text*, Clearing House Publication no. 32, 1971.

(b) No person, whether acting under color of law or otherwise, shall intimidate, threaten, or coerce, or attempt to intimidate, threaten, or coerce any person for voting or attempting to vote, or intimidate, threaten, or coerce, or attempt to intimidate, threaten, or coerce any person for urging or aiding any person to vote or attempt to vote, or intimidate, threaten, or coerce any person for exercising any powers or duties under section 3(a), 6, 8, 9, 10, or 12(e).

(c) Whoever knowingly or willfully gives false information as to his name, address, or period of residence in the voting district for the purpose of establishing his eligibility to register or vote, or conspires with another individual for the purpose of encouraging his false registration to vote or illegal voting, or pays or offers to pay or accepts payment either for registration to vote or for voting shall be fined not more than $10,000 or imprisoned not more than five years, or both: *Provided, however,* That this provision shall be applicable only to general, special, or primary elections held solely or in part for the purpose of selecting or electing any candidate for the office of President, Vice President, presidential elector, Member of the United States Senate, Member of the United States House of Representatives, or Delegates or Commissioners from the territories or possessions, or Resident Commissioner of the Commonwealth of Puerto Rico.

(d) Whoever, in any matter within the jurisdiction of an examiner or hearing officer knowingly and willfully falsifies or conceals a material fact, or makes any false, fictitious, or fraudulent statements or representations, or makes or uses any false writing or document knowing the same to contain any false, fictitious, or fraudulent statement or entry, shall be fined not more than $10,000 or imprisoned not more than five years, or both.

Section 12

(a) Whoever shall deprive or attempt to deprive any person of any right secured by section 2, 3, 4, 5, 7, or 10 or shall violate section 11(a) or (b), shall be fined not more than $5,000, or imprisoned not more than five years, or both.

(b) Whoever, within a year following an election in a political subdivision in which an examiner has been appointed (1) destroys, defaces, mutilates, or otherwise alters the marking of a paper ballot which has been cast in such election, or (2) alters any official record of voting in such election tabulated from a voting machine or otherwise, shall be fined not more than $5,000, or imprisoned not more than five years, or both.

DOCUMENT 28.4

South Boston High School

Phyllis Ellison

I didn't know much about South Boston High School at the time. I didn't know what I was getting myself into, that South Boston High School was part of busing

Source: From Henry Hampton and Steve Fayer, *Voices of Freedom: An Oral History of the Civil Rights Movement from the 1950s through the 1980s* (New York: Bantam Books, 1990), pp. 600–601.

or desegregation, I just knew that I was going to attend South Boston High School. My mother's reaction was I was *not* going to attend South Boston High School, that I would go to a Catholic school. And I let her know that my friends were going to South Boston High and I wanted to attend there. I said I would quit school if I had to go to a Catholic school, because I wanted to be with my friends and none of my friends could go to Catholic school because of affordability.

I remember my first day going on the bus to South Boston High School. I wasn't afraid because I felt important. I didn't know what to expect, what was waiting for me up the hill. We had police escorts. I think there was three motorcycle cops and then two police cruisers in front of the bus, and so I felt really important at that time, not knowing what was on the other side of the hill.

Well, when we started up the hill you could hear people saying, "Niggers go home." There were signs, they had made a sign saying, "Black people stay out. We don't want any niggers in our school." And there were people on the corners holding bananas like we were apes, monkeys. "Monkeys get out, get them out of our neighborhood. We don't want you in our schools." So at that time it did frighten me somewhat, but I was more determined then to get inside South Boston High School, because of the people that were outside.

When I got off the bus, first of all I felt important, because of the news media that was there. [Television reporter] Natalie Jacobson out in front of your school getting the story on your school. So I felt really important going through the metal detectors and making sure that no one could come into the school armed. I felt like this was a big deal to me, to attend South Boston High School.

I felt like I was making history, because that was the first year of desegregation and all the controversies and conflicts at that time. I felt that the black students there were making history.

DOCUMENT 28.5

Missing Emmett

Emmett and I were getting ready to go on our vacation. We were excited because we were driving to Omaha where some of my cousins lived. We'd set our date which was less than a week away.

But Emmett heard that Uncle Mose was in town and two of the boys that he grew up with, Uncle Mose's grandsons. They were going back to Mississippi. That's what he wanted to do. It messed up our plans completely. After a lot of pressure, my mother and I decided it would be all right to let Emmett go to Mississippi.

About three days into Mississippi, they went into a little country store. This was Money, Mississippi. They had games on the front porch and you could buy pop and candy, little junk. The boys were playing checkers and Emmett decided

Source: Interview with Mamie Mobley, in Studs Terkel, *Race: How Blacks and Whites Think and Feel about the American Obsession* (New York: New Press, 1992), pp. 20–21.

to go in the store and buy something. His young cousin went into the store with him. Emmett bought bubble gum and some candy.

As they came out of the store, according to the accounts I heard from some of the boys, someone asked Emmett, "How did you like the lady in the store?" They said Emmett whistled his approval. The word got back to the two men, the husband and the half-brother of that husband—oh, my goodness, Roy Bryant and Big Jim, W. J. Milam [She carefully spells out the name]: M-I-L-A-M.

When they heard about it, it just escalated into something all out of hand. When the younger man, Bryant, hesitated to follow up on it, his half-brother, Big Jim, said, "If you won't, I will." In order to make a man out of his younger brother, he pushed the issue.

It was about 2:30 the following Sunday morning that these two men stormed into my uncle's house and took my son out at gunpoint. And the rest, we don't know what really happened, but we do know how the body looked when it was finally discovered three days later. He had been shot, he had been beaten, they had wired a gin-mill fan around his neck. When the sheriff pulled Emmett from the water, the only way my uncle recognized him was by the ring on his finger.

I was successful in getting the body back to Chicago and it was then, when I looked at Emmett, I could not believe that it was even something human I was looking at. I was forced to do a bit-by-bit analysis on his entire body to make really sure that that was my son. If there was any way to disclaim that body, I would have sent that body back to Mississippi. But it was without a doubt Emmett.

Have you ever seen any pictures? Have you ever seen what he looked like? I will show you them before you go.

There was a trial. The men said they questioned Emmett and they decided he was not the boy, so they pointed him back to my uncle's house and let him go on foot. It doesn't take much to understand. You can look through certain things and see whether or not they're true.

They were acquitted within one hour and five minutes. The jury was all-male, all-white.

Mose Wright, my mother's brother-in-law, pointed out Bryant and Milam as the two men who came for Emmett: "Thar's them." It took unprecedented courage. Nothing like that had ever happened in the South before. That was an old black man, sixty-five years old. He stayed in the area until he was rescued by some civil-rights group and put under surveillance. One night he slept in the graveyard behind his church. He was a minister. He slept under the cotton house one night. He never spent another night in that house. No one did.

Emmett would have been forty-eight this year. I have no grandchildren. He was my only child. You can see coming up the walk, I could really use a grandkid to shovel snow. I often think about that. I like to have a garden and in the springtime, I'm trying to dig . . . So I have to depend on whoever passes by and finally get someone to help me in the spring and again in the winter. We just sort of have to hope somebody comes along when there's been a snow.

DOCUMENT 28.6

A Christmas Letter of Hope

The Volunteers in Service to America (VISTA), organized in the form of a domestic Peace Corps. Young adults were encouraged to sign up for a year, paid a
minimal salary, and after a brief training program, were sent to areas of the
country which needed their idealism, enthusiasm, and wisdom. Whether their
assignment was an Indian reservation or a rural slum, the VISTA trainees confronted poverty and its consequences in a most intense form. And all too frequently the Negro was to be found among the impoverished.

Muriel Hamilton graduated from Oberlin College in June 1965 and joined
the VISTA program. In a 1965 Christmas letter, she explained her job, her hopes,
her frustrations, and her despairs. Her letter is significant not only for these but
also because as a Negro she represents the concerned action-oriented youth
whose involvement today will shape tomorrow.

Piney Point, Florida, migrant labor camp (complete with outdoor privy, mud,
snakes, rats, and 10 million mosquitoes) was home for six weeks of training last
summer. We studied the migrant farm worker's way of life by reading and hearing about it from "authorities" and by living in conditions like those of the
worker and his family all across the country. If we hadn't been convinced before-
hand of the complexity of the problem we were about to tackle, the training period left us no doubts. By mid-August we had given up our quick, sure solutions;
much of our wistful idealism was gone; but we were more determined than ever
to try our hands at breaking the vicious, dehumanizing cycle of poverty and
hopelessness which chains millions of men to lives of misery and futility.

My year's assignment is to work with the Community Action Fund Migrant Program which operates in 15 counties of central Florida. This organization has been funded by the Office of Economic Opportunity to deal with the
social, political, and economic situations of migrant families. This has rarely
been done before, hence the great difficulty of knowing where to begin the task
of merely understanding the problems, to say nothing of their solutions. Our
basic program is divided into various areas of education: preschool day care
and training, youth tutorial and guidance, adult literacy, home management,
sanitation, and citizenship. We try to offer service to the entire family from
dawn, when parents bring their tots to the day care center, to far into the night,
when classes are held after work is done.

However, before the program can get off the ground, the people must see
some value to themselves in becoming a part of it. And here is where the Volunteer has a unique and crucial role. How do you convince a boy to stay in
school when his family needs the $9/day he can make picking tomatoes? Or
should you *try* to convince him? How can you ask a mother to come to literacy

Source: Muriel Hamilton's Christmas letter of hope, in Leslie H. Fishell, Jr., and Benjamin Quarles, *The
Negro American: A Documentary History* (Glenview, IL: Scott, Foresman, 1967), pp. 535–36.

class after a 10-hour day of back-breaking labor plus the usual household chores? What do you tell a father who can find no escape from his misery other than drink or who refuses to allow his wife to practice birth control in spite of the unfed children already thin from malnutrition? What can we, as strangers to them and their situations, offer that will be meaningful, not just another fly-by-night promise?

Literally hundreds of such dilemmas face us continually and must be overcome before any formal projects can be successful. To help answer what seem to be unanswerable questions, VISTA's live in the community which they hope to serve and try to gain the confidence of the people so that these problems can be faced together. Solutions are not made in Washington or Tallahassee or even in our Bradenton office, but develop out of community meetings or quiet talks on front porches. This "grass-roots" approach seems cumbersome and slow, yet in my opinion it is the only way to get to the heart of the problems and to deal honestly with the poor as thinking, feeling human beings rather than as statistics in someone's random survey. This change in attitude about poor people is by far the most important aspect of the entire war on poverty and the gauge by which to judge its success or failure.

Since about 80% of the East Coast Migrant Stream are American Negroes (the rest are Mexicans and Puerto Ricans) the problems they face are simply more severe versions of those faced by most American Negroes. When one has no money, his lack of educational opportunities, decent housing, financial credit, and the overall opportunity to improve his living standard and self-respect are magnified to almost insurmountable problems. Every part of the farm laborer's environment tells him that he is no good and he soon begins to believe it himself. Much of my energy is spent in trying to *make* people want a better life, to overcome the bitter lessons of the past. As I try to help to find a solution to these situations, I am constantly faced with the decision of whether the answers should come by greasing up the wheels of the present mechanisms of society (e.g., make welfare less dependent on residence, get a few kids into vocational training programs, tutor a bit after school) or by working for major changes in the machine itself (e.g., a minimum wage law for farm workers, more sympathetic local and state officials, etc.). I can't answer that question yet; I hope to be more able to in the next several months.

My days are filled with many activities—teaching remedial reading, knocking on doors, talking to anyone who will give me an ear, addressing clubs, planning recreation programs and clean-up campaigns, writing letters to people and groups who might be able to help. There's never a dull moment. These are days of frustration, excitement, optimism and pessimism, small joys and deep sorrows, and then amazement at the true beauty of friendship and gentle love which can blossom in even the most barren situations of poverty.

29

Hubris

No sooner had the United States begun to realize its capabilities as a world power, perhaps even a "super" power, than it began to experience its limitations on the world stage. Perhaps it was pride and youthfulness that contributed to the sort of hubris that ensnared the nation in the 1960s and 1970s. An older and quite experienced Dwight D. Eisenhower, veteran of two world wars, once warned the nation of becoming too comfortable with the "military industrial complex." He also declined the opportunity to influence another part of the world by remaining guardedly cautious about involvement in Southeast Asia and what was then known as French Indochina. But President Kennedy, a much younger veteran of the Second World War, inspired the nation with grand rhetoric that suggested a generous and open-ended commitment of American treasure and blood throughout the world. That commitment nearly precipitated World War III through the Cuban missile crisis. Though the resolution of that conflict can be viewed as a great diplomatic victory for Kennedy and American Cold War strategies, it surely also influenced the desire and resolve of Kennedy and others to resist "aggression" elsewhere.

Hubris comes in many forms. It might be seen in the American desire to orchestrate world events thousands of miles away; it might also be apparent in the laudable but unrealistic domestic social aspirations of Lyndon Johnson and his Great Society programs. Material wealth and desire to do good may have suggested the possibility of reaching Johnson's goals, but that same wealth might appear to be simple materialism nurturing the seeds of social complacency. Consider the perspective revealed in the Port Huron Statement, for example.

A Pandora's box of cultural clashes and social dislocations seems to have broken open during the 1960s, embroiling Americans of all classes and persuasions in reconsideration of values and loyalties. The "Ballad of Joe Hill" represented to some American youth in the 1960s both a revival of earlier struggles against the limitations on liberty and restrictions on the pursuit of *happiness; it could also be seen as the commencement of a new quest for a freer America. These views are further illustrated in the "Manifesto Addressed to the President of the United States from the Youth of America."*

DOCUMENT 29.1

Dwight D. Eisenhower Ponders Involvement in Vietnam

Reviewing the entire episode in retrospect, I find that four questions merit consideration:

(1) Why, with the superiority in manpower and resources available, were the French unable to win?

(2) Why was the very considerable amount of material American aid not more effective in helping the French?

(3) Why, when the French were in difficulty and the interests of the Free World affected, at least indirectly, were the successive French governments unwilling to take logical and reasonable steps to bring United States' and other support to their assistance?

(4) What lessons or benefits, if any, accrued to the Free World as a result?

I am convinced that the French could not win the war because the internal political situation in Vietnam, weak and confused, badly weakened their military position. I have never talked or corresponded with a person knowledgeable in Indochinese affairs who did not agree that had elections been held as of the time of the fighting, possibly 80 per cent of the population would have voted for the Communist Ho Chi Minh as their leader rather than Chief of State Bao Dai. Indeed, the lack of leadership and drive on the part of Bao Dai was a factor in the feeling prevalent among Vietnamese that they had nothing to fight for. As one Frenchman said to me, "What Vietnam needs is another Syngman Rhee, regardless of all the difficulties the presence of such a personality would entail."

In the earlier stages of the conflict, the fighting was mostly conducted where rough terrain made it impossible to seek out the enemy and bring him to a pitched battle. Later, even when the battle lines became so located that the *groupes mobiles* could be effective, there still existed within the Red River Delta a condition in which the French could control even the main roads for only about two or three hours a day. The rest of the time all lines of communication were in the hands of the Vietminh. This meant that the mass of the population supported the enemy. With such a feeling prevalent, it was inevitable that the French should find it impossible to retain the loyalty of their Vietnamese troops.

In addition to the miserable political situation, the French military activities were puzzling. Most perplexing was taking up the position at Dien Bien Phu. True, the position was strong enough to inflict heavy Vietminh casualties; but in the long run, giving up mobility in favor of occupying an inaccessible static position, dominated by high ground surrounding, was certainly not normal practice.

Source: From Dwight D. Eisenhower, *Mandate for Change, 1953–1956* (New York: Doubleday & Company, 1963), pp. 372–74.

Had the French been able to establish political and military cooperation with the Vietnamese, the Navarre Plan probably would have worked. Unfortunately, this did not occur. In a press conference held by General Navarre shortly after the fall of Dien Bien Phu, he reportedly stated that one of the difficulties in the defense of that bastion had been inability of Asiatics to withstand artillery fire. A Vietnamese reporter asked General Navarre how it was that the Vietminh themselves, who were Asiatics, had been so successful in learning how to stand up under French artillery fire. At that point the Asiatic reporters in the meeting got up and left.

With this unsound relationship between the Asiatics and the French, it is not difficult to answer the second question: American aid could not cure the defect in the French-Vietnamese relationship and therefore was of only limited value. The decision to give this aid was almost compulsory. The United States had no real alternative unless we were to abandon Southeast Asia.

We will never know, of course, how much United States aid did to forestall a military disaster worse than the one which actually did occur. The French might have been pushed from the Red River Delta into the sea, with the loss of additional thousands of lives, and the rapid spread of Communism in the region. Willingness to fight for freedom, no matter where the battle may be, has always been a characteristic of our people, but the conditions then prevailing in Indochina were such as to make unilateral American intervention nothing less than sheer folly.

Had the circumstances lent themselves to a logical use of military force, the task of explaining to the American public the necessity for sacrifice would have been an acceptable one. But the losses would have been heavy, and because there never arose a situation justifying intervention, speculation as to "might have beens" is—as always—scarcely more than an exercise in futility.

Air strikes in support of Dien Bien Phu would not have been effective. But American air intervention in case of Communist employment of MIGs in the Red River Delta would certainly have been so. Had the Chinese adopted a policy of regular air support for the Vietminh, we would have assuredly moved in to eliminate this blatant aggression from without. This would have necessitated striking Chinese airfields and would have created some risk of general war with China. As it was, I feel confident that our capability to operate in this fashion had a decisively deterrent effect on the Chinese.

The strongest reason of all for United States refusal to respond by itself to French pleas was our tradition of anticolonialism. This tradition, violated—almost accidentally—for a time in the nineteenth and early twentieth centuries, was born in the circumstance of our own national birth in 1776. Our deep conviction about colonialism has often brought us embarrassment in dealings with our friends in Western Europe, whose histories as colonialists are largely alien to our history. But the standing of the United States as the most powerful of the anticolonial powers is an asset of incalculable value to the Free World. It means that our counsel is sometimes trusted where that of others may not be. It is essential to our position of leadership in a world wherein the majority of the nations have at some time or another felt the yoke of colonialism. Never, throughout the long and sometimes frustrating search for an effective means of defeating the communist struggle for power in Indochina, did we lose sight of the importance of America's moral position.

Much good, along with much sadness, came out of the Indochinese struggle. It accelerated the independence of Laos and Cambodia and South Vietnam by measures which the French implemented in their desperation during the last days of the conflict; this complete independence, with the removal of French troops, paved the way to an understanding among the free nations of Southeast Asia. It alerted those nations to the dangers of international Communism and finally convinced our European allies, the British and French, of the need for cooperative action in that region. This new realization culminated in the formation of one of our most important regional alliances, the Southeast Asia Treaty Organization.

DOCUMENT 29.2

John F. Kennedy's Inaugural Address

January 20, 1961

. . . Let every nation know, whether it wishes us well or ill, that we shall pay any price, bear any burden, meet any hardship, support any friend, oppose any foe to assure the survival and the success of liberty.

This much we pledge—and more.

To those old allies whose cultural and spiritual origins we share, we pledge the loyalty of faithful friends. United, there is little we cannot do in a host of cooperative ventures. Divided, there is little we can do—for we dare not meet a powerful challenge at odds and split asunder.

To those new states whom we welcome to the ranks of the free, we pledge our word that one form of colonial control shall not have passed away merely to be replaced by a far more iron tyranny. We shall not always expect to find them supporting our view. But we shall always hope to find them strongly supporting their own freedom—and to remember that, in the past, those who foolishly sought power by riding the back of the tiger ended up inside.

To those peoples in the huts and villages of half the globe struggling to break the bonds of mass misery, we pledge our best efforts to help them help themselves, for whatever period is required—not because the communists may be doing it, not because we seek their votes, but because it is right. If a free society cannot help the many who are poor, it cannot save the few who are rich.

To our sister republics south of our border, we offer a special pledge—to convert our good words into good deeds—in a new alliance for progress—to assist free men and free governments in casting off the chains of poverty. But this peaceful revolution of hope cannot become the prey of hostile powers. Let all

Source: From John F. Kennedy, Inaugural Address, January 20, 1961. In *Public Papers of the Presidents of the United States.* Washington, DC: United States Government Printing Office, 1962.

our neighbors know that we shall join with them to oppose aggression or subversion anywhere in the Americas. And let every other power know that this Hemisphere intends to remain the master of its own house.

To that world assembly of sovereign states, the United Nations, our last best hope in an age where the instruments of war have far outpaced the instruments of peace, we renew our pledge of support—to prevent it from becoming merely a forum for invective—to strengthen its shield of the new and the weak—and to enlarge the area in which its writ may run.

Finally, to those nations who would make themselves our adversary, we offer not a pledge but a request: that both sides begin anew the quest for peace, before the dark powers of destruction unleashed by science engulf all humanity in planned or accidental self-destruction.

We dare not tempt them with weakness. For only when our arms are sufficient beyond doubt can we be certain beyond doubt that they will never be employed.

But neither can two great and powerful groups of nations take comfort from our present course—both sides overburdened by the cost of modern weapons, both rightly alarmed by the steady spread of the deadly atom, yet both racing to alter that uncertain balance of terror that stays the hand of mankind's final war.

So let us begin anew—remembering on both sides that civility is not a sign of weakness, and sincerity is always subject to proof. Let us never negotiate out of fear. But let us never fear to negotiate.

Let both sides explore what problems unite us instead of belaboring those problems which divide us.

Let both sides, for the first time, formulate serious and precise proposals for the inspection and control of arms—and bring the absolute power to destroy other nations under the absolute control of all nations.

Let both sides seek to invoke the wonders of science instead of its terrors. Together let us explore the stars, conquer the deserts, eradicate disease, tap the ocean depths and encourage the arts and commerce.

Let both sides unite to heed in all corners of the earth the command of Isaiah—to "undo the heavy burdens . . . (and) let the oppressed go free."

And if a beach-head of cooperation may push back the jungle of suspicion, let both sides join in creating a new endeavor, not a new balance of power, but a new world of law, where the strong are just and the weak secure and the peace preserved.

All this will not be finished in the first one hundred days. Nor will it be finished in the first one thousand days, nor in the life of this Administration, nor even perhaps in our lifetime on this planet. But let us begin.

In your hands, my fellow citizens, more than mine, will rest the final success or failure of our course. Since this country was founded, each generation of Americans has been summoned to give testimony to its national loyalty. The graves of young Americans who answered the call to service surround the globe.

Now the trumpet summons us again—not as a call to bear arms, though arms we need—not as a call to battle, though embattled we are—but a call to bear the burden of a long twilight struggle, year in and year out, "rejoicing in hope, patient in tribulation"—a struggle against the common enemies of man: tyranny, poverty, disease and war itself.

Can we forge against these enemies a grand and global alliance, North and South, East and West, that can assure a more fruitful life for all mankind? Will you join in that historic effort?

In the long history of the world, only a few generations have been granted the role of defending freedom in its hour of maximum danger. I do not shrink from this responsibility—I welcome it. I do not believe that any of us would exchange places with any other people or any other generation. The energy, the faith, the devotion which we bring to this endeavor will light our country and all who serve it—and the glow from that fire can truly light the world.

And so, my fellow Americans: ask not what your country can do for you—ask what you can do for your country.

My fellow citizens of the world: ask not what America will do for you, but what together we can do for the freedom of man.

DOCUMENT 29.3

John F. Kennedy's Cuban Missile Crisis Speech

. . . The 1930s taught us a clear lesson; aggressive conduct, if allowed to go unchecked and unchallenged, ultimately leads to war. This nation is opposed to war. We are also true to our word. Our unswerving objective, therefore, must be to prevent the use of these missiles against this or any other country, and to secure their withdrawal or elimination from the Western Hemisphere.

Our policy has been one of patience and restraint, as befits a peaceful and powerful nation, which leads a worldwide alliance. We have been determined not to be diverted from our central concerns by mere irritants and fanatics. But now further action is required—and it is under way; and these actions may only be the beginning. We will not prematurely or unnecessarily risk the costs of worldwide nuclear war in which even the fruits of victory would be ashes in our mouth—but neither will we shrink from that risk at any time it must be faced.

Acting, therefore, in the defense of our own security and of the entire Western Hemisphere, and under the authority entrusted to me by the Constitution as endorsed by the resolution of the Congress, I have directed that the following initial steps be taken immediately:

Source: From John F. Kennedy, "Cuban Missile Crisis," in Janet Podell and Steven Anzovin, eds., *Speeches of the American Presidents* (New York: H. W. Wilson Co., 1988), pp. 614–15.

First: To halt this offensive buildup, a strict quarantine on all offensive military equipment under shipment to Cuba is being initiated. All ships of any kind bound for Cuba from whatever nation or port will, if found to contain cargoes of offensive weapons, be turned back. This quarantine will be extended, if needed, to other types of cargo and carriers. We are not at this time, however, denying the necessities of life as the Soviets attempted to do in their Berlin blockade of 1948.

Second: I have directed the continued and increased close surveillance of Cuba and its military buildup. The foreign ministers of the OAS, in their communique of October 6, rejected secrecy on such matters in this hemisphere. Should these offensive military preparations continue, thus increasing the threat to the hemisphere, further action will be justified. I have directed the armed forces to prepare for any eventualities; and I trust that in the interest of both the Cuban people and the Soviet technicians at the sites, the hazards to all concerned of continuing this threat will be recognized.

Third: It shall be the policy of this nation to regard any nuclear missile launched from Cuba against any nation in the Western Hemisphere as an attack by the Soviet Union on the United States, requiring a full retaliatory response upon the Soviet Union.

Fourth: As a necessary military precaution, I have reinforced our base at Guantanamo, evacuated today the dependents of our personnel there, and ordered additional military units to be on a standby alert basis.

Fifth: We are calling tonight for an immediate meeting of the Organ of Consultation under the Organization of American States, to consider this threat to hemispheric security and to invoke articles 6 and 8 of the Rio Treaty in support of all necessary action. The United Nations Charter allows for regional security arrangements—and the nations of this hemisphere decided long ago against the military presence of outside powers. Our other allies around the world have also been alerted.

Sixth: Under the Charter of the United Nations, we are asking tonight that an emergency meeting of the Security Council be convoked without delay to take action against this latest Soviet threat to world peace. Our resolution will call for the prompt dismantling and withdrawal of all offensive weapons in Cuba, under the supervision of U.N. observers, before the quarantine can be lifted.

Seventh and finally: I call upon Chairman Khrushchev to halt and eliminate this clandestine, reckless, and provocative threat to world peace and to stable relations between our two nations. I call upon him further to abandon this course of world domination, and to join in an historic effort to end the perilous arms race and to transform the history of man. He has an opportunity now to move the world back from the abyss of destruction—by returning to his government's own words that it had no need to station missiles outside its own territory, and withdrawing these weapons from Cuba—by refraining from any action which will widen or deepen the present crisis—and then by participating in a search for peaceful and permanent solutions.

DOCUMENT 29.4

Lyndon Johnson's "Great Society" Program

. . . The challenge of the next half century is whether we have the wisdom to use that wealth to enrich and elevate our national life, and to advance the quality of our American civilization.

Your imagination, your initiative, and your indignation will determine whether we build a society where progress is the servant of our needs, or a society where old values and new visions are buried under unbridled growth. For in your time we have the opportunity to move not only toward the rich society and the powerful society, but upward to the Great Society.

The Great Society rests on abundance and liberty for all. It demands an end to poverty and racial injustice, to which we are totally committed in our time. But that is just the beginning.

The Great Society is a place where every child can find knowledge to enrich his mind and to enlarge his talents. It is a place where leisure is a welcome chance to build and reflect, not a feared cause of boredom and restlessness. It is a place where the city of man serves not only the needs of the body and the demands of commerce but the desire for beauty and the hunger for community.

It is a place where man can renew contact with nature. It is a place which honors creation for its own sake and for what it adds to the understanding of the race. It is a place where men are more concerned with the quality of their goals than the quantity of their goods.

But most of all, the Great Society is not a safe harbor, a resting place, a final objective, a finished work. It is a challenge constantly renewed, beckoning us toward a destiny where the meaning of our lives matches the marvelous products of our labor.

So I want to talk to you today about three places where we begin to build the Great Society—in our cities, in our countryside, and in our classrooms.

Many of you will live to see the day, perhaps 50 years from now, when there will be 400 million Americans—four-fifths of them in urban areas. In the remainder of this century urban population will double, city land will double, and we will have to build homes, highways, and facilities equal to all those built since this country was first settled. So in the next 40 years we must rebuild the entire urban United States.

Aristotle said: "Men come together in cities in order to live, but they remain together in order to live the good life." It is harder and harder to live the good life in American cities today.

The catalog of ills is long: there is the decay of the centers and the despoiling of the suburbs. There is not enough housing for our people or transportation for our traffic. Open land is vanishing and old landmarks are violated.

Source: From Lyndon Johnson, "'Great Society' Program," in Janet Podell and Steven Anzovin, eds., *Speeches of the American Presidents* (New York: H. W. Wilson Co., 1988), pp. 635–36.

Worst of all expansion is eroding the precious and time honored values of community with neighbors and communion with nature. The loss of these values breeds loneliness and boredom and indifference.

Our society will never be great until our cities are great. Today the frontier of imagination and innovation is inside those cities and not beyond their borders.

New experiments are already going on. It will be the task of your generation to make the American city a place where future generations will come, not only to live but to live the good life.

I understand that if I stayed here tonight I would see that Michigan students are really doing their best to live the good life.

This is the place where the Peace Corps was started. It is inspiring to see how all of you, while you are in this country, are trying so hard to live at the level of the people.

A second place where we begin to build the Great Society is in our countryside. We have always prided ourselves on being not only America the strong and America the free, but America the beautiful. Today that beauty is in danger. The water we drink, the food we eat, the very air that we breathe, are threatened with pollution. Our parks are overcrowded, our seashores overburdened. Green fields and dense forests are disappearing.

A few years ago we were greatly concerned about the "Ugly American." Today we must act to prevent an ugly America.

For once the battle is lost, once our natural splendor is destroyed, it can never be recaptured. And once man can no longer walk with beauty or wonder at nature his spirit will wither and his sustenance be wasted.

A third place to build the Great Society is in the classrooms of America. There your children's lives will be shaped. Our society will not be great until every young mind is set free to scan the farthest reaches of thought and imagination. We are still far from that goal.

Today, eight million adult Americans, more than the entire population of Michigan, have not finished five years of school. Nearly 20 million have not finished eight years of school. Nearly 54 million—more than one-quarter of all America—have not even finished high school.

Each year more than 100,000 high school graduates, with proved ability, do not enter college because they cannot afford it. And if we cannot educate today's youth, what will we do in 1970 when elementary school enrollment will be five million greater than 1960? And high school enrollment will rise by five million. College enrollment will increase by more than three million.

In many places, classrooms are overcrowded and curricula are outdated. Most of our qualified teachers are underpaid, and many of our paid teachers are unqualified. So we must give every child a place to sit and a teacher to learn from. Poverty must not be a bar to learning, and learning must offer an escape from poverty.

But more classrooms and more teachers are not enough. We must seek an educational system which grows in excellence as it grows in size. This means better training for our teachers. It means preparing youth to enjoy their hours of leisure as well as their hours of labor. It means exploring new techniques of teaching, to find new ways to stimulate the love of learning and the capacity for creation.

These are three of the central issues of the Great Society. While our government has many programs directed at those issues, I do not pretend that we have the full answer to those problems.

But I do promise this: We are going to assemble the best thought and the broadest knowledge from all over the world to find those answers for America. I intend to establish working groups to prepare a series of White House conferences and meetings—on the cities, on natural beauty, on the quality of education, and on other emerging challenges. And from these meetings and from this inspiration and from these studies we will begin to set our course toward the Great Society.

The solution to these problems does not rest on a massive program in Washington, nor can it rely solely on the strained resources of local authority. They require us to create new concepts of cooperation, a creative federalism, between the national capital and the leaders of local communities.

DOCUMENT 29.5

Port Huron Statement

Students for a Democratic Society

1962

Courtesy Office of Sen. Tom Hayden.

INTRODUCTION: AGENDA FOR A GENERATION

We are people of this generation, bred in at least modest comfort, housed now in universities, looking uncomfortably to the world we inherit.

When we were kids the United States was the wealthiest and strongest country in the world: the only one with the atom bomb, the least scarred by modern war, an initiator of the United Nations that we thought would distribute Western influence throughout the world. Freedom and equality for each individual, government of, by, and for the people—these American values we found good, principles by which we could live as men. Many of us began maturing in complacency.

As we grew, however, our comfort was penetrated by events too troubling to dismiss. First, the permeating and victimizing fact of human degradation, symbolized by the Southern struggle against racial bigotry, compelled most of us from silence to activism. Second, the enclosing fact of the Cold War, symbolized by the presence of the Bomb, brought awareness that we ourselves, and

Source: Available at www.voiceoftheturtle.org/library/porthuron.shtml.

our friends, and millions of abstract "others" we knew more directly because of our common peril, might die at any time. We might deliberately ignore, or avoid, or fail to feel all other human problems, but not these two, for these were too immediate and crushing in their impact, too challenging in the demand that we as individuals take the responsibility for encounter and resolution. . . .

Our work is guided by the sense that we may be the last generation in the experiment with living. But we are a minority—the vast majority of our people regard the temporary equilibriums of our society and world as eternally-functional parts. In this is perhaps the outstanding paradox: we ourselves are imbued with urgency, yet the message of our society is that there is no viable alternative to the present. Beneath the reassuring tones of the politicians, beneath the common opinion that America will "muddle through," beneath the stagnation of those who have closed their minds to the future, is the pervading feeling that there simply are no alternatives, that our times have witnessed the exhaustion not only of Utopias, but of any new departures as well. Feeling the press of complexity upon the emptiness of life, people are fearful of the thought that at any moment things might thrust out of control. They fear change itself, since change might smash whatever invisible framework seems to hold back chaos for them now. For most Americans, all crusades are suspect, threatening. The fact that each individual sees apathy in his fellows perpetuates the common reluctance to organize for change. The dominant institutions are complex enough to blunt the minds of their potential critics, and entrenched enough to swiftly dissipate or entirely repel the energies of protest and reform, thus limiting human expectancies. Then, too, we are a materially improved society, and by our own improvements we seem to have weakened the case for further change. . . .

WHAT IS NEEDED?

. . . It is necessary that America make disarmament, not nuclear deterrence, "credible" to the Soviets and to the world. That is, disarmament should be continually avowed as a national goal; concrete plans should be presented at conference tables; real machinery for a disarming and disarmed world—national and international—should be created while the disarming process itself goes on. . . .

4. Experiments in disengagement and demilitarization must be conducted as part of the total disarming process. These "disarmament experiments" can be of several kinds, so long as they are consistent with the principles of containing the arms race and isolating specific sectors of the world from the Cold War power-play. First, it is imperative that no more nations be supplied with, or locally produce, nuclear weapons. . . .

The Industrialization of the World

Many Americans are prone to think of the industrialization of the newly developed countries as a modern form of American noblesse, undertaken sacrificially for the benefit of others. On the contrary, the task of world industrialization, of eliminating the disparity between have and have-not nations, is as important as any issue facing America. The colonial revolution signals the end of an era for the old Western powers and a time of new beginnings for most of the people of the earth. In the course of these upheavals, many problems will emerge: American policies must be revised or accelerated in several ways.

   a. The United States' principal goal should be creating a world where hunger, poverty, disease, ignorance, violence, and exploitation are replaced as central features by abundance, reason, love, and international cooperation. To many this will seem the product of juvenile hallucination: but we insist it is a more realistic goal than is a world of nuclear stalemate. Some will say this is a hope beyond all bounds: but it is far better to us to have positive vision than a "hard headed" resignation. Some will sympathize, but claim it is impossible: if so, then, we, not Fate, are the responsible ones, for we have the means at our disposal. We should not give up the attempt for fear of failure.

   b. We should undertake here and now a fifty-year effort to prepare for all nations the conditions of industrialization. Even with far more capital and skill than we now import to emerging areas, serious prophets expect that two generations will pass before accelerating industrialism is a worldwide act. . . .

   c. We should not depend significantly on private enterprise to do the job. Many important projects will not be profitable enough to entice the investment of private capital. The total amount required is far beyond the resources of corporate and philanthropic concerns. The new nations are suspicious, legitimately, of foreign enterprises dominating their national life. World industrialization is too huge an undertaking to be formulated or carried out by private interests. Foreign economic assistance is a national problem, requiring long range planning, integration with other domestic and foreign policies, and considerable public debate and analysis. Therefore the Federal government should have primary responsibility in this area. . . .

5. America should show its commitment to democratic institutions not by withdrawing support from undemocratic regimes, but by making domestic democracy exemplary. Worldwide amusement, cynicism and hatred toward the United States as a democracy is not simply a communist propaganda trick, but an objectively justifiable phenomenon. If respect for democracy is to be international, then the significance of democracy must emanate from American [sic] shores, not from the "soft sell" of the United States Information Agency.

6. America should agree that public utilities, railroads, mines, and plantations, and other basic economic institutions should be in the control

of national, not foreign, agencies. The destiny of any country should be determined by its nationals, not by outsiders with economic interests within. We should encourage our investors to turn over their foreign holdings (or at least 50% of the stock) to the national governments of the countries involved.

7. Foreign aid should be given through international agencies, primarily the United Nations. The need is to eliminate political overtones, to the extent possible, from economic development. The use of international agencies, with interests transcending those of American or Russian self-interest, is the feasible means of working on sound development. Second, internationalization will allow more long-range planning, integrate development plans adjacent countries and regions may have, and eliminate the duplication built into national systems of foreign aid. Third, it would justify more strictness of supervision than is now the case with American foreign aid efforts, but with far less chance of suspicion on the part of the developing countries. Fourth, the humiliating "hand-out" effect would be replaced by the joint participation of all nations in the general development of the earth's resources and industrial capacities. Fifth, it would eliminate national tensions, e.g. between Japan and some Southeast Asian areas, which now impair aid programs by "disguising" nationalities in the common pooling of funds. Sixth, it would make easier the task of stabilizing the world market prices of basic commodities, alleviating the enormous threat that decline in prices of commodity exports might cancel out the gains from foreign aid in the new nations. Seventh, it would improve the possibilities of non-exploitative development, especially in creating "soft-credit" rotating-fund agencies which would not require immediate progress or financial return. Finally, it would enhance the importance of the United Nations itself, as the disarming process would enhance the UN as a rule-enforcement agency.

8. Democratic theory must confront the problems inherent in social revolutions. For Americans concerned with the development of democratic societies, the anti-colonial movements and revolutions in the emerging nations pose serious problems. We need to face these problems with humility: after 180 years of constitutional government we are still striving for democracy in our own society. We must acknowledge that democracy and freedom do not magically occur, but have roots in historical experience; they cannot always be demanded for any society at any time, but must be nurtured and facilitated. We must avoid the arbitrary projection of Anglo-Saxon democratic forms onto different cultures. Instead of democratic capitalism we should anticipate more or less authoritarian variants of socialism and collectivism in many emergent societies. . . .

As students, for a democratic society, we are committed to stimulating this kind of social movement, this kind of vision and program is campus and community across the country. If we appear to seek the unattainable, it has been said, then let it be known that we do so to avoid the unimaginable.

DOCUMENT 29.6

Ballad of Joe Hill

I dreamed I saw Joe Hill last night
Alive as you and me
Says I, "But Joe, you're ten years dead,"
"I never died," says he, "I never died," says he.

"In Salt Lake, Joe, by God," says I
Him standing by my bed,
"They framed you on a murder charge."
Says Joe, "But I ain't dead," says Joe, "But I ain't dead."

"The copper bosses shot you, Joe,
They killed you, Joe," says I.
"Takes more than guns to kill a man,"
Says Joe, "I didn't die," says Joe, "I didn't die."

And standing there as big as life
And smiling with his eyes
Joe says, "What they forgot to kill
Went on to organize, went on to organize."

"Joe Hill ain't dead," he says to me,
"Joe Hill ain't never died.
Where workingmen are out on strike
Joe Hill is at their side, Joe Hill is at their side."

"From San Diego up to Maine
In every mine and mill
Where workers strike and organize,"
Says he, "You'll find Joe Hill," says he, "You'll find Joe Hill."

Source: "Ballad of Joe Hill," lyrics as recorded by Earl Robinson, Reeves Sound Studios, New York, NY, January 8, 1940; reprinted in Ronald D. Cohen and Dave Samuelson, liner notes for *Songs for Political Action*, Bear Family Records BCD 15720 JL, 1996, p. 72. © 1938 Leeds Music, Inc., New York, NY.

DOCUMENT 29.7

Manifesto Addressed to the President of the United States from the Youth of America

DANIEL E. TIJERINA

This, Mr. President, is to tell you how I feel about the problems now facing the United States, particularly our struggle for justice in the Southwestern states.

Source: Excerpted from Alan Rinzler, ed., *Manifesto Addressed to the President of the United States from the Youth of America* (New York: Macmillan Company, 1970), pp. 189–93, 83–85, 226–28.

Here in the state of New Mexico we have an organization that is led by my father, Reis Lopez Tijerina. We are fighting for what we know is ours here in the Southwest, our land grants left to us by our Spanish and Indian ancestors. We, the Indo-Espano people, are followers and believers of what is right, and we have not been brainwashed or whitewashed in the schools of the United States. We have been trying to fight in the courts for these land grants which do belong to us, but the government doesn't even bother to look into the Treaty of Guadalupe, which was signed on February 2, 1848, by the United States and Mexico.

Mr. President, I ask not for me but for my people that you look into the Treaty of Guadalupe Hidalgo. I think it is only just that you do this because our people have been put down long enough. I assure you that if the legal papers of the Treaty of Guadalupe have not been changed or destroyed, you will find that these grants do legally belong to us. We are not a people of violence, but we do believe in justice. If this problem is not looked into, I assure you that the United States will become just like North and South Vietnam. We will fight for our rights until we have won or died. We are not like some of these others that are always rioting or demonstrating for better jobs, better pay and things like that. All we want is what belongs to us legally, the land left to us by our forefathers, which was protected by the Treaty of Guadalupe.

The Anglos came and cheated and stole and killed for these land grants. Some homesteaded the land, some bought it for fifty cents an acre, and when our people didn't want to sell, they forced out their cattle and burned their crops. Sometimes they would kill the man of the house and force his woman to sell. And now that we have finally gotten started organizing to gain our rights here in New Mexico, the Minutemen and the John Birch Society are trying to stop us. I believe that these organizations have members who are policemen and rich people like bankers and big businessmen. That is why it is hard for us to progress rapidly. . . .

On June 5 we were invited to a picnic at a member's ranch in Canjilon. While at the picnic, a rumor went around that some of the men were going to make a citizen's arrest. They were going to arrest the district attorney who had stopped the meeting we were supposed to have had on the third day of June. The men who had been arrested a couple of days before were being arraigned. So a group of people got together there at the picnic and went to the court house in Tierra Amarilla to make a citizen's arrest. When a few of them walked into the court house, a state policeman went for his gun. When the men saw the policeman reach for his gun, they shot him. After they shot him, many others started shooting. Then they looked all over for the district attorney but they couldn't find him. So the men got into their cars and trucks and went back to the picnic at Canjilon.

Within a few hours the National Guard and state policemen came with their army tanks and helicopters. I guess they wanted to have a little war there. But like I say, we're not people of violence unless forced into it. We were surrounded by state policemen with carbines and shotguns. We were all told to step into a clearing and sit on the ground where there was horse shit and cow shit. Afterward they took the few rifles that we had. Then we were all called out of the corrals. They searched us and took our names, just like a captured enemy in war. Then they sent us all back into the corrals. We had been cooking potatoes when they got there. It started raining and they didn't let us tend our food.

We were held at the corral for two days and a night and the National Guard wouldn't let us accept blankets from people who were offering them to us. We had to ask for permission to use the bathroom. But afterward, my father was freed because, Mr. President, ours is a just cause.

Mr. President, it is only right that you look into our problem. It is not right that our people go on being treated this way. Our people need to learn the truth in schools. The Treaty of Guadalupe Hidalgo says that teachers in the state of New Mexico have to know both English and Spanish culture and language. But the majority do not. We need to be taught our Spanish culture in our schools. The schools teach about Davy Crocket and Lewis and Clark, but they don't teach about our Spanish heroes, like Mario Leyba, who you probably never even heard of.

Well, Mr. President, just like our country needs us, we need our country. We need justice here in the United States, not in Vietnam. At the age of eighteen we have to go to Vietnam to die like animals or go to jail if we won't. But at the age of eighteen we can't even vote for anything. Why is it, Mr. President, that we can die at eighteen but we can't vote? Those are the kinds of things you should worry about first before sending us to any war.

God made people to help each other, not fight against each other. If all the countries can't unite in peace, why don't you try to get peace here by satisfying your own people, not Koreans or Vietnamese.

But the one thing I ask of you most, Mr. President, is to look into our problem of land grants. After we get our rights I would be more than glad to fight in a just war for the United States.

KASOUNDRA KASOUNDRA

WE, THE PEOPLE OF THE UNITED STATES, IN ORDER TO FORM A MORE PERFECT PIE CRUST, ESTABLISH JUSTICE, INSURE DOMESTIC TRANQUILITY, PROVIDE FOR ALL THE GENERAL WELFARE, AND SECURE THE BLESSINGS WHICH ENHANCE OUR POSTERIOR AND ENABLE US OUR MOST GLORIOUS CONSTIPATION, THEREFORE RESOLVE THAT:

there must be a new diet of allegiance,
a hunger that will bring us to terms as gentlemen and women,
a wish to retire to the country,
of a maid to bring us news of oysters and fish,
of the servants we become to our influence divine
with our particular misfortunes so little,
off to the country to bake our bread,
to get ourselves straight,
to no longer neglect the manners we were given.

I want an end, a conclusion to any further constipation.
I want ideals to have a new sense of gracefulness,

something delivered from the caress of the apples
with a casting out of rotten entrées.
There is time to observe manners of the young and old,
for our manners have accomplished little for our lives.
Advanced in sophistication, we conduct the dinner sitting
with less and less articulation . . . the policy of our lives is as
badly handled as our country.
We should become primitive in this land of frozen chicken.
There is richness in becoming aware of others and with
the sharing of the new opulence around our bread
also is heard a conversation with a new heart.
Does the country bring a renaissance of the family we have lost?
It is so simple, so simple that all of the table grace
that has left our fingers could be easily found again.
I must go to all places that are green,
it could be the first time for a peace of mind.
I will keep sending you flowers and strawberries until all of you join me . . .

THE UNANIMOUS DECLARATION OF INTERDEPENDENCE

When, in the course of evolution, it becomes necessary for one species to de-nounce the notion of independence from all the rest and to assume among the powers of the earth, the interdependent station to which the natural laws of the cosmos have placed them, a decent respect for the opinions of all mankind requires that they should declare the conditions which impel them to assert their interdependence.

We hold these truths to be self-evident—that all species have evolved with equal and unalienable rights; that among these are Life, Liberty and the pursuit of Happiness. That to insure these rights, nature has instituted certain principles for the sustenance of all species, deriving these principles from the capabilities of the planet's life-support system. That whenever any behavior by members of one species becomes destructive of these principles, it is the function of other members of that species to alter or abolish such behavior and to reestablish the theme of interdependence with all life, in such a form and in accordance with those natural principles, that will effect their safety and happiness. Prudence, indeed, will dictate that cultural values long established should not be altered for light and transient causes, that mankind is more disposed to suffer from asserting a vain notion of independence than to right themselves by abolishing that culture to which they are now accustomed. But when a long train of abuses and usurpations of these principles of interdependence, evinces a subtle design to reduce them, through absolute despoliation of the planet's fertility, to a state of ill will, bad health, and great anxiety, it is their right, it is their duty, to throw off such notions of independence from other species and from the life support system, and to provide new guards for the reestablishment of the security and maintenance of these principles. Such has been the outlet and patient suffrage of all species, and such is now the necessity which constrains the species Homo sapiens to reassert the principles of interdependence. The history of the present notion of independence is a history of repeated injuries and usurpations, all having in direct effect the establishment of an absolute tyranny over Life. To prove this, let facts be submitted to a candid world.

1. People have refused to recognize the roles of other species and the importance of natural principles for growth of the food they require.
2. People have refused to recognize that they are interacting with other species in an evolutionary process.
3. People have failed the waters that all life partakes of.
4. People have transformed the face of the earth to enhance their notion of independence from it, and in so doing have interrupted many natural processes that they are dependent upon.
5. People have contaminated the common household with substances that are foreign to the life processes which are causing many organisms great difficulties.
6. People have massacred and extincted fellow species for their feathers and furs, for their skins and tusks.
7. People have persecuted most persistently those known as coyote, lion, wolf and fox because of their dramatic role in the expression of interdependence.
8. People are proliferating in such an irresponsible manner as to threaten the survival of all species.
9. People have warred upon one another, which has brought great sorrow to themselves and vast destruction to the homes and the food supplies of many living things.

People have denied others the right to live to completion their interdependencies to the full extent of their capabilities.

We, therefore, among the mortal representatives of the eternal process of life and evolutionary principles, in mutual humbleness, explicitly stated, appealing to the ecological consciousness of the world for the rectitude of our intentions, do solemnly publish and declare that all species are interdependent; that they are all free to realize these relationships to the full extent of their capabilities; that each species is subservient to the requirements of the natural processes that sustain all life. And for the support of this declaration, with a firm reliance on all other members of our species who understand their consciousness as a capability, we mutually pledge to assist all of us and our brothers to interact in order to realize a life process that manifests its maximum potential of diversity, vitality and planetary fertility to ensure the continuing of life on earth.

30

Crisis of Confidence

This chapter begins with a powerful visual presentation: two photographs whose images have been etched in the minds of millions of Americans. The first photograph further galvanized sentiment against the war in Vietnam, as the United States appeared to be party to cruel and barbaric behavior reminiscent of its first Asian war in the Philippines. The second photograph demonstrates that the war in Vietnam had flowed back to the United States when Ohio National Guardsmen fired on students at Kent State University in northeastern Ohio, killing and wounding dozens. The second picture seems to capture the helplessness and the despair of a nation that did not know how to extricate itself from foreign entanglements or to reconcile internal differences.

When President Nixon announced the achievement of a cease-fire in Vietnam, it offered hope that American soldiers were returning the fate of Vietnam over to the Vietnamese and themselves to American shores. A little more than a year later, Nixon himself became a casualty of a complex confluence of history and personality, forcing him to resign the presidency as a result of the infamous Watergate affair. In doing so, however, he reaffirmed his commitment to achieving world peace and demonstrated pride in ending America's involvement in the Vietnam conflict. Despite Richard Nixon's public hopes that the South Vietnamese government would be able to sustain itself and achieve democracy and prosperity, President Ford tersely announced the withdrawal of American personnel from Saigon just before the complete collapse of the South Vietnamese government and the final victory of the Vietnamese Communist party in unifying the country. Thus a huge investment of American blood and treasure spanning almost two decades ended ignominiously without honor. America's cause, if not America, had been defeated. Not too long after America's agonizing relationship with Vietnam, President Ford also sought to set to rest another agonizing chapter of American history with regard to Asian Americans and the Second World War. He signed a presidential proclamation [4417] that formally terminated President Franklin Roosevelt's Executive Order

9066, which had served as the enabler of the internment of Japanese residents and Japanese-American citizens during World War II.

The cultural seismic tremors that shook America in the 1970s came from a wide array of epicenters. President Jimmy Carter, who defeated Gerald Ford partially because of Ford's pardon of Nixon, saw the death of Elvis Presley as the loss of another symbol of what America was and could be. A succession of musical genres and styles that had been washing across the country and capturing America's youth with the regularity of tides had become a fundamental pillar of American civilization. Elvis Presley, who combined African American musical components with other southern musical traditions, seemed to illustrate the possibilities of cultural combination and fusion. But then, suddenly, the "king" died, perhaps as a result of his lifestyle that had become intertwined with self-destructive behavior associated with the rock and roll world. Truth, whether it emanated from lyrics or lifestyles, again seemed irrelevant.

Perhaps a greater and more fundamental shock to the American system was the nuclear accident and near disaster at Three Mile Island. This represented a double shock because it challenged Americans' faith in technology and science and in their government leaders, who were perceived to have been ineffectual in a crisis and possibly misleading in their representation of the true gravity of that crisis to the public. Such was the situation and the climate when President Carter prepared to speak to the nation in 1979. Ostensibly the speech was to be about the "oil" crisis that had resulted from an Arab oil boycott. Reacting to American support of Israel, Arab countries had refused to sell oil to the United States. President Carter believed that the issues and challenges facing the nation were more fundamental than long lines at the gas pumps.

DOCUMENT 30.1

Two Photographs: Vietnam and Kent State

The Napalm Girl: Kim Phuk

Source: Nick Ut, photographer, "The Napalm Girl: Kim Phuk," June 8, 1972.

Mary Vecchio Over the Body of Jeffrey Miller

Source: © John Filo/Valley News Dispatch. John Filo, photographer, Mary Vecchio over the body of Jeffrey Miller, May 4, 1970.

DOCUMENT 30.2

Peace with Honor

Richard M. Nixon

A cease-fire, internationally supervised, will begin at 7 p.m., this Saturday, January 27, Washington time.

Within 60 days from this Saturday, all Americans held prisoners of war throughout Indochina will be released. There will be the fullest possible accounting for all of those who are missing in action.

During the same 60-day period, all American forces will be withdrawn from South Vietnam.

The people of South Vietnam have been guaranteed the right to determine their own future, without outside interference.

By joint agreement, the full text of the agreement and the protocols to carry it out will be issued tomorrow.

Throughout these negotiations we have been in the closest consultation with President Thieu and other representatives of the Republic of Vietnam. This settlement meets the goals and has the full support of President Thieu and the Government of the Republic of Vietnam, as well as that of our other allies who are affected.

The United States will continue to recognize the Government of the Republic of Vietnam as the sole legitimate government of South Vietnam.

We shall continue to aid South Vietnam within the terms of the agreement, and we shall support efforts by the people of South Vietnam to settle their problems peacefully among themselves.

We must recognize that ending the war is only the first step toward building the peace. All parties must now see to it that this is a peace that lasts, and also a peace that heals—and a peace that not only ends the war in Southeast Asia but contributes to the prospects of peace in the whole world.

This will mean that the terms of the agreement must be scrupulously adhered to. We shall do everything the agreement requires of us, and we shall expect the other parties to do everything it requires of them. We shall also expect other interested nations to help insure that the agreement is carried out and peace is maintained.

As this long and very difficult war ends, I would like to address a few special words to each of those who have been parties in the conflict.

First, to the people and Government of South Vietnam: By your courage, by your sacrifice, you have won the precious right to determine your own future, and you have developed the strength to defend that right. We look forward to working with you in the future—friends in peace as we have been allies in war.

To the leaders of North Vietnam: As we have ended the war through negotiations, let us now build a peace of reconciliation. For our part, we are prepared

Source: From Richard M. Nixon, "Peace with Honor," radio-television broadcast, January 23, 1973, in *Public Papers of the Presidents of the United States: Richard Nixon, 1973* (Washington, DC: Government Printing Office, 1975), pp. 19–20.

to make a major effort to help achieve that goal. But just as reciprocity was needed to end the war, so too will it be needed to build and strengthen the peace.

To the other major powers that have been involved even indirectly: Now is the time for mutual restraint so that the peace we have achieved can last.

And finally, to all of you who are listening, the American people: Your steadfastness in supporting our insistence on peace with honor has made peace with honor possible. I know that you would not have wanted that peace jeopardized. With our secret negotiations at the sensitive stage they were in during this recent period, for me to have discussed publicly our efforts to secure peace would not only have violated our understanding with North Vietnam, it would have seriously harmed and possibly destroyed the chances for peace. Therefore, I know that you now can understand why, during these past several weeks, I have not made any public statements about those efforts.

The important thing was not to talk about peace, but to get peace—and to get the right kind of peace. This we have done.

Now that we have achieved an honorable agreement, let us be proud that America did not settle for a peace that would have betrayed our allies, that would have abandoned our prisoners of war, or that would have ended the war for us but would have continued the war for the 50 million people of Indochina. Let us be proud of the 2½ million young Americans who served in Vietnam, who served with honor and distinction in one of the most selfless enterprises in the history of nations. And let us be proud of those who sacrificed, who gave their lives so that the people of South Vietnam might live in freedom and so that the world might live in peace.

DOCUMENT 30.3

Richard Nixon's Resignation

From the discussions I have had with Congressional and other leaders, I have concluded that because of the Watergate matter, I might not have the support of the Congress that I would consider necessary to back the very difficult decisions and carry out the duties of this office in the way the interests of the Nation will require.

I have never been a quitter. To leave office before my term is completed is abhorrent to every instinct in my body. But as President, I must put the interests of America first. America needs a full-time President and a full-time Congress, particularly at this time with problems we face at home and abroad.

To continue to fight through the months ahead for my personal vindication would almost totally absorb the time and attention of both the President and the Congress in a period when our entire focus should be on the great issues of peace abroad and prosperity without inflation at home.

Source: Excerpted from Richard Nixon, resignation speech, radio-television broadcast, August 8, 1974, *Public Papers of the Presidents of the United States: Richard Nixon, 1974* (Washington, D.C.: Government Printing Office, 1975), pp. 627–29.

Therefore, I shall resign the Presidency effective at noon tomorrow. Vice President Ford will be sworn in as President at that hour in this office. . . .

For more than a quarter of a century in public life, I have shared in the turbulent history of this era. I have fought for what I believed in. I have tried, to the best of my ability, to discharge those duties and meet those responsibilities that were entrusted to me.

Sometimes I have succeeded and sometimes I have failed, but always I have taken heart from what Theodore Roosevelt once said about the man in the arena, "whose face is marred by dust and sweat and blood, who strives valiantly, who errs and comes short again and again because there is not effort without error and shortcoming, but who does actually strive to do the deed, who knows the great enthusiasms, the great devotions, who spends himself in a worthy cause, who at the best knows in the end the triumphs of high achievements and who at the worst, if he fails, at least fails while daring greatly."

I pledge to you tonight that as long as I have a breath of life in my body, I shall continue in that spirit. I shall continue to work for the great causes to which I have been dedicated throughout my years as a Congressman, a Senator, Vice President, and President, the cause of peace, not just for America but among all nations—prosperity, justice, and opportunity for all of our people.

There is one cause above all to which I have been devoted and to which I shall always be devoted for as long as I live.

When I first took the oath of office as President 5½ years ago, I made this sacred commitment: to "consecrate my office, my energies, and all the wisdom I can summon to the cause of peace among nations."

I have done my very best in all the days since to be true to that pledge. As a result of these efforts, I am confident that the world is a safer place today, not only for the people of America but for the people of all nations, and that all of our children have a better chance than before of living in peace rather than dying in war.

This, more than anything, is what I hoped to achieve when I sought the Presidency. This, more than anything, is what I hope will be my legacy to you, to our country, as I leave the Presidency.

To have served in this office is to have felt a very personal sense of kinship with each and every American. In leaving it, I do so with this prayer: May God's grace be with you in all the days ahead.

DOCUMENT 30.4

Withdrawal from Vietnam

Gerald R. Ford

During the past week, I had ordered the reduction of American personnel in the United States mission in Saigon to levels that could be quickly evacuated

Source: Gerald R. Ford, statement following evacuation of United States personnel from the Republic of Vietnam, April 29, 1975, in *Public Papers of the Presidents of the United States: Gerald Ford, 1975,* book 2, *January 1 to July 17, 1975* (Washington, DC: Government Printing Office, 1977), p. 605.

during an emergency, while enabling that mission to continue to fulfill its duties.

During the day on Monday, Washington time, the airport at Saigon came under persistent rocket as well as artillery fire and was effectively closed. The military situation in the area deteriorated rapidly.

I therefore ordered the evacuation of all American personnel remaining in South Vietnam.

The evacuation has been completed. I commend the personnel of the Armed Forces who accomplished it as well as Ambassador Graham Martin and the staff of his mission, who served so well under difficult conditions.

This action closes a chapter in the American experience. I ask all Americans to close ranks, to avoid recrimination about the past, to look ahead to the many goals we share, and to work together on the great tasks that remain to be accomplished.

DOCUMENT 30.5

Proclamation 4417: An American Promise

Gerald R. Ford

February 19 is the anniversary of a very, very sad day in American history. It was on that date in 1942 that Executive Order 9066 was issued resulting in the uprooting of many, many loyal Americans. Over 100,000 persons of Japanese ancestry were removed from their homes, detained in special camps, and eventually relocated.

We now know what we should have known then—not only was that evacuation wrong but Japanese-Americans were and are loyal Americans. On the battlefield and at home the names of Japanese-Americans have been and continue to be written in America's history for the sacrifices and the contributions they have made to the well-being and to the security of this, our common Nation.

Executive Order 9066 ceased to be effective at the end of World War II. Because there was no formal statement of its termination, there remains some concern among Japanese-Americans that there yet may be some life in that obsolete document. The proclamation [4417] that I am signing here today should remove all doubt on that matter.

I call upon the American people to affirm with me the unhyphenated American promise that we have learned from the tragedy of that long ago experience—forever to treasure liberty and justice for each individual American and resolve that this kind of error shall never be made again.

Source: Gerald R. Ford, remarks upon signing a proclamation concerning Japanese-American internment during World War II, February 19, 1976, in *Public Papers of the Presidents of the United States: Gerald Ford, 1975, 1976* (Washington, DC: Government Printing Office, 1978), p. 366.

DOCUMENT 30.6

Death of Elvis Presley

Jimmy Carter

Elvis Presley's death deprives our country of a part of itself. He was unique and irreplaceable. More than 20 years ago, he burst upon the scene with an impact that was unprecedented and will probably never be equaled. His music and his personality, fusing the styles of white country and black rhythm and blues, permanently changed the face of American popular culture. His following was immense, and he was a symbol to people the world over of the vitality, rebelliousness, and good humor of his country.

Source: Jimmy Carter, "Death of Elvis Presley," August 17, 1977, in the *Public Papers of the Presidents of the United States,* Book II—June 25 to December 31, 1977 (Washington, D.C.: Government Printing Office).

DOCUMENT 30.7

Three Mile Island

Bill Whittock:

The accident occurred around four o'clock in the morning on Wednesday, March 28. I was sleeping and became aware of this explosive release of steam over at the plant. There was a roar, a *terrific* roar. It woke me up and I jumped out of bed. I looked across the river and saw the column of steam that was escaping. It roared for about five minutes. It stopped and then it started to roar again.

About the second time, it eased off until there was just a relatively small column of steam which just kept hissing pretty near all morning. I went back to sleep because the plant had erupted about ten times before and I thought it was just an ordinary disturbance like we've been going through for the last several years.

About seven o'clock when I got up I heard on the radio that there had been a radioactive release. Then I went uptown to get the mail. I could sense a metallic taste in the air when I got outside. I asked up at the marina if the people up there had sensed this taste. Two of them did.

About nine-thirty a helicopter came in and landed up here in the field. There was a TV crew that came down. That was when I began to realize that it was pretty serious.

* * *

Source: Excerpted from Robert Leppzer, *Voices from Three Mile Island: The People Speak Out* (Trumansburg, NY: Crossing Press, 1980), pp. 1, 16–18.

Fran Cain:

Q.: Do you ever worry about the dosages of radiation that you might have received living so close to the plant?

Yes I do continually. During the accident I was worried about the animals, I was worried about the child, I was worried about the home—what was going to happen if a meltdown were to occur. I still live in fear. I have nightmares. I have not really slept well. Nerve-wise, all I have to do is look out my dining room window and see Unit 2 of Three Mile Island, directly across the street.

When I started my poodle business, I was very green. It has taken me thirteen years to get where I am now, producing champion dogs. My main objective over the years has been to improve the toy poodle strain. I'm deeply hurt because this has disrupted my life. It has affected me both mentally and physically. Nerves are one thing. I have been ill. Whether it's gall bladder, hernia or what, my body keeps acting up continually, so much so that I cannot operate my grooming shop alone. I've had to call in extra help. I get only a commission out of my own business, believe it or not, because I am not able, physically or mentally, to do the grooming by myself any more.

I can't concentrate on my work. My mind will go back to what is going on over on the island—how truthful they're being to us, whether they're lying some more, what they are doing with the water, if anything is escaping. This goes through my mind continually, night and day.

I don't feel safe. If I leave my house for the day to go shopping or to go into Harrisburg or do something on business, I'm constantly thinking, if there's anything wrong over there, am I going to be able to get back to get my dogs out of here?

Q.: How has the accident changed your life?

I feel that I am endangered continually, even now after the accident, as I was at the beginning. I have one daughter in tenth grade who concerns me. I've called realtors in. I've been in touch with Mr. Arnold, Vice-President of Met. Ed. He offered to help and sent a representative in. I told him I definitely want to move. He said they would come back but they haven't done anything.

I have a problem because I have a kennel of twenty-three to twenty-five dogs and have to relocate in an area where it's zoned agricultural. If it weren't for that, if it were just my husband and my daughter and myself, I would pick up and I would be long gone. I would not stay here. The homes that are being sold down here are being sold at a loss. I heard about one man down the street who got $10,000 less than what he was actually asking. I can't afford to do that.

Q.: So you feel like you're in a real bind?

Definitely in a bind. I would like to get out. During the accident, we evacuated the kennel for approximately nine days. I went to the NRC and they told us to move all the breeding stock out because of the proximity to the plant. The bill was over $1,000. I submitted a claim to American Nuclear Insurance.

Q.: Did you receive reimbursement?

No. None at all. I have the letter. It stated that "I *may* have sustained a substantial loss." Well, I definitely did. They have never reimbursed me one dime.

I have a "FOR SALE" sign on my home, but it's very hard for me to relocate. Because of the dogs, I'd have to find land that was zoned agricultural. I really feel we are trapped here. Financially, I just cannot walk out of this house and relocate. It's almost impossible the way mortgage and interest rates are today.

Q.: Have you had a hard time getting offers from people to buy your house?

Yes. Somebody made the remark they'd give me $10,000 for it. (laughs) The homes in this vicinity today are worth about $55,000. I have a business, my grooming shop, that I would have to sell also when I sell the home. I have between $85 and $90,000 tied up here between the home and the business.

Q.: What have you been offered for it?

The only offer I had was for $10,000.

Q.: That was the only one?

Yes.

Q.: And other than that, nobody wants to buy your house?

That's right.

Q.: So what are you going to do?

Wait it out and see what takes place across the road.

DOCUMENT 30.8

"Malaise" Speech

Jimmy Carter

Ten days ago I had planned to speak to you again about a very important subject—energy. For the fifth time I would have described the urgency of the problem and laid out a series of legislative recommendations to the Congress. But as I was preparing to speak, I began to ask myself the same question that I now know has been troubling many of you. Why have we not been able to get together as a nation to resolve our serious energy problem?

It's clear that the true problems of our Nation are much deeper—deeper than gasoline lines or energy shortages, deeper even than inflation or recession.

Source: Excerpted from Jimmy Carter, "Malaise" speech, 1979. In *Public Papers of the Presidents of the United States*, Book II—June 23 to December 31, 1979. Washington, D.C.: Government Printing Office. Available at www.rightwingnews.com/speeches/carter.php.

And I realize more than ever that as President I need your help. So, I decided to reach out and listen to the voices of America. . . .

But after listening to the American people I have been reminded again that all the legislation in the world can't fix what's wrong with America. So, I want to speak to you first tonight about a subject even more serious than energy or inflation. I want to talk to you right now about a fundamental threat to American democracy.

I do not mean our political and civil liberties. They will endure. And I do not refer to the outward strength of America, a nation that is at peace tonight everywhere in the world, with unmatched economic power and military might.

The threat is nearly invisible in ordinary ways. It is a crisis of confidence. It is a crisis that strikes at the very heart and soul and spirit of our national will. We can see this crisis in the growing doubt about the meaning of our own lives and in the loss of a unity of purpose for our Nation.

The erosion of our confidence in the future is threatening to destroy the social and the political fabric of America.

The confidence that we have always had as a people is not simply some romantic dream or a proverb in a dusty book that we read just on the Fourth of July. It is the idea which founded our Nation and has guided our development as a people. Confidence in the future has supported everything else—public institutions and private enterprise, our own families, and the very Constitution of the United States. Confidence has defined our course and has served as a link between generations. We've always believed in something called progress. We've always had a faith that the days of our children would be better than our own.

Our people are losing that faith, not only in government itself but in the ability as citizens to serve as the ultimate ruler and shapers of our democracy. As a people we know our past and we are proud of it. Our progress has been part of the living history of America, even the world. We always believed that we were part of a great movement of humanity itself called democracy, involved in the search for freedom, and that belief has always strengthened us in our purpose. But just as we are losing our confidence in the future, we are also beginning to close the door on our past.

In a nation that was proud of hard work, strong families, close-knit communities, and our faith in God, too many of us now tend to worship self-indulgence and consumption. Human identity is no longer defined by what one does, but by what one owns. But we've discovered that owning things and consuming things does not satisfy our longing for meaning. We've learned that piling up material goods cannot fill the emptiness of lives which have no confidence or purpose.

The symptoms of this crisis of the American spirit are all around us. For the first time in the history of our country a majority of our people believe that the next 5 years will be worse than the past 5 years. Two-thirds of our people do not even vote. The productivity of American workers is actually dropping, and the willingness of Americans to save for the future has fallen below that of all other people in the Western world.

As you know, there is a growing disrespect for government and for churches and for schools, the news media, and other institutions. This is not a message of happiness or reassurance, but it is the truth and it is a warning.

These changes did not happen overnight. They've come upon us gradually over the last generation, years that were filled with shocks and tragedy.

We were sure that ours was a nation of the ballot, not the bullet, until the murders of John Kennedy and Robert Kennedy and Martin Luther King, Jr. We were taught that our armies were always invincible and our causes were always just, only to suffer the agony of Vietnam. We respected the Presidency as a place of honor until the shock of Watergate.

We remember when the phrase "sound as a dollar" was an expression of absolute dependability, until 10 years of inflation began to shrink our dollar and our savings. We believed that our Nation's resources were limitless until 1973, when we had to face a growing dependence on foreign oil.

These wounds are still very deep. They have never been healed.

Looking for a way out of this crisis, our people have turned to the Federal Government and found it isolated from the mainstream of our Nation's life. Washington, D.C., has become an island. The gap between our citizens and our Government has never been so wide. The people are looking for honest answers, not easy answers; clear leadership, not false claims and evasiveness and politics as usual.

What you see too often in Washington and elsewhere around the country is a system of government that seems incapable of action. You see a Congress twisted and pulled in every direction by hundreds of well-financed and powerful special interests. You see every extreme position defended to the last vote, almost to the last breath by one unyielding group or another. You often see a balanced and a fair approach that demands sacrifice, a little sacrifice from everyone, abandoned like an orphan without support and without friends.

Often you see paralysis and stagnation and drift. You don't like it, and neither do I. What can we do?

First of all, we must face the truth, and then we can change our course. We simply must have faith in each other, faith in our ability to govern ourselves, and faith in the future of this Nation. Restoring that faith and that confidence to America is now the most important task we face. It is a true challenge of this generation of Americans.

31

Standing Tall

Like the script of a television show or movie, Ronald Reagan, tall, confident, even inspiring, defeated President Carter in 1980. Reagan promised to bring America back to its former status as an unchallengeable super power and the bastion of truth, freedom, and democracy worldwide. Within the folds and wrinkles of Reagan's public imagery were economic policies and predilections that had long been at the core of the Republican Party's economic policy reactor. Among these was a desire to liberate business from the fetters of restrictive governmental controls in order to unlock prosperity for the whole nation. In the process, a new trend was unleashed, bringing into public favor the idea of smaller, less intrusive government, which empowered businesses through deregulation. In the process, corporate executives who utilized short-term strategies for quick profits were becoming new American heroes. The result was a shake-up in American corporations that benefited a few and jettisoned many from their previously held ideas about work and economic security. Ultimately, though, Reagan seems to have had as much influence on American culture as American economics as suggested by the selection by Sidney Blumenthal and Thomas Byrne Edsall.

Many have claimed Reagan's policies had a direct impact on the break-up of the Communist bloc and the ending of the Cold War. Whether he or others are given the credit or blame for this ultimately, President Bush, in his address to the nation on the 26th anniversary of the assassination of President Kennedy, was right in noting that Thanksgiving 1989 was going to be conducted in a different world than all the others for the previous 40 years. The end of the Cold War and America's victory in the Gulf War, however, could not keep George Bush in the White House. William Jefferson Clinton won the election of 1992 and proceeded to realign and retool the Democratic Party as well as politics in America. Clinton, a Democrat, was almost as effective as Reagan, now a Republican icon, had been in reshaping the political landscape. Republicans, striving to regain lost ground, responded with the "Contract with America."

Throughout these years, an epidemic was beginning to spread across the globe and invade the United States as well. It became a household word in the eighties, known simply as AIDS. Few people even knew its full name, acquired immune deficiency syndrome. AIDS the disease was initially misunderstood, as its victims, the medical community, and even governmental agencies attempted to make sense of it and devise treatment programs and search for a cure. In the meantime, its appearance on the pathological landscape may have had significant impact on the social behavior of Americans.

Standing tall in the saddle and coming back from defeatism and self-doubt seemed to be prescriptions for curing the ails of America. But the metaphor of "standing tall" and the reality of life in contemporary America for Native Americans had quite different implications. Reyna Green illustrates this as she tries to use humor as a salve for Native American pain and an instructive device to inspire reflection from another group's perspective.

DOCUMENT 30.1

Hostile Takeovers

Statement of Alvah H. Chapman, Jr.,
Chairman and CEO, Knight-Ridder, Inc.

Mr. CHAPMAN. Senator Proxmire, my name is Alvah Chapman. I'm the chairman and CEO of Knight-Ridder. We are a $2 billion communications company. Among other things, we publish newspapers in Akron, OH, where Mr. Mercer's company is headquartered and I am quite familiar with the situation that he was describing earlier and support his comments very strongly.

I would like to say that I am here not out of any concern or threat that might be coming to our company. Our company has 44 percent of our shares in the hands of our founding families, our officers, directors, and employees of our company. We don't feel that we are a potential target.

I am here as a concerned American businessman about what's happening to American business and what's happening to the economy of our country because of this takeover activity. And I'd like to make some comments about that.

I have prepared longer comments which presumably will be in the record but in your interest I will try to shorten this to the 5 minutes that you have requested.

The CHAIRMAN. Without objection, your statement will be printed in full in the record.

Mr. CHAPMAN. Thank you, sir.

Source: From Alvah H. Chapman, Jr., testimony before the Committee on Banking, Housing, and Urban Affairs, U.S. Senate, 100th Congress, 1st Session, "Examination of the need for reform of the procedures and practices of insider trading, financing of hostile take-overs and their effect on the economy and international competitiveness," January 28, March 4, and April 8, 1987 (Washington, DC: Government Printing Office, 1987).

MOCKERY OF TRADITIONAL VALUES

Some people say that the hostile takeover craze is a spur to good management. I say just the opposite is true. Hostile takeovers are the strongest incentive to bad management in America today. Takeover mania has made a mockery of traditional American values.

Americans have long been proud of the free enterprise system and risk rewards that it produces. When a new product was conceived, it was produced with quality and efficiency. Markets were sought, companies were built, jobs were created, communities were benefited, and the national economy was strengthened.

Most companies that succeeded were managed for the long term. Now the corporate raiders are trying to turn the American economy into a money game. Hostile takeovers create no new wealth but merely shift ownership and replace equity with large amounts of debt.

The threat and/or reality of hostile takeovers without an orderly process to protect shareholders' interest encourages management to concentrate on the short term to the detriment of long-term development and growth.

Speculators may make quick, short-term profit, but at what cost? Employees may lose jobs, pension rights, and other benefits. Communities are disrupted. Major companies are sold off and sometimes closed as though the U.S. economy were a large Monopoly game.

Restructured companies rarely have budgets for research or start new businesses or contribute to the local United Way. The long-term investments rarely get priority.

One of my major concerns is that the human toll in takeovers is often ignored. How many of the takeover artists have ever visited a company, ever talked to an employee group, ever looked into the eyes of the people whose craftsmanship and ability and commitment built a company over many years?

There was an article in the December 14 *Los Angeles Times* which I will not describe in great detail, but it was written by a writer named John Lawrence. He talked about a young manager who was building his career and all of a sudden he was out of a job because the division in which he was involved decided that it couldn't be continued because they were under a threat of a takeover and had to close it down.

The human concern is a real concern of mine and to Peter Drucker, whose reputation in American business certainly needs no enhancement from me. Let me share with you Peter Drucker's comments.

Quoting from his recent book,

In the case of takeovers, Drucker adds, the only rationale is to enrich somebody who has nothing to do with the performance of the enterprise and who quite admittedly has not the slightest interest in it. And this goes against the grain of employees who feel that the hostile takeover treats them as chattel and not as a resource, let alone as human beings.

So much for the damaging effects on companies and the people who work for them. I contend the takeover trend is equally damaging to the economy as a whole. I have great concern about using a national resource—namely, debt—in a way that creates no new jobs, no new businesses, and no lasting value of any kind.

We all know that total U.S. corporate debt has increased alarmingly in recent years. It's now $1.2 trillion, according to an article I read in the current issue of *Time*.

DOCUMENT 31.2

Reaganite Culture

Ronald Reagan sought to use his presidency to do more than cut taxes and increase the military budget. From the beginning, his handlers spoke of their ultimate goal of fostering a political realignment that would lock in Republican power on the presidential level into the twenty-first century. To make this an enduring feat, they sought to control more than the dynamic of elections; they wanted to transform society as well. Reagan seemed ideal to serve as the instrument for this ambitious venture. He was, after all, more than a pure-bred politician; he had descended to politics from the ether of popular culture. In his first race, he finessed the "actor issue" by casting himself as a "citizen-politician," asserting his lack of qualification precisely as his salient qualification. He aspired to be the enchanting ruler of society, over which he would spread "stardust." But the White House political directorate thought little about culture, which in any case was not as malleable as the White House press corps. The Reagan managers never went beyond public relations, never beyond acts such as negotiating for a cover photo on *Parade* magazine of the oldest president in a white T-shirt lifting weights.

At its height, before the Iran-contra scandal, Reaganism put the country in a warm bath, which may have had a short-term therapeutic effect. This was not a continuation of what Harold Rosenberg called "the tradition of the new," a tradition that is more than twentieth-century modernism: it is the cultural essence of American progress. Nostalgia was at the center of the Reaganite aesthetic, which fed upon the cultural debris of the past. Because it was inherently backward-looking, Reaganism had no redemptive power and was ultimately disabling. There was no cultural realignment on which to rest a presumptive political realignment. . . .

Source: Excerpted from Sidney Blumenthal and Thomas Byrne Edsall, eds., *The Reagan Legacy* (New York: Pantheon Books, 1988), pp. 259–60, 284–85.

Another current that flourished under Reagan was that of evangelism. It was more than simply a religious expression; it was political and cultural, too. Reagan's chief contribution to this development was encouragement. "I endorse you," he told a convention of right-wing religious broadcasters. Though he claimed to be "born again" and occasionally regaled visitors with stream-of-consciousness chat about Armageddon, Reagan's attachment to the creed seemed entirely political and rhetorical. As he noted during the 1984 campaign, he never attended church because of fear of terrorist attack. His children showed no evidence of religious training or interest, though Patti did marry her yoga instructor.

The cultural explosion of the evangelicals was partly made possible by modern telecommunications. There were television shows, cable networks, radio stations, "Christian" pop singers like Amy Grant, and "Christian" record labels. Novel means advanced the old-time religion. Though some "Christian" music was presented in the form of MTV-like videos, the chief style was kitsch. For example, the mainstay programming of the Christian Broadcasting Network was not "The 700 Club," the talk show hosted by the network's owner, the Reverend Pat Robertson, but old television series from the 1950s. Apparently, kitsch in black and white was traditional culture.

The enemy, according to the religious right, was a demonic secular humanism, which encompassed most of contemporary American culture. Curiously, Reagan and Reaganism were seen as standing apart, somehow untainted. The president, of course, rhetorically supported the religious-right agenda, lending it legitimacy. But the movement's acceptance of him went beyond the political. To them, he was a cultural hero. The fundamentalists assailed the popular culture as profane, but a creature of neokitsch was seen as sacred. Perhaps because Reagan seemed to fit the category of black-and-white kitsch, he was regarded as a defender of the traditional. The host of "Death Valley Days" and "General Electric Theater" was the moral guardian of My Little Margie and Lassie.

The neokitsch aesthetic—the true Reaganite aesthetic—had few self-conscious exponents (apart from Ron Reagan). It was ironic that it did not claim advocates among those who argued most strongly for the return to the past as the source of virtue and cultural coherence. It was even more revealing that the so-called traditionalists neglected to sustain a criticism of Reaganite culture.

DOCUMENT 31.3

Breaking Down the Berlin Wall

George Bush

On other Thanksgivings, the world was haunted by the images of watchtowers, guard dogs, and machineguns. In fact, many of you had not even been born

Source: From George Bush, Thanksgiving address to the nation, November 22, 1989, in *Public Papers of the Presidents of the United States: George Bush, 1989*, book 2, *July 1 to December 31, 1989* (Washington, DC: Government Printing Office, 1990), pp. 1581–82.

when the Berlin Wall was erected in 1961. But now the world has a new image, reflecting a new reality: that of Germans, East and West, pulling each other to the top of the wall, a human bridge between nations; entire peoples all across Eastern Europe bravely taking to the streets, demanding liberty, pursuing democracy. This is not the end of the book of history, but it's a joyful end to one of history's saddest chapters.

Not long after the wall began to open, West German Chancellor Kohl telephoned, and he asked me to give you, the American people, a message of thanks. He said that the remarkable change in Eastern Europe would not be taking place without the steadfast support of the United States—fitting praise from a good friend. For 40 years, we have not wavered in our commitment to freedom. We are grateful to our American men and women in uniform, and we should also be grateful to our postwar leaders. You see, we helped rebuild a continent through the Marshall plan; and we built a shield, NATO, behind which Americans, Europeans could forge a future in freedom.

For so many of these 40 years, the test of Western resolve, the contest between the free and the unfree, has been symbolized by an island of hope behind the Iron Curtain: Berlin. In the 1940's, West Berlin remained free because Harry Truman said: Hands off! In the 1950's, Ike backed America's words with muscle. In the 1960's, West Berliners took heart when John F. Kennedy said: "I am a Berliner." In the 1970's, Presidents Nixon, Ford, and Carter stood with Berlin by standing with NATO. And in the 1980's, Ronald Reagan went to Berlin to say: "Tear down this wall!" And now we are at the threshold of the 1990's. And as we begin the new decade, I am reaching out to President Gorbachev, asking him to work with me to bring down the last barriers to a new world of freedom. Let us move beyond containment and once and for all end the cold war.

We can make such a bold bid because America is strong and 40 years of perseverance and patience are finally paying off. More recently, quiet diplomacy, working behind the scenes, has achieved results. We can now dare to imagine a new world, with a new Europe, rising on the foundations of democracy. This new world was taking shape when my Presidency began with these words: "The day of the dictator is over." And during the spring and summer we told the people of the world what America believes and what America wants for the future. America believes that "liberty is an idea whose time has come in Eastern Europe." America wants President Gorbachev's reforms, known as *perestroika*, to succeed. And America wants the Soviets to join us in moving beyond containment to a new partnership. Some wondered if all this was realistic. And now, though we are still on the course set last spring, events are moving faster than anyone imagined or predicted.

Look around the world. In the developing nations, the people are demanding freedom. Poland and Hungary are now fledgling democracies—a non-Communist government in Poland and free elections coming soon in Hungary. And in the Soviet Union itself, the forces of reform under Mikhail Gorbachev are bringing unprecedented openness and change. But nowhere in the world today, or even in the history of man, have the warm hearts of men and women triumphed so swiftly, so certainly, over cold stone as in Berlin, indeed, in all of East Germany. If I may paraphrase the words of a great poet, Robert Frost: There is certainly something in us that doesn't love a wall.

DOCUMENT 31.4

Contract with America

As Republican Members of the House of Representatives and as citizens seeking to join that body we propose not just to change its policies, but even more important, to restore the bonds of trust between the people and their elected representatives.

That is why, in this era of official evasion and posturing, we offer instead a detailed agenda for national renewal, a written commitment with no fine print.

This year's election offers the chance, after four decades of one-party control, to bring to the House a new majority that will transform the way Congress works. That historic change would be the end of government that is too big, too intrusive, and too easy with the public's money. It can be the beginning of a Congress that respects the values and shares the faith of the American family.

Like Lincoln, our first Republican president, we intend to act "with firmness in the right, as God gives us to see the right." To restore accountability to Congress. To end its cycle of scandal and disgrace. To make us all proud again of the way free people govern themselves.

On the first day of the 104th Congress, the new Republican majority will immediately pass the following major reforms, aimed at restoring the faith and trust of the American people in their government:

FIRST, require all laws that apply to the rest of the country also apply equally to the Congress;

SECOND, select a major, independent auditing firm to conduct a comprehensive audit of Congress for waste, fraud or abuse;

THIRD, cut the number of House committees, and cut committee staff by one-third;

FOURTH, limit the terms of all committee chairs;

FIFTH, ban the casting of proxy votes in committee;

SIXTH, require committee meetings to be open to the public;

SEVENTH, require a three-fifths majority vote to pass a tax increase;

EIGHTH, guarantee an honest accounting of our Federal Budget by implementing zero base-line budgeting.

Source: Contract with America, 1994. Available at www.nationalcenter.org/ContractwithAmerica.html.

DOCUMENT 31.5

America in the Age of AIDS

Elinor Burkett

Nobody talked about AIDS, but that was hardly surprising. By the late 1980s, America seemed intent on ignoring dozens of problems, from crumbling highways to the burgeoning number of homeless. The truth of poverty, racism and corporate greed was disguised in euphemism. The reality of a plague was a mere whisper.

But the silence shrouding AIDS was more deafening in Miami than in other epicenters of infection. Miami wasn't squalid enough to provide a convincing backdrop for a plague. Trim young bodies in skimpy bikinis and sundresses paraded along Ocean Drive. Even the senior citizens sported tans as they carried tennis rackets to the courts.

By the time the first young victims of a new virus were being buried, Miami had also become the Cuban miracle, a sleepy backwater converted into the capital of Latin America by the drive of almost a million immigrants intent on proving Fidel Castro wrong. Ultramodern skyscrapers had begun to shade a downtown that just a decade earlier looked like a provincial city in the Dominican Republic. The port of Miami was packed with cruise ships competing for docking space with cargo ships signaling the city's arrival as the import-export center of Latin America.

No one was eager to acknowledge the misery beneath the makeup: that the young men driving Jaguar convertibles around town were paying their cellular phone bills with drug money; that the black community had missed out on the 1960s and still languished in virtual segregation; that the lack of a state income tax had left education, medical care and a wide range of social services on the level of that of rural Mississippi.

Miami, of all American cities, excelled at illusion.

The epidemic leached into a city of taboos, the most important of which forbade unpleasant truths. Miami was certainly not unique in its aversion to reality, but it enforced compliance to fantasy with singular viciousness. Those who didn't understand the city's first commandment—Thou shalt not speak the truth about certain issues—needed only to hear about the Miami radio announcer who had dared to praise some of Castro's reforms and was blown up, and left paralyzed, in response.

AIDS touched all of the city's rawest nerves. It first hit Little Haiti, a community still scarred by the terrors that had been Haiti's national history. It then grabbed hold of gay men whose nascent attempts to organize themselves had careened from a stunning victory in 1977, when Dade County commissioners passed one of the nation's first anti-discrimination laws, to a demoralizing

Source: Excerpted from Elinor Burkett, *The Gravest Show on Earth: America in the Age of AIDS* (Boston: Houghton Mifflin, 1995), pp. 1–4.

defeat in the face of the anti-gay hysteria whipped up by Anita Bryant. AIDS began to claim African American men, who pretended to be heroin addicts rather than admit to homosexuality.

The virus spread through a city with no meaningful history of free speech; denial reached fever pitch. What Hispanic and Haitian tradition did not quiet, a brand of Catholicism still untouched by the liberalizing precepts of Vatican II did. So when the first young Cuban men succumbed to the new disease, their mothers maintained their decorum and insisted that their sons had been devastated by cancer. When the first young Cuban women developed the odd pneumonias, no one dared talk about how common bisexuality was among Hispanic men.

On the surface, the city responded brilliantly. Largely because of the efforts of a young physician, Dr. Margaret Fischl, Miami's only public hospital developed a research program that quickly became one of the nation's principal AIDS research sites, well funded by the federal government and pharmaceutical companies. Across the street, the Veterans Administration Medical Center reached out to its infected constituency—mostly the homeless and the drug addicted—with a treatment program so sophisticated that the well-insured fought for access to its services. A group of lesbian and gay physicians responded to their community's need almost instantly, setting up specialized AIDS practices and keeping abreast of even the most experimental treatments.

Two brothers, both infected with HIV, talked their parents into converting their popular sports bar into Body Positive, an AIDS resource center where gay men could go for seminars on new treatments, advice on everything from housing to Social Security, or a cup of coffee and an hour of comfort. A young Puerto Rican graduate of an overseas medical school opened a center to promote AIDS awareness in the Hispanic community. And the city's Haitian population formed its own AIDS coalition to mobilize Haitian physicians against the epidemic and to fight the branding of Haitians as "high risks" for AIDS.

But as with so much else in AIDS, these were little more than illusions. . . .

Body Positive was racked by three years of the same kind of infighting that divided AIDS service organizations all across America; it didn't succumb, but it barely survived. And the Hispanic AIDS center became a constant source of suspicion when it moved out of a poor minority neighborhood into an affluent Anglo suburb. When the local chapter of the AIDS activist group ACT UP received $25,000 from a national fundraising campaign, it held no demonstrations. It bought no newspaper ads, printed no eye-catching fliers, forced no change in the city's policy of ignoring AIDS. ACT UP used the money to buy certificates of deposit. The People with AIDS Coalition kicked one long-time member off its board after he missed the group's annual retreat. The fact that he had been caring for his best friend, who was dying of AIDS, was not deemed a valid excuse. Refugees terrified that immigration officials would discover that they were HIV positive and deport them refused to seek medical assistance. Quacks peddling everything from lemons to electric therapy treatments preyed on the vulnerable, untouched by state health enforcement officials.

And the party continued on Miami Beach, where Gay America went to take a vacation from safe sex.

During my first year or two in the city, I thought the problems were unique to Miami—and vowed to shake things up. I naively thought that if I told the truth the problems would disappear. I was seriously deluded. The problems weren't so much indifference to the plight of the sick as a dozen competing agendas—political, economic, scientific and social—that had nothing to do with the growing number of obituaries of thirty-five-year-olds. But that truth, about AIDS and America, unfolded slowly in story after story.

DOCUMENT 31.6

Native American Ironic Humor

Rayna Green (Cherokee)

So I tried to think about what use Indian scholars like myself can be to Indian people. And I thought of all kinds of things. You know, we write all the time and do research and I'm grateful that Owanah and Ohoyo gave me the chance to do something that would actually get out to Indian people: the bibliography on Native women. Most of the things I write get published in places that no one will ever read them and so I'm always grateful for the chance to do something that will be useful to Indian people. I want to tell you about a few of those things that scholars, young Indian scholars, like myself, and one much better than I am, are involved in and there's some very exciting things. I want to share those with you.

One of those things, for example, we are involved in, a number of us are now consulting for some new TV series, Norman Lear, who has produced the soap, *Maude*—all these TV situation comedies—now we are producing Indian TV situation comedies. I really am so excited about this. Just think, Indian people will be on television. They won't be saying, "Um, my people call it Mazola." We have been changing this to actually produce real Indian commercials. Toni Eagleshield is going to come out and she is going to say, "You people call them mushrooms, my people call them magic." She's going to have a little white powder in one spoon and she's going to say, "My people call it . . . (Smiling and deeply sniffing.) We've been thinking of giving her a glue tube, but we decided that would be tacky. We know you will share in the excitement of these new commercials. We really believe we can sell the products. We're marketing a commercial fry bread mix very soon. Owanah doesn't know it yet but she's going to pose for it. She's going to be the Indian Aunt Jemima. We knew you'd be happy about that.

But the two things that excite us most are two serials we're working on. Charlie Hill and some of us are working on a Navajo soap opera. It's about a

Source: Excerpted from Ronald K. Burke, ed., *American Public Discourse: A Multicultural Perspective* (Lanham, MD: University Press of America, 1992), pp. 24–27.

modest little Navajo family, a bunch of sheepherders, and it's called *Yazzie and Harriet*. The most exciting one is an Indian science fiction serial. It's (called) *Skin Trek*. We're very excited about that too. The computer is an old Indian man that calls everyone "my son" and leads them all astray, regularly. "Yes, my son, go two million miles, turn right . . . " Well, that's one of the things we're involved in doing. . . .

But the thing I'm most excited about recently is the grand project. This is a multi-million dollar project, it's been funded by all the major foundations in the country. It's very exciting. As you know, all over the country, the Cherokee Nation and many of the Indian nations all over the country have established their own museums. I've done a great deal of museum consulting for the National Endowment and for the tribal museums, for the Indian Museum Association. But I had found a real lack of a particular kind of museum that I really feel we need. And this is going to be a major cultural institution. I want to tell you about it because I am so thrilled to be part of this. This idea, I have to give credit, was originally hatched up by the ex-chairman of the Winnebago tribe, (Louis) LaRose, and myself, late one night in a serious scholarly discussion in Albuquerque. Basically what we want to develop is a unique, cultural institution. I know you will be thrilled. This is an institution that is meant for Indian people. It is something we've been needing for a long time. Its something that is particularly needed to meet a very special, critical need. The museum is called *Museum of the Plains White Person*. It meets this critical need that I spoke of. It's very serious. You see, we began to be very worried. As you know their (White people's) culture is dying out. Very soon, very soon there will be very few White persons. We worry about this. What will the last surviving White person do when they have no one to ask what their language was like, what their customs and clothes were like. So, we began to worry about this and we came up with the idea of the *Museum of the Plains White Person*. As I said, it's been met with great reception all over the country. Foundations have rushed to pour money in. Indian people have given money for it. I can't tell you how many shawl and blanket raffles have gone on to pay for this museum. And I want to tell you something about the museum and perhaps this will inspire some of you to go to those few White people that you know are living out there and quickly acquire artifacts from them before they disappear. Because, you know, they don't know how to take care of them. We worry about this. It's quite serious.

The first big collection that we are working on, and this is really inspiring, is the bone collection. As you know, all museums have to have a bone collection. We have begun a national campaign to acquire the bones of famous White people. We want little Indian children to be able to come in and study these and Indian scholars want to pore over them, the different skull shapes and so forth. And, of course, when we do acquire them we will acquire them permanently. As you know, they cannot be given back once they have been handled. We do need to study them for years. And so we are acquiring these. We have just acquired, I think, what is a quite moving find. One of the most important ones. We have just acquired the bones of John Wayne. As you realize what great significance this can have for the scholars, what a study of his bones will tell us about these people and what their lives were like. Well, so that's very important.

There are a number of other famous bones that we want to acquire and I am sure you can begin to guess whose we have our sights on. It's going to be thrilling. The collection will be quite large, of course. We have planned to make the collection as large as it needs to be with as many samples. So, we are going to begin a massive grave excavation all over the country. We have, through our legal offices, which have become very sophisticated, as you know, acquired clear title to at least 80 percent of all the graves in White cemeteries all over the country. We plan to move in with steam shovels right away. We've acquired Mr. Peabody's big coal shovel which did strip mining up at Northern Cheyenne in order to begin and it's going to be an amazing project.

I'll tell you a few things about some of the other collections that I think are quite exciting. We are going to have collections of their food, for example— their food ways. We are going to reconstruct a McDonald's in its entirety. In that we're going to have true-to-life plastic exhibits of white bread, mayonnaise, iceberg lettuce and peanut butter which will be everywhere—smeared all over everything. Primarily stuck to the roof of everyone's mouth. We are going to have several exhibits about their customs. We want to have some performing arts there and we have found the last of a number of White people who know their dances and songs and who have preserved these intact and we are going to have everyday, living exhibits of the two-step, the fox-trot, the disco and other dances. This is going to be very exciting when children come to visit, particularly.

We have acquired exhibits of their costumes. In fact, in the condominium that we are going to reconstruct in its entirety, inside the museum, there will be a typical little family with the gentleman in the three-piece suit and a briefcase and the other artifacts of their civilization.

We have found one very unusual thing that I do want to tell you about. It's an archaeological remain that we have found somewhat in the vicinity of what used to be called "Los Angeles." It's very interesting. It proves that their culture was very flighty. They seemed to change rulers quite regularly. It's kind of interesting. In fact, we found an archaeological artifact that indicates that they changed rulers regularly. It's a big thing they used to call a neon sign—and it says "Queen for a Day." We are going to do some more excavation to determine just how they did depose their rulers and how they transferred power.

Well, I think you'll agree that this is one of the most exciting things that Indian people have done—one of the most exciting contributions that we could make. As young Indian scholars we are deeply pleased to be able to make this. I should tell you something about the Board of Trustees. It will be composed entirely of distinguished Indian people and one little old White lady from Nebraska who speaks no Indian languages. However, she is going to be the representative for the total culture as we feel that anyone of her age and status would be able to speak for all of them. We know they'll be pleased to have a representative. We did find her the other day and we plan to spray and fix her permanently so she will remain on the board.

32

Rainbows and Webs

The world has been shaped by technological innovations throughout this period. Now in the 21st century more advanced forms of communication have emerged, including a vast communication network of e-mail and instant messaging and virtual realities. All of this is partly the result of Department of Defense research conducted in the 1960s; an early report from that agency reveals that even then some of the implications of the work were foreseen. By the same token a different sort of "virtual" reality and electronic community has appeared on the landscape and become perhaps the hope and, at times, the bane of Native Americans. The casino movement, the creative utilization of tribal lands and, in some cases, antiquated "rights" of sovereignty have provided never before imagined revenue streams for some of the most impoverished people in America. As Native Americans bank the money that Anglo-Americans, pursuing dreams of quick riches and the easy life, may throw at them, the question of poetic balance is inescapable. For many tribal groups, it is, in a real way, "The return of the buffalo."

If Native Americans are searching for new ways to relate to the Anglo World, African Americans are also assessing their place in the mix. To say that progress has been made in sharing more life, liberty, and happiness with African America is an understatement. The Civil Rights movement and time itself have brought about legal, political, economic, and social transformations, as illustrated in the interviews Studs Terkel conducted in 1989 and 1990. In fighting hatred and intolerance, Morris Dees, the founder of the Southern Poverty Law Center, began to use civil suits creatively to bring justice for victims of hate. But Mr. Dees does not feel that his successes have solved the problem; the struggle against hatred must continue.

The status and position of women in America has improved as well. At the beginning of this period, American women suffered under legal statutes that denied them fundamental rights of property ownership and the right to vote. As victories were won to unlock rights both economic and political, the battle lines

have now moved to areas less obvious, clouded by competing rights and re-
sponsibilities. Such is the case with abortion and a woman's right to be the sole
voice in decisions regarding her body. Issues of life, liberty, and the pursuit of
happiness have been on the table numerous times as the Supreme Court has
been asked to decide complicated issues regarding competing rights.

Finally, the last two documents also illustrate significant cultural transfor-
mations since the Civil War; yet they also suggest the persistence of human
habits. The light of this inquiry has been refracted through the lens of "Life, Lib-
erty and the Pursuit of Happiness." When that phrase was first coined, the
phrase "pursuit of happiness" was a euphemism for the pursuit of property—the
assumption being that property was the major ingredient in the pursuit of hap-
piness. Since the inception of this nation, Americans have consistently and en-
thusiastically sought property. In so doing, an engine of prosperity has been
assembled from self-interest and combined individual activity. Distressingly,
there have been all too many instances where the pursuit of happiness in the
form of property has meant simply the pursuit of greed. The government of the
United States, powerful enough to solve issues of shared governance with states
and reign supreme through victory in the Civil War, has been an arena where the
propriety of government restraint of human desires—in this case greed—has
been debated and acted upon. For the common good, another rule, regulation,
and control has been instituted to protect the public from unscrupulous, greedy
individuals who would seek profit from financial finagling, if not outright fraud.

But the "pursuit of happiness" has in the years since the Civil War also
come to take on another, cultural meaning. Contemporary Americans seem to
understand the truth and value of that phrase as the "right to BE happy." In pur-
suing happiness and resisting restraints on individual happiness, American cul-
ture and society face many challenges balancing individual freedoms with
collective responsibilities. Though young people have the legal right to con-
sume alcohol, the last article suggests some of the consequences of the exer-
cise of that right. And that may suggest another truism—namely that the
overexercise of any right, privilege, ability, capability, or power, indeed
overindulgence itself, may be one of the major challenges stretching and test-
ing the ability of the United States of America "to secure these rights," through
governments "deriving their just powers from the consent of the governed . . . "

DOCUMENT 32.1

The Early Days of ARPANET

Somewhat expectedly, the network has facilitated a social change in the United
States computer research community. It has become *more convenient* for geographically separated groups to perform collaborative research and development. The ability to easily send files of text between geographically remote

Source: From Defense Advanced Research Projects Agency, *A History of the Arpanet: The First
Decade,* Report 4799, Boit Beranek and Newman, Inc., Arlington, VA, April 1, 1981.

groups, the ability to communicate via messages quickly and easily, and the ability to collaboratively use powerful editing and document production facilities has changed significantly the "feel" of collaborative research with remote groups. Just as other major improvements in human communication in the past have resulted in a change in the rate of progress, this social effect of the ARPANET may finally be the largest single impact of the ARPANET development.

A non-trivial question of considerable importance to the country is *why* the ARPANET project has been so successful. It would certainly be nice if the same formula could be applied to other pressing national needs. While timing, accident, and luck must not be discounted, it is possible to identify several possible contributing factors:

- Despite the fact that the ARPANET was a government project and further despite the fact that it was run within the Defense Department, it was possible, at least initially, to free the research and development from some of the constraints which often seriously hamper other activities. First, the project was entirely unclassified. Second, the provision of network service was for a very long time provided to government contractors as a "free good"; this allowed people to experiment with the use of the network without being forced to make early and probably ill-advised cost/benefit decisions. Third, despite, a valid government and Defense Department concern about unauthorized use of government facilities, it was possible to build the ARPANET without complex administrative procedures for access control. Finally, the ARPANET did not have to interconnect directly with other existing communication systems; it was possible to explore line protocols and interface standards *de novo*, in the best ways that could be devised. Thus, the ARPANET program was incredibly free of "artificial" requirements and was able to concentrate intensively on the primary required research and development. Much later in the project, after success had been assured, it was relatively easy to reopen consideration of some of these issues; and at the current time, for example, the Defense Communications Agency is charging user groups for network access, and there have been experiments (using private line interfaces) in the transmission of classified data over the ARPANET, and research was done on how to implement network login procedures, etc., etc.
- A very convenient fact was the common DARPA support of both the "network authority" and the initial early group of network users. It was possible for DARPA to strongly encourage a cooperative attitude and cooperative engineering at the time in the project when such cooperation was most critically necessary.

In sum, the project was an illustration of what can be accomplished with strong technically sophisticated central management, adequate resources, and a clear-headed undeviating concentration on the central research and development issues.

The largest single surprise of the ARPANET program has been the incredible popularity and success of network mail. There is little doubt that the techniques of network mail developed in connection with the ARPANET program are going to sweep the country and drastically change the techniques used for intercommunication in the public and private sectors.

DOCUMENT 32.2

Native American Casinos

Testimony of Arlyn Ackley, Sr., Tribal Chairman Sokaogon Chippewa Community

Mr. Chairman, Members of the Committee, my name is Arlyn Ackley, Sr., Tribal Chairman of the Mole Lake Band of the Lake Superior Chippewa Tribe. Our Sokaogon Chippewa Community is located at the Mole Lake Indian Reservation in Northern Wisconsin. Mole Lake is the smallest, poorest Tribe in Wisconsin. It is located in the State's Northeastern region within Forest County. . . .

With the County's economy dominated by the recession sensitive forest products and tourism industries, few Tribal members found gainful employment. These conditions are further documented by high unemployment rates of Tribal members throughout a 30-year period. Before gaming, Reservation unemployment was 84%; it still is at 35%. Furthermore, as late as 1988 only 5% of the on-reservation adult members had an income above $7,000 annually. Despite poor economic conditions Tribal members have continued to return to the reservation. Many Tribal members living in urban centers were displaced by the Midwest's economic restructuring in the 1980's. Others returned home to escape urban poverty and violence. In effect, the BIA relocation programs of the 1950's and 1960's are now working in reverse. Within the last 30 years, the reservation's population has increased 369%. Given the Tribe has an enrollment population of 1,128, future service population increases are highly likely.

A number of years ago, Mole Lake established a small gaming enterprise which has provided jobs for some of our people and created a small stream of income for Tribal programs. Indian gaming jobs are not for everyone who needs a job, but they have provided some hope for some of our people. Yet, we are still at the bottom economically. We cannot meet even the most basic needs of our people. And every day the Tribe faces new challenges that require immediate attention.

The federal government's historic failure to meet its trust responsibility has created a 140-year backlog of reservation infrastructure needs for transportation, housing, education, health care, and business development. To address

Source: From Arlyn Ackley, Sr., Testimony before the Committee on Government Reform and Oversight, House of Representatives, 105th Congress, 2nd Session, January 21, 22, 28, and 29, 1998, "The Department of the Interior's Denial of the Wisconsin Chippewa's Casino Applications," vol. 1, (Washington, DC: Government Printing Office, 1998).

these unmet needs and provide basic services to our growing Tribal population, Mole Lake has adopted a strategy of concurrently developing Tribal economic, governmental, and social infrastructure.

The Tribe supports all efforts to expand and diversify the region's economic base as long as the new employment opportunities are created in non-polluting, self-sustaining industries. Net profits from gaming have been targeted for use through a BIA approved plan. Mole Lakes net gaming revenues are allocated as follows.

- 30.5% for funding Tribal governmental operations and programs such as food distribution, Tribal courts, environmental protection, day care, and housing;
- 25.0% to support health programs, clinic expansion, human services, and education;
- 12.5% for Tribal economic development;
- 1.5% to supplement local fire protection and municipal services;
- 0.5% for donation to charitable organizations; and
- 30.0% for per capita distribution under formal guidelines established by the Tribal government and approved by the BIA.

Unfortunately, net gaming revenues are scarce. The Tribe's isolation from urban markets and the region's seasonal tourism economy greatly limit gaming's profitability on the reservation. Furthermore, being located within one of the poorest counties in the State leaves little chance for development of local gaming markets. While some Tribes may have the good fortune of considerable gaming revenue, Mole Lake is not one of them. Our limited revenues have enabled us to build a health clinic; however, we are unable to hire a doctor. Our daycare, which, we are trying to replace, is a veritable fire trap. We have a long list of Tribal members waiting to get decent housing. We have two and three families living in single family homes. Our needs are the unmet basic needs of Tribal members, not merely increasing income for individual members. While the BIA approved plan provides for a per capita payment to be made to Tribal members, there was no payment this year and last year the total payment was one hundred and ninety four dollars ($194.00).

In this context, when our Tribe was invited to join the Red Cliff and Lac Courte Oreilles Bands of Lake Superior Chippewa in a joint gaming venture, our Tribal Council decided to participate. This appeared as an opportunity to benefit ourselves and to help two other Tribes who were also located a great distance from gaming markets. However, before we joined the venture, I personally called the Tribal leaders of the surrounding Tribes and asked if they had any problems with Mole Lake participating in this venture. No Tribe at that time offered any opposition.

Once we decided to join the venture, we put forth a maximum effort utilizing what limited resources we had. I personally made contact with the BIA agency in Ashland to insure that we were taking all of the necessary steps to properly put this land in to trust. Any problems that were identified were immediately addressed by our staff and the agency. After a good deal of effort, we finally were able to satisfy the agency. Our proposal was approved (at least the part the agency was responsible for) and forwarded to the BIA Area Office in Minneapolis.

There the process seemed almost to start over, but our staffs continued to work closely with all the appropriate people in reviewing and analyzing the data necessary to complete every phase of our application. In order to once again insure that we were doing everything properly, my staff and I, along with representatives of the other Tribes, went to Minneapolis to meet with the BIA Area staff. We were instructed that not only did we have to complete the environmental study, but we had to provide a thirty (30) day period for others to comment on our actions. We did *everything* as we were asked to do. Finally, our application was approved and forwarded to the BIA Central Office in Washington D.C. I have served as Tribal Chairman for many years and my experience has been that once we received approval at the Area Office, it should have been a formality for this land to be placed in trust. I believe this because the Area Office is the closest and most familiar with the Tribes that could be affected by any trust application. In this particular case, the Area Office is literally "just across the river" from the City of Hudson, Wisconsin. I felt this proximity was an even greater benefit to our Tribes, since the Area Office would definitely be aware of any possible "detriment" to the local communities and surrounding Tribes.

There could have been some small areas in which we or the Area Office could have made a mistake, but the trust responsibility of the Federal government to the Tribes obligates the government to assist us and to provide us an opportunity to correct any errors that we may have made. I instructed my staff to make themselves available to the Central Office to answer any questions, which they did. We knew that the Area Office would have thoroughly examined all of the technical details of putting land in trust. There would be additional concerns raised by the Indian Gaming office of Interior. The Interior staff did in fact ask us to clarify several points, including one that would assure our Tribe of a right-of-way to the property. The technical staff at Interior worked closely with the Tribal staff and did not ever indicate to them that there would be any problem that could not be corrected. When no problems were disclosed but no approval was forthcoming, I began to wonder what the hold up was. I personally made a trip to the Department of Interior and met with Mr. Skibine, who told me that he had just been appointed to head the Indian Gaming Management Staff and would review it as soon as possible. After more time had passed with no communication or action, I returned for a second meeting with Mr. Skibine. It was at this time he informed me that John Duffy had met with the Minnesota Congressional delegation and some Tribes who were opposing our application and had granted them an additional comment period. We would not have known about this additional period unless we had inquired about the delay.

We suffered through this period and were led to believe by Interior staff that no new problems had been identified and that competition alone would not be enough to be considered detrimental to surrounding Tribes. Environmental problems had been looked at several times. As for local opposition, a local referendum had been passed approving of gaming at the dog track and no subsequent referendum has rescinded the local approval. Every indication was that there was nothing of significance that would prevent our placing the land into trust. We believed we had met every requirement and had done everything that the Interior staff required of us.

You can understand my shock and indignation when our application was turned down, especially when my staff working with the Department of Interior's Indian Gaming staff were not told of any item that would cause our application to be rejected. There are two factors that are very relevant in this case. First, Interior just has not turned down applications that had been approved without reservations by the Area Office. Second, Interior should at least have provided us an opportunity to correct any problems that they found. These two principles were violated; we were given a final decision without recourse. I still question why were we not given opportunity to correct or at least respond to possible problems.

DOCUMENT 32.3

Race: The American Obsession

C. P. ELLIS

When the news came over the radio that Martin Luther King was assassinated, I got on the telephone and began to call other Klansmen. We just had a real party at the service station. Really rejoicin' 'cause that sonofabitch was dead. Our troubles are over with. They say the older you get, the harder it is for you to change. That's not necessarily true. Since I changed, I've set down and listened to tapes of Martin Luther King. I listen to it and tears come to my eyes, 'cause I know what he's sayin' now. I know what's happenin'. . . .

What worries me is that racism is getting worse. In the last ten years, the White House has been promoting it. It has become more open. There was a time when it was getting better, but these last two administrations have set it back. With Reagan and Bush, it's like a nod to say okay, try it again. And it's being tried.

I don't think anybody is born full of hate, born a racist. At the Democratic Convention, the cameras zoomed in on one Klansman. He was saying, "I hope Jesse Jackson gets AIDS and dies." I felt sympathy for him. That's the way my old friends used to think. Me, too. And my father.

After I left the Klan, I felt guilt, isolation, rejection. I wound up getting counseling. I was getting calls from former Klan friends, "You betrayed us." I began to question myself. But now at sixty-three, with this new light, I feel good about myself.

Source: Excerpted from interviews C. P. Ellis and Howard Clement in Studs Terkel, *Race: How Blacks and Whites Think and Feel about the American Obsession* (New York: New Press, 1992), pp. 278–86.

Sometimes I see my old Klan friends. Sometimes they speak to me, sometimes they don't. I don't worry about it. I wish them well; they're human beings. I think some of them changed a little bit.

But they're not willing to come out with it. They're afraid to change their own life because they're afraid of life. It would have been easier for me if I had gone on being a member of the Klan. It's been a struggle. Any change is.

My children have all changed along with me. They were with me when I was in the Klan and they painfully left with me. Now they feel the way I do. We used to say the word "nigger." Not anymore. When my oldest son came home with a black girl, I was shocked at first. It wasn't serious; he married somebody else. But when I met her, I felt like I was a great liberal. I don't like the word "liberal." I like the word "progressive."

Most of my friends in Durham are progressive, but there's an economic barrier. Their station is higher than mine. I don't feel comfortable in their homes. Sometimes I find myself standing in the corner in a social gathering and that ought not to be. But the black people in my union are progressive, too. I feel comfortable with them. . . .

I have the same fundamental beliefs I've had for a long time. But it's hard to find a church out here that preaches the social gospel. I'm visiting churches now trying to find one. I believed Christ cared about poor people. That's something I learned after I left the Klan. I do a lot of riding, and I do most of my thinking on the road, when I'm on to my next meeting.

I think Christ was a god in the flesh. He cares about individuals, he cares about how we're treated. It's got to bother Him to see people hungry, to see people under the bridges, homeless, starving. I think if He came back today, he'd be extremely disappointed.

HOWARD CLEMENT

In the sixties, Durham was evolving into a more open community. Black people were being elected to public office for the first time. In '74, I became chairman of the local Democratic Party. My father, who himself had run for Congress against Mendel Rivers, had switched to the Republican Party. He suggested that I switch, too.

The fact is I was becoming more conservative myself on some issues. I began to question: Why was I a Democrat? I don't see how they helped the black community improve its conditions. We were actually retrogressing. The Democrats talked a good game but they seldom delivered. They had us in a bag. In 1984, I switched to the Republicans.

That created quite a stir because at the time I was a member of the Durham City Council. Everybody figured my career had come to an end. It was a city of twenty-five Democrats to one Republican. I've run for election three times and have been successful each time.

In 1989, we elected our first black mayor, Chester Jenkins. I backed the conservative white, Strawbridge. Our slate was thrashed, except for me. The truth is, Jenkins didn't ask for my support. He did all he could to disavow any association with me. One newspaper put me to the right of Jesse Helms. Of course I openly supported Harvey Gantt against Helms.

I perceive myself as a moderate Republican. I favor affirmative action, though I have never supported it vocally. There's a bit of unfairness in it that Helms used to his advantage. I will never openly oppose affirmative action. I see it as a way to level the playing field, but there must be some other way. What it is, I don't know.

It's funny, isn't it? C. P. Ellis has become more liberal and I've become more conservative. I'll never forget that 1970 parents' meeting. When he got up and bitterly complained about his son's lack of educational opportunity, of bad housing, and no jobs for people like him, I remembered black people saying the exact same things.

I had sat down with them, in those neighborhoods, teaching these mothers how to express themselves when they went before the school board or the city council. I thought they should learn to speak for themselves. At first, they were too embarrassed because they didn't have the words. Three or four nights a week, I'd go down and meet with these mothers and their children. It was a real education for me.

I'll never forget one night at a housing project. A six-year-old boy, muddy and grimy, was pulling at my tie. His mother said, "Get away from Mr. Clement, you're messing up his tie." That night she called me up to apologize. "You're the first black man my son has ever seen with a shirt and tie on."

When C. P. Ellis, a poor white Klansman, got up with his litany of complaints, I was hearing all these black mothers. During his appearance at the city council, he was trying to get the black picketers off the streets. He called us scalawags. There he was in his overalls and dirty shoes and there I was in my three-piece suit, button-down shirt, and he was calling me trash. I had a negative opinion of him then. That was before I began to understand how things worked.

The white bankers, the power structure, never seen openly with C. P. Ellis, would be calling him at night, giving him money, telling him what to do. After we became friends, he confided in me. He started turning when the same people who called him at night would avoid him on the street. I would walk down the same street and shake hands with him. It confused him.

At that meeting, I said, "C. P., we're brothers." That statement hit the news like a fire hitting dry straw. My father read about it in the *Washington Post*. I had called a Klansman my brother! When he ran for Congress in '48, the Klan had done everything to frighten him. I'll never forget, I was fourteen at the time. They'd follow our cars, throw bricks through our window. My father had to sleep with a shotgun by his bed. Now I was calling a Kleagle of the Klan brother. A lot of my black friends thought I'd gone cuckoo, too. [*Chuckles.*] I feel now that was one of the best things I've ever done.

I'll never forget the expression on C. P.'s face. He was stunned. "What that nigger callin' me brother for?" [*A prolonged laugh.*] That episode drew us and

Ann Atwater together. Ann has slowed down considerably. She has not been well. At that time, she was big, black, and bad. [*Laughs.*] She frightened everybody. C. P., too.

DOCUMENT 32.4

Fighting Hate

Eighteen months earlier we had bankrupted the United Klans of America (UKA), the KKK group responsible for some of the most heinous crimes of the civil rights era. Our involvement had been triggered by a murder—the lynching of a nineteen-year-old black man named Michael Donald in Mobile in 1981. After one member of the UKA was convicted of the killing and a second pleaded guilty, we filed a civil lawsuit on behalf of Michael's mother against several members of the UKA and, most significantly, the organization itself.

Our theory—admittedly novel—was that the UKA, like any corporation, should be held liable for the acts of its agents when those agents were acting to further the organization's goals. By securing secret Klan documents and demonstrating that the UKA had a long history of using violence to advance its stated goal, the "God-given supremacy of the white race," we were able to persuade an all-white jury to deliver a landmark $7 million verdict for Mrs. Donald in February 1987. Unable to come up with the money, the Klan organization was forced to satisfy the judgment by turning over its national headquarters to Mrs. Donald. She sold the building and used the proceeds to move out of public housing for the first time in her adult life.

This had been my most important case in twenty-five years as a lawyer. My parents were tenant cotton farmers in Montgomery County. I had picked cotton side by side with blacks and had as many black friends as white when I was growing up. Still, it had taken a long time before I questioned the segregation that had been in place well before my birth in 1936.

Some of the UKA's past actions that we focused on at the Donald trial had special significance to me. After Imperial Wizard Bobby Shelton's thugs beat the Freedom Riders in Montgomery in 1961, I represented a neighbor with ties to the Klan who was accused of assaulting a newsman during the riot. As I left the courthouse, I was confronted by two black men, who asked me how I could work for a violent racist. I'd always thought of myself as a friend to blacks, sympathetic to their lot, but these honest inquisitors forced me to consider whether my actions reflected my thoughts. Then and there I decided that no one would ever again have to ask where I stood.

Two years later the UKA's infamous bombing of a Birmingham church moved me to take my first public stance against the violence of the civil rights

Source: From Morris Dees and Steve Fiffer, *Hate on Trial: The Case against America's Dangerous Neo-Nazi* (New York: Villard Books, 1993), pp. 10–11.

era. On the Sunday after the tragedy, I asked my neighbors in our Pike Road Baptist Church to join in prayer for the families of the four black girls who had died in the blast and to send money to help rebuild the church. My fellow Christians' angry rejection of my plea caused me to leave what I saw as a hypocritical church. This started a split with old friends, who soon ostracized me and, worse, my family.

DOCUMENT 32.5

Women's Reproductive Rights

Liberty finds no refuge in a jurisprudence of doubt. Yet 19 years after our holding that the Constitution protects a woman's right to terminate her pregnancy in its early stages, *Roe* v. *Wade,* 410 U. S. 113 (1973), that definition of liberty is still questioned. Joining the respondents as *amicus curiae,* the United States, as it has done in five other cases in the last decade, again asks us to overrule *Roe.* See Brief for Respondents 104-117; Brief for United States as *Amicus Curiae* 8. . . .

After considering the fundamental constitutional questions resolved by *Roe,* principles of institutional integrity, and the rule of *stare decisis,* we are led to conclude this: the essential holding of *Roe* v. *Wade* should be retained and once again reaffirmed.

It must be stated at the outset and with clarity that *Roe*'s essential holding, the holding we reaffirm, has three parts. First is a recognition of the right of the woman to choose to have an abortion before viability and to obtain it without undue interference from the State. Before viability, the State's interests are not strong enough to support a prohibition of abortion or the imposition of a substantial obstacle to the woman's effective right to elect the procedure. Second is a confirmation of the State's power to restrict abortions after fetal viability, if the law contains exceptions for pregnancies which endanger a woman's life or health. And third is the principle that the State has legitimate interests from the outset of the pregnancy in protecting the health of the woman and the life of the fetus that may become a child. These principles do not contradict one another; and we adhere to each. . . .

Men and women of good conscience can disagree, and we suppose some always shall disagree, about the profound moral and spiritual implications of terminating a pregnancy, even in its earliest stage. Some of us as individuals find abortion offensive to our most basic principles of morality, but that cannot control our decision. Our obligation is to define the liberty of all, not to mandate our own moral code. The underlying constitutional issue is whether the State can resolve these philosophic questions in such a definitive way that a woman lacks all choice in the matter, except perhaps in those rare circumstances in which the pregnancy is itself a danger to her own life or health, or is the result of rape or incest. . . .

Source: Excerpted from Supreme Court of the United States, [Nos. 91-744 and 91-902] *Planned Parenthood of Southeastern Pennsylvania, et al., v. Robert P. Casey, et al., etc.,* June 29, 1992.

Our law affords constitutional protection to personal decisions relating to marriage, procreation, contraception, family relationships, child rearing, and education. *Carey* v. *Population Services International*, 431 U. S., at 685. Our cases recognize "the right of the individual, married or single, to be free from unwarranted governmental intrusion into matters so fundamentally affecting a person as the decision whether to bear or beget a child." *Eisenstadt* v. *Baird, supra,* at 453 (emphasis in original). Our precedents "have respected the private realm of family life which the state cannot enter." *Prince* v. *Massachusetts*, 321 U. 5. 158, 166 (1944). These matters, involving the most intimate and personal choices a person may make in a lifetime, choices central to personal dignity and autonomy, are central to the liberty protected by the Fourteenth Amendment. At the heart of liberty is the right to define one's own concept of existence, of meaning, of the universe, and of the mystery of human life. Beliefs about these matters could not define the attributes of personhood were they formed under compulsion of the State.

These considerations begin our analysis of the woman's interest in terminating her pregnancy but cannot end it, for this reason: though the abortion decision may originate within the zone of conscience and belief, it is more than a philosophic exercise. Abortion is a unique act. It is an act fraught with consequences for others: for the woman who must live with the implications of her decision; for the persons who perform and assist in the procedure; for the spouse, family, and society which must confront the knowledge that these procedures exist, procedures some deem nothing short of an act of violence against innocent human life; and, depending on one's beliefs, for the life or potential life that is aborted. Though abortion is conduct, it does not follow that the State is entitled to proscribe it in all instances. That is because the liberty of the woman is at stake in a sense unique to the human condition and so unique to the law. The mother who carries a child to full term is subject to anxieties, to physical constraints, to pain that only she must bear. That these sacrifices have from the beginning of the human race been endured by woman with a pride that ennobles her in the eyes of others and gives to the infant a bond of love cannot alone be grounds for the State to insist she make the sacrifice. Her suffering is too intimate and personal for the State to insist, without more, upon its own vision of the woman's role, however dominant that vision has been in the course of our history and our culture. The destiny of the woman must be shaped to a large extent on her own conception of her spiritual imperatives and her place in society.

It should be recognized, moreover, that in some critical respects the abortion decision is of the same character as the decision to use contraception, to which *Griswold* v. *Connecticut, Eisenstadt* v. *Baird,* and *Carey* v. *Population Services International,* afford constitutional protection. We have no doubt as to the correctness of those decisions. They support the reasoning in *Roe* relating to the woman's liberty because they involve personal decisions concerning not only the meaning of procreation but also human responsibility and respect for it. As with abortion, reasonable people will have differences of opinion about these matters. One view is based on such reverence for the wonder of creation that any pregnancy ought to be welcomed and carried to full term no matter how difficult it will be to provide for the child and ensure its well-being. Another is that the inability to provide for the nurture and care of the infant is a cruelty to the child and an anguish to the parent. These are intimate views with infinite variations, and their deep, personal character underlay our decisions in *Griswold, Eisenstadt,* and *Carey.* The same concerns are present when the woman confronts the reality that, perhaps despite her attempts to avoid it, she has become pregnant.

It was this dimension of personal liberty that *Roe* sought to protect, and its holding invoked the reasoning and the tradition of the precedents we have discussed, granting protection to substantive liberties of the person. *Roe* was, of course, an extension of those cases and, as the decision itself indicated, the separate States could act in some degree to further their own legitimate interests in protecting pre-natal life. The extent to which the legislatures of the States might act to outweigh the interests of the woman in choosing to terminate her pregnancy was a subject of debate both in *Roe* itself and in decisions following it.

While we appreciate the weight of the arguments made on behalf of the State in the case before us, arguments which in their ultimate formulation conclude that *Roe* should be overruled, the reservations any of us may have in reaffirming the central holding of *Roe* are outweighed by the explication of individual liberty we have given combined with the force of *stare decisis.*

DOCUMENT 32.6

Truth in Accounting

U.S. Securities and Exchange Commission: File No. 4-460: Order Requiring the Filing of Sworn Statements Pursuant to Section 21(a)(1) of the Securities Exchange Act of 1934

In light of recent reports of accounting irregularities at public companies, including some large and seemingly well-regarded companies, the purpose of the Commission's investigation is to provide greater assurance to the Commission and to investors that persons have not violated, or are not currently violating, the provisions of the federal securities laws governing corporate issuers' financial reporting and accounting practices, and to aid the Commission in assessing whether it is necessary or appropriate in the public interest or for the protection of investors for the Commission to adopt or amend rules and regulations governing corporate issuers' reporting and accounting practices and/or for the Commission to recommend legislation to Congress concerning these matters.

Source: United States Securities and Exchange Commission, "File No. 4-460: Order Requiring the Filing of Sworn Statements Pursuant to Section 21(a)(1) of the Securities Exchange Act of 1934." Available at www.sec.gov./rules/other/4-460.htm.

As part of this investigation, the Commission believes it necessary to require written statements, under oath, from senior officers of certain publicly traded companies, identified in *the list* attached hereto (the "Companies"), with revenues during their last fiscal year of greater than $1.2 billion, that file reports with the Commission pursuant to the Securities Exchange Act of 1934, regarding the accuracy of their Companies' financial statements and their consultation with the Companies' audit committees.

Accordingly, pursuant to Section 21(a) of the Securities Exchange Act, it is:

ORDERED, that the principal executive officer and principal financial officer of each of the Companies shall either (a) file a statement in writing, under oath, in the form of *Exhibit A* hereto, or (b) file a statement in writing, under oath, describing the facts and circumstances that would make such a statement incorrect. In either case, such statement shall further declare in writing, under oath, whether or not the contents of the statement have been reviewed with the Company's audit committee, or in the absence of an audit committee, the independent members of the Company's board of directors. Such sworn statement shall be delivered for publication in written form to Jonathan G. Katz, Secretary, Securities and Exchange Commission, 450 Fifth Street, N.W., Washington, DC 20549 by the close of business on the first date that a Form 10-K or Form 10-Q of such Company is required to be filed with the Commission on or after August 14, 2002.

By the Commission.

DOCUMENT 32.7

Fatal College Daze

1,400 Deaths Blamed on College Drinking

WASHINGTON—Drinking by U.S. college students contributes to 1,400 deaths, a half million injuries and 70,000 sexual assaults a year, according to a three-year review of existing studies released Tuesday by the National Institute on Alcohol Abuse and Alcoholism.

The study also found that 2.1 million students—one-fourth of college students aged 18 to 24—drove under the influence of alcohol during the last year.

"The harm that college students do to themselves and others as a result of excessive drinking exceeds what many would have expected," said Ralph Hingson, professor of social behavioral sciences at Boston University's School of Public Health and the study's lead author.

In addition to the study, published in the March issue of the Journal of Studies on Alcohol, the institute's Task Force on College Drinking issued a companion report that offers suggestions on how to curb the problem of college-age

Source: Johanna Neuman, "1,400 Deaths Blamed on College Drinking," *Chicago Tribune*, April 10, 2002, p. 10.

drinking. The 59-page report recommends changing the culture of drinking at U.S. colleges."

Mark Goldman, co-chairman of the task force that produced the report, says the study and the report together document how severe the problem is.

"Our society has always dealt with this with a wink and a nod, as a rite of passage," said Goldman, distinguished research professor of psychology at the University of South Florida. "But the statistics that Ralph Hingson has put together are stunning to all of us, even the most seasoned researchers."

The task force, in an unusual twist, brought together scientific researchers who had been studying the problem and university presidents who had been dealing with the results. The 36-member group, which also included students, took a pragmatic tack, suggesting solutions tailored to specific schools and involving the larger community around the school.

"This is one of those cases of squeezing the balloon," said Goldman. "A dry campus just drives the problem off campus. The community has to be on the same page."

The task force was formed several years ago, after Scott Krueger, an 18-year-old freshman at the Massachusetts Institute of Technology, died after a weekend of drinking at a fraternity.

Credits

Chapter 18

Frank Collinson: Excerpted from *Life in the Saddle* by Frank Collinson, edited by Mary Whatley Clarke, pp. 31-41. Copyright © 1963 by the University of Oklahoma Press. Reprinted by permission.

Ida B. Wells (on lynchings in the South): From Ida B. Wells, "Mob Rule in New Orleans," 1900, reprinted in *Southern Horrors and Other Writings: The Anti-Lynching Campaign of Ida B. Wells, 1892-1900,* Jacqueline Jones Royster, ed., pp. 206-207, published by Bedford/St. Martin's.

Chapter 20

Photograph of Flatiron Building, New York, 1902: © Howard Davis/Greatbuildings.com. Used with permission.

Chapter 22

Miriam E. Tefft, Bisbee AZ: From "Last of the Vigilantes" from the Miriam E. Tefft Biographical File. Reprinted by permission of Arizona Historical Society, Tucson, AZ.

Chapter 24

Alfred P. Sloan, Jr.: Excerpts from Alfred P. Sloan, Jr., *My Years With General Motors*, pp. 150-152. © 1963 by Alfred P. Sloan. Reprinted by permission of the Harold Matson Co., Inc.

Middletown: Excerpts from MIDDLETOWN: A STUDY IN CONTEMPORARY AMERICAN CULTURE by Robert S. Lynd & Helen Merrell Lynd, pp. 253-259, 269-271, copyright 1929 by Harcourt, Inc. and renewed 1957 by Robert S. and Helen M. Lynd, reprinted by permission of the publisher.

Malcolm Cowley: From Malcolm Cowley, *Exile's Return: A Narrative of Ideas* by Malcolm Cowley, pp. 69-76. Copyright © 1934 W.W. Norton & Company, Inc. Used by permission of W.W. Norton & Company.

Chapter 25

Photo, image of distress: Photograph from *Let Us Now Praise Famous Men* by James Agee & Walker Evans. Copyright © 1941 by James Agee and Walker Evans. Copyright © renewed 1969 by Mia Fritsch Agee and Walker Evans. Reprinted by permission of Houghton Mifflin Company. All rights reserved.

Robert S. McElvaine letters: From DOWN AND OUT IN THE GREAT DEPRESSION: LETTERS FROM THE FORGOTTEN MAN by Robert S. McElvaine, pp. 57-58, 117, 162, 179-180. Copyright © 1983 by the University of North Carolina Press. Used by permission of the publisher.

Woody Guthrie's "Tom Joad": TOM JOAD, words and music by Woody Guthrie, TRO © Copyright 1960, (renewed) and 1963 (renewed) Ludlow Music, Inc., New York, NY. Used with permission.

San Francisco longshoreman's strike, 1934: From *Highlights of a Fighting History: 60 Years of the Communist Party*, Bart, Bassett, Weinstone & Zipser (eds.), pp. 114-115. Copyright © 1979 by International Publishers. Reprinted by permission of International Publishers Company and by United Electrical, Radio & Machine Workers of America.

Chapter 26

Poem, E.B. White: From E.B. White, "The Meaning of Democracy," July 3, 1943. Reprinted by permission of Mrs. Allene White.

William Manchester: From William Manchester, Preamble to *Goodbye, Darkness: A Memoir of the Pacific War*, pp. 3-7. Copyright © 1979 by William Manchester. Reprinted by permission of Don Congdon Associates, Inc.

Poems "August 6" and "Flames": From Sankichi, Toge in *Hiroshima Three Witnesses*, Richard H. Minear (ed. & trans.), pp. 306-307, 311-312. Copyright © 1990 Princeton University Press. Reprinted by permission of Princeton University Press.

Chapter 27

Arthur Miller excerpt: From "All My Sons," copyright 1947, renewed © 1975 by Arthur Miller, from ARTHUR MILLER'S COLLECTED PLAYS by Arthur Miller, pp. 78-84. Used by permission of Viking Penguin, a division of Penguin Putnam Inc. and by International Creative Management, Inc.

Marilyn R. Allen: Excerpts from Miss Marilyn R. Allen, *Alien Minorities and Mongrelization*, pp. 28-32, 43-44. Copyright © 1949 Meador Publishing Company, Boston.

Ferdinand Lundberg and Marynia F. Farnham: Pages 201-202, 236-241 from MODERN WOMAN: THE LOST SEX by Ferdinand Lundberg and Marynia F. Farnham. Copyright © 1947 by Ferdinand Lundberg and Marynia F. Farnham. Reprinted by permission of HarperCollins Publishers Inc.

Harry S. Truman on the beginning of the Korean War: From Harry S. Truman, *Memoirs by Harry S. Truman, Volume Two: Years of Trial and Hope*, Doubleday & Company, Inc., 1956. Reprinted by permission of Margaret Truman Daniel.

Chapter 28

Henry Hampton and Steve Fayer (Myrlie Evers Remembers): From VOICES OF FREEDOM by Henry Hampton and Steve Fayer, pp. 153-155, copyright © 1990 by Blackside, Inc. Used by permission of Bantam Books, a division of Random House, Inc.

Henry Hampton and Steve Fayer (Phyllis Ellison): From VOICES OF FREEDOM by Henry Hampton and Steve Fayer, pp. 600-601, copyright © 1990 by Blackside, Inc. Used by permission of Bantam Books, a division of Random House, Inc.

Mamie Mobley: Copyright © 1992 *Race: How Blacks and Whites Think and Feel About the American Obsession*, pp. 20-21, by Studs Terkel. Reprinted with permission of The New Press.

Chapter 29

Excerpt from Dwight D. Eisenhower: From *Mandate for Change 1953-1956* by Dwight David Eisenhower, pp. 374-376, copyright © 1963 by Dwight David Eisenhower. Used by permission of Doubleday, a division of Random House, Inc.

Words to "Ballad of Joe Hill": JOE HILL, Music by Earl Robinson, Words by Alfred Hayes. Copyright © 1938 Universal - MCA Music Publishing, renewed by Music Sales Corporation (ASCAP). International copyright secured. All rights secured. Used with permission.